EXCESSIVE USE OF FORCE

EXCESSIVE USE OF FORCE

One Mother's Struggle Against Police Brutality and Misconduct

Loretta P. Prater

WITHDRAWN

ROWMAN & LITTLEFIELD
Lanham • Boulder • New York • London

Published by Rowman & Littlefield
A wholly owned subsidiary of The Rowman & Littlefield Publishing Group, Inc.
4501 Forbes Boulevard, Suite 200, Lanham, Maryland 20706
www.rowman.com

Unit A, Whitacre Mews, 26-34 Stannary Street, London SE11 4AB

British Library Cataloguing in Publication Information Available

Library of Congress Cataloging-in-Publication Data
Names: Prater, Loretta P.
Title: Excessive use of force: one mother's struggle against police
    brutality and misconduct / Loretta P. Prater.
Description: Lanham : Rowman & Littlefield, [2018] | Includes index.
Identifiers: LCCN 2017031630 (print) | LCCN 2017045702 (ebook) |
    ISBN 9781538108017 (electronic) | ISBN 9781538108000 (cloth : alk.
    paper)
Subjects: LCSH: Police brutality—United States. | Discrimination in law
    enforcement—United States. | African American men—Family
    relationships. | Mothers and sons—United States. | Wrongful death
    United States.
Classification: LCC HV8141 (ebook) | LCC HV8141 .P72 2018 (print)
    | DDC 363.2/32—dc23
LC record available at https://lccn.loc.gov/2017031630

♾™ The paper used in this publication meets the minimum requirements
of American National Standard for Information Sciences—Permanence of
Paper for Printed Library Materials, ANSI/NISO Z39.48-1992.

Printed in the United States of America

*This book is dedicated to the memory of our beloved son,
the late Leslie Vaughn Prater, and in honor of
Stefan DeWitt Prater, our remaining pride and joy.
We love our sons very much and they will forever
live inside our hearts.*

CONTENTS

ACKNOWLEDGMENTS

The first acknowledgment is to my immediate family. My husband, Dwight, while dealing with his own feelings of loss, has stood by my side, provided strength when I was weak in grief, and supported me in all of my endeavors. I certainly could not have endured the emotional pain or written this book without him. I recognize that not only did Dwight lose Leslie, but, in many ways, he also lost the woman he married. I will never be the same. Our younger son, Stefan, shares in our grief. Stefan's relationship, with his older brother and only sibling, is different from, but enlightened by, the mother-and-child relationship. There is a kind of a sacred bond between African American men and their mothers, as can be further explored in Keith Brown's book, *Sacred Bond: Black Men and Their Mothers*, and demonstrated by Stefan's relationship with me.

I must acknowledge Lucille and Willie Pinkard, the loving maternal grandparents who raised me. Without them, I would not be the person I am today or have the fortitude to write this book. Other family members were instrumental in my journey in completing the manuscript. My aunt Louise Arnold, who has been like a devoted older sister to me and had a close relationship with Leslie and deep love for him, and my mother, the late Willie Mae Smith, provided words of encouragement that helped to sustain me during these difficult times. Cousins Ronald and Dollie

Montgomery and Dorothy and Alvin Winton are among extended family members who provided encouragement. The numerous ways in which they helped me are too many to name.

I have also been blessed to have supportive in-laws who stood beside us during our darkest days, including many years after Leslie's death. Dwight's brother Herman and his wife, Lawanda; his brother Michael and his late wife, Kathy; and Dwight's sisters, Terry and Andrea, have provided strength to us. They marched with us, attended numerous meetings in Chattanooga, and collected information helpful to our case. Dwight's brother Marion and his late wife Barbara, from Las Vegas, were unable to participate in the ceremonies in Chattanooga, but they provided moral support through their cards, calls, and prayers. Their son Anthony, one of Leslie's favorite cousins, sent a beautiful message that was read at Leslie's funeral. I must also recognize Stefan's wife, Heather, and his friend Rick Bakewell, for the emotional support they provided to him. Heather also provided the book cover picture.

Many friends supported us emotionally, spiritually, and physically by their presence. The late Ingrid Peter, prior to her death in April 2012, attended all of the memorials, marches, and Chattanooga City Council meetings and listened to me describe my heartache during countless long-distance phone calls. Our former pastor, Rev. Paul A. McDaniel, provided support and spiritual guidance during our initial and continued grieving process. The presence and encouragement of friends Johnny and Juanita Holloway, Dr. Phyllis Bell Miller, attorney Emma Jones, and the late Dr. Marcia Riley will always be remembered. Many other friends and relatives, as well as people who hardly knew us personally, forwarded expressions of sympathy and concern, which helped to sustain us.

I would like to thank my publisher, Rowman & Littlefield, and editor Kathryn Knigge. I certainly appreciate the significant assistance of my primary book reviewer and dear friend, Marsha Haskell. I consider her to be my literary angel. Other reviewers included Dr. Tom Linares, Dr. Vida Mays, Dr. Robert Polack, Judy Zabike, Jeanice Scott, Vera Campbell-Jones, Dr. Francisco Barrios, Joycelyn Phillips, Johnny Holloway, Dr. Morris Jenkins, Dr. Festus Obiakor, former police chief Carl Kinnison, and attorney Al Spradling. Further assistance was provided by Dr. Jeremy Ball and Dr. Linda Heitman. I thank Dr. Susan Swartwout

for her superior technical assistance. I would like to express appreciation to attorneys Nick Brustin, John Wolfe, Amelia Roberts, and Barry
Scheck for their support of this project. To all of the other supporters
and friends of our family who have offered encouragement and prayers,
I say thank you. Your words helped me to continue the journey.

Lastly, I would like to thank all of my former English and grammar
teachers from elementary school and beyond. Those outstanding educators stimulated my interest in writing and facilitated the foundation
for my ability to write, and are partly responsible for my enjoyment and
appreciation of the written word. A special note of thanks is extended
to Mrs. Christine Simmons Hicks, my twelfth-grade English teacher
at Howard High School in Chattanooga, Tennessee. This may sound
odd, but I really loved those English term paper assignments, which I
consider an early precursor to my doctoral dissertation and subsequent
writing projects.

PROLOGUE

I don't know where to start. There were so many times when I would say to myself, "Today is the day that I will devote to writing the book, and I will do absolutely nothing else today." Then conveniently, other things would intervene and postpone my good intentions. Maybe it was work, a telephone call that I initiated, volunteer obligations, or just an unlimited number of various excuses to keep me from sitting at the computer and working on this book. I had to question myself, "Why the avoidance?" Was this something that I really wanted to do or just something I should be doing? I knew the answer. I learned years ago that humans are programmed to welcome pleasure, repeat the circumstances that are pleasurable, and avoid pain. I anticipated that writing this book would bring pain, and possibly intensify it. So, I chose the route of avoidance. I knew that I would have to uncover some feelings that I had tried to bury for the past thirteen years. However, I also remained convinced that this book must be written. In my opinion, only I could write this story. Maybe I was being selfish, thinking that only my perception of the events should be reported. Of course, I will also include some sentiments and reflections of other family members who were close to Leslie.

I always felt that there was a special mother-son bond between Leslie and me, maybe because I carried him in my body for nine months.
I have heard other mothers of sons express this feeling as well. I am
not the mother of any daughters, so I don't have an alternative frame
of reference, although Nancy Friday's book about mother-daughter
relationships seems to suggest that there is also a unique bond between
mothers and daughters.[1] Could Keith Brown be right in suggesting that
African American men and their mothers share a special attachment? In
Brown's book, he shared a sentiment from Washington Irving that there
is an enduring tenderness in the love of a mother for a son that transcends all other affections of the heart. From my experience, I certainly
would not dispute that claim.[2]

I will ask for forgiveness in advance for being selfish and writing in
the first person, but this is my story, from the viewpoint of an angry
black mother. I said to one of my reviewers that I didn't want people to
think that I was just an angry black woman. He pointed out to me that,
although the book had substance, I *was* an angry black woman. I had
to admit that he was correct. Stefan, my younger son, is a good writer.
I hope that one day he will write his story too, but this is my journey
toward survival. I am uncertain if I will ever get there, but I know that
the sleepless nights and numerous spontaneous incidents of fighting
back the tears are indications that I have not arrived yet.

Over several years, I talked with several people about my plans to
write this book. I received a lot of encouragement during those conversations but never put "pen to paper." I spoke with other book authors,
read books focused on the "how-to" of writing books, and talked to
numerous people about my ideas. I also collected a lot of information
that I knew I wanted to include in the book. I have boxes of "stuff,"
probably enough raw data for two or three books. Yet I had still not
begun this project in earnest. Sometimes I received conflicting suggestions. I was told to find a publisher first and then let the assigned editor
guide me through the process. Then I was told to write the book first
and then shop for a publisher. I was also advised that I needed to get
an agent first. People sent me information on self-publishing and writing e-books. Additionally, I received a variety of suggestions about the
audience I should address. I was totally open to suggestions and sincere
in my requests for input. However, the inundation of well-intended

solicited advice and information can stifle the process. I had written a number of published book chapters and journal articles, but this anticipated manuscript would be my first attempt as the sole author of a book. Because there are so many facets to this story, I became more confused than ever in regard to where to start and how to proceed. Finally, I had the privilege of meeting noted author and successful entrepreneur Clifton L. Taulbert. His first book, *When We Were Colored*, is among my private collection of works focused on African Americans.[3] The personal account of his journey through childhood and his reflections of those times were very inspiring to me. At the time that I finished reading his book, I never thought I would have the opportunity of actually meeting him.

My meeting with Mr. Taulbert was unanticipated. I attended the Delta Regional Authority Leadership conference in Little Rock, Arkansas, in November 2011, seven years after Leslie's death. Mr. Taulbert was one of the speakers on a guest panel. Fortunately, I had a chance to talk with him at the end of his session. Maybe it was divine intervention that we were able to meet. When I briefly discussed with him my dilemma and confusion in identifying the audience for the book, he said to me, "Write the book as though you were the audience, and it is written as a book that you would want to read." At that moment, it was as though clarity instantly surfaced! That was the best advice I could have received, because I immediately thought, "Yes, I can do that." After all the years of struggling with where to begin and how to proceed, his direct statement made the path so clear, and yet so simple. I would write the book for me, Leslie's mother. If no publisher would publish it, I would self-publish. If no one wanted to read it, I would read it. Thank you, Clifton Taulbert.

INTRODUCTION

One spring Saturday afternoon on the campus of the University of Missouri in Columbia, I sat communing with nature and being entertained merely watching people of all ages, sizes, and ethnicities walking by. The warm, friendly breeze reminded me of many past spring afternoons when I would sit enjoying the beautiful flowers and swaying trees, fanning the yellow jackets that seemed to be attracted to my perfume. And yet, as was so often the case, my thoughts drifted and focused on reflections of Leslie. My thirty-seven-year-old son Leslie could not enjoy the flowers. He could not see the trees. He could not even feel frustration with the interference of the yellow jackets. Leslie would not ever see another spring on Earth. He would never again laugh and talk with his friends, the people he enjoyed so much.

Leslie was a person filled with life and love. People enjoyed just being around him, drawn to him by his extroverted personality and his kind demeanor. Everyone expressed affection toward him. I know you have heard people describe a personality by saying, "When he walks into a room, it lights up," or "He never met a stranger." Well, that was Leslie.

My mind drifted more as I continued daydreaming about Leslie. During such times, I would often reflect upon Mary Dawson Hughes's poem "You're My Guest in Thought."[1] In her poem, she discusses how you can visit deceased loved ones daily through daydreaming. From her writing, I am especially warmed by the following passage:

> For though my daydreams bring you near
> I wish that you were really here
> But what reality cannot change
> My dreams and wishes can arrange
> And through my wishing you'll be brought
> To me each day, a guest in thought.

Just observing those young people, many of whom were the age that Leslie would have been, I immediately felt immense grief, the kind that just appears and takes over your emotions, your thoughts. Now, I often refer to these experiences as a "meltdown," as part of the grief process. I recently had a meltdown episode when on an outing with friends to see the movie *Fruitvale Station*, about the 2009 shooting death of unarmed, twenty-two-year-old Oscar Grant in Oakland, California. I had to go out and sit in the lobby. It was just too painful, and all too familiar, to watch scenes depicting the merciless and unjustifiable killing of an unarmed young man by a BART police officer at Fruitvale Station.[2] You may be familiar with Elizabeth Kübler-Ross's five stages of grief: denial, anger, bargaining, depression, and acceptance.[3] Each day, I struggle with one or more of these stages, trying to be a survivor, rather than a victim. With Leslie's death, I am often stuck between denial and anger. Certainly, after thirteen years, I have not reached acceptance.

As I sat on the campus of the University of Missouri and reflected on Leslie, I suddenly felt the resurgence of anger. The contrast between my anger and the rainbow of flowers glowing in the warm sunshine on a beautiful campus seemed very surreal. What was the source of that anger? It was that the last persons his eyes looked upon were those who cared nothing for him, people who, I believe, hated him for no reason. I am still angry with those individuals, identified as public servants. These people did not even know him, had never met him, but they demonstrated such disdain for him that, by their unwarranted aggressive behavior, they denied Leslie his constitutional right to life. I believe that they would have treated an animal with more respect.

How often have we read of police officers or other first responders taking great personal risks in rescuing a dog or a cat from a distressing

or potentially dangerous situation? One can face criminal charges for
shooting a dog, for example.[4] I am pleased that the lives of animals are
saved, but I would expect no less concern or assistance when public servants encounter a human being in distress. We only have one physical
life on Earth; at least that is my belief. Unfortunately, Leslie's cry for
help was answered with death.

The amazing irony in how Leslie's life ended is that he had such a
high regard for human beings, even those who were labeled as undesir-
able by some societal, stereotypical standards. We all have a purpose in
life. Maybe Leslie's life was to serve as a model of the demonstration of
unconditional love and true friendship. I recall saying to him on numerous occasions, "Everyone who smiles in your face is not your friend," or
"Those guys are not friends." His constant reply was "Oh Mother, he's
OK" or "They're cool."

As I continued my observation of people's interactions—walking,
talking, laughing—more anger consumed me. Again, I had to ask myself, "Why am I so angry?" I think it was because I strongly felt that
Leslie's life was unfairly taken, stolen from him and from us, the people
who loved him so much. The ironic thing is that I remain convinced, as
documented by two autopsy reports, that Leslie's life was taken by people who were expected, and paid by taxpayers, to serve and protect him.
His constitutional rights were violated and dismissed. In accordance
with the Fourteenth Amendment of the United States Constitution,
Leslie was deprived of life and liberty and denied protection under the
law. He was unarmed and helpless at the time of his death, causing no
harm to any individual. Leslie's life ended on January 2, 2004, in Chattanooga, Tennessee.

Leslie represents so many other homicide victims whose circumstances of death remain virtually unknown to society. No, there was not
a video that was shown on national news. The incident was not an international viral webcast feature or blog. No, there was not a march led
by national civil rights advocates like Al Sharpton or Jessie Jackson. No,
we were not interviewed by CNN, nor did we appear on the national
evening news broadcasts of ABC, NBC, or CBS affiliates. We did send
information to the producers of 20/20 and the Oprah Winfrey Show
in an effort to attract national attention to this case, but we received
no response. Leslie's death only attracted the interest of local news

reporters. Those who caused Leslie's death were not held accountable. Justice was denied.

This book will tell the story of our struggle for justice in the wrongful death of our son. To date, I have been unable to find any other book that was authored solely by a mother in a similar circumstance. One book that comes close is *My Heart Will Cross This Ocean*, coauthored by Craig Wolff and Kadiatou Diallo, the mother of slain, unarmed Amalou Diallo. Their book is a memoir that includes the death of her son by police officers in New York City in 1999.[5] Lezley McSpadden, the mother of Michael Brown, coauthored a book with Lyah Beth LeFlore. Her book, *Tell the Truth and Shame the Devil*, is a biography of her life and the account of Michael's death by gunfire in Ferguson, Missouri.[6] It is my hope that other families with experiences of police brutality will be helped and comforted by my sharing of these very personal events. Although no situation is identical to another, there are many common occurrences when lay citizens challenge the authority and inappropriate actions of police officers. Our experience is one of many, among a long history of unjust, wrongful deaths and injuries perpetrated by law enforcement officers.

For researchers who read this book, I feel an obligation to briefly discuss the unique research model used in this project. I chose to use triangulation, which is a technique used in the social sciences to indicate that two or more methods are used. The advantage of this integrative methodological approach is that a more detailed picture of a situation can be accomplished.[7] The four types of triangulation are data, investigator, theoretical, and methodological.[8] In this project, I used the methods of secondary analysis of quantitative research, interviews, data analysis, and participant observer to gain information. Participant observation is the process of enabling researchers to learn about those activities.[9] Unlike some other social scientists, I was already a member of one of the families of concern. I thus felt the need for multiple sources to address this complex issue and to add validity to the hypothesis that police brutality is a real social justice issue with real consequences. It is anticipated that the use of triangulation will also widen the reader's understanding of this pertinent social phenomenon.

0

HOMICIDE OR NATURAL CAUSES

How Did Leslie Vaughn Prater Die?

I understand that life is a precious, fragile gift. More than ever, I understand that one will stop living and transition to death in an instant. Nothing protects us from the inevitability of death, not youth, physical well-being, social status, or popularity. Death is the ultimate equalizer. Without any discrimination, death will eventually claim all lives. Babies die; people in seemingly good health die; and, yes, movie stars, politicians, and the wealthy die. There are all types of circumstances, natural and unnatural, that cause death. There are diseases such as heart disease, cancer, and diabetes that may claim a life, with heart attack being the number one cause of death in America, including for women.[1] In fact, at least one in four women will die of a heart attack.[2] Accidents claim many lives daily, especially car accidents among our youth. Worldwide, traffic accidents are the leading cause of death for all youth over the age of ten.[3] But there is an exception. For African American males, homicide is the leading cause of death. Researcher Dr. Charles H. Hennekens reported that the number of homicide deaths among African American males exceeds those resulting from car accidents, suicides, and diseases combined. Dr. Hennekens further found that, in America, young black men are six times more likely to die from homicide than young white men.[4]

There are numerous other factors that can cause a tragic end to life. During the warm months, drownings and boating accidents add to these tragic numbers. Sometimes people die from strange circumstances, such as a sinkhole opening[5] or a terrific mudslide.[6]

Unfortunately, we cannot discount the fact that acts of violence from various means end the lives of people in our communities, within all age ranges. These occurrences of homicide are especially prevalent during weekends and in urban settings. Of no surprise is that increasing numbers are the result of injuries inflicted from firearms. These shootings can occur anywhere. Persons die from gunshot wounds while in their homes, shopping in the mall, or working in an elementary school. Memories still linger of the horrible 2013 shootings of children, some as young as five years old, at Sandy Hook Elementary School in Connecticut.[7] It seems that almost daily, there is some incident of a shooting of innocent people, whether on a military base, in a park filled with children, in a movie theater, or merely on the street. For example, on April 13, 2014, in Kansas City, there was an arrest for the fatal shooting of Dr. William Lewis Corporon and his fourteen-year-old grandson, Reat Griffin Underwood. These killings were identified as a hate crime, because the assailant believed, erroneously, that the victims were Jewish.[8]

So, what happened to Leslie Vaughn Prater, a thirty-seven-year-old African American male? Simply stated, Leslie stopped breathing. The question that I propose is "What caused him to stop breathing?" In Alan D. Wolfelt's "Mourner's Bill of Rights," among the ten items listed is the right to search for meaning.[9] Thirteen years after Leslie's death, I am still searching.

I believe that Leslie, an African American male, was the victim of a twenty-first-century version of a lynching, which I equate with the all-too-common occurrence of death by police brutality. In addition to law enforcement officers, I would include armed lay citizens who get away with murder by using the "stand-your-ground defense" after killing unarmed young black males. I know that the law doesn't only apply to unarmed African American males killed by white persons, but these are the cases that are most publicized, especially when there is no conviction rendered. It appears that more states are interested in passing stand-your-ground laws. Sadly, Missouri passed a stand-your-ground provision in 2016, during the same year of legislative approval to carry concealed firearms without a permit.[10] In general, a stand-your-ground law is a justification in a criminal case whereby defendants can "stand their ground" and use force without retreating in order to protect and defend themselves or others against threats or perceived threats.[11]

In Florida, Trayvon Martin and Jordan Davis, both unarmed seventeen-year-old African American males, were murdered by gunfire. Attorneys for the white male adult killers used the stand-your-ground defense. A shocking verdict of "not guilty" was rendered for George Zimmerman in Trayvon's death.[12] In the case of Jordan Davis, Michael Dunn was initially not charged in the killing of Jordan but was convicted of attempted murder in the shootings of Jordan's three friends, who survived. The Davis case is known as the "Loud Music" murder trial. Jordan was killed because he refused to turn down his music, as Dunn, a white man, demanded. Dunn returned to court to be tried for Jordan's murder, independent of the attempted murder charges, which carried a minimum sentence of twenty years for each conviction, plus fifteen years for the felony charge. Tonyaa Weathersbee provided an interesting analysis of the verdict in her reporting of the Davis/Dunn case. She stated, "What the verdict says is that in this nation, in the 21st Century, some white men still believe they have the right to intrude into the space of young black men and make demands. And if the black man is unarmed, with no weapon except his words, those white men can still kill him and call it self-defense. All they need is for a jury to buy it."[13] Fortunately, the jury in the murder trial did not buy it. On October 1, 2014, Michael Dunn was found guilty of the first-degree murder of Jordan Davis.[14] Subsequently, he was sentenced to life in prison.

I will submit a controversial proposal that our unarmed black sons are being lynched. Why would I think that the concept of lynching could even be applied in Leslie's death? It is because common features of lynching include group participation in the death, which is motivated by twisted notions of justice or racial hatred.[15] There is a history of lynching in America. Between 1882 and 1946, there were at least five thousand recorded lynchings in the United States.[16] No one knows how many other lynchings were not recorded.

I propose that lynching is alive and well today. I acknowledge that, as a cause of death, there are fewer people hanging from trees in 2017 than in prior years, but there is more than one way for a group to kill unarmed people.[17] Moreover, traditional lynching still happens. Just ask the families of Frederick Jermaine Carter, lynched in 2010,[18] and Johnny Lorenzo Clark, the victim of a lynching in 2012.[19] Contemporary forms of lynching include burning, beating, shooting, and dragging people attached to motor vehicles. Death can still result from these cruel and outlandish actions. James Byrd Jr., an African American, lost his life in Texas after he was tied to a pickup truck and dragged until he died. His murder was considered a federal hate crime.[20]

In cases in which the cause of death is a mystery or not easily determined, or there is speculation that a crime was committed, it is common for autopsies to be performed. In the case of Leslie's death, an autopsy was immediately ordered by police officials. On the evening of January 2, 2004, the Chattanooga Police Department fingerprinted Leslie, prior to releasing the body to the medical examiner. Is there a rational explanation for why this action was taken? My belief is that the Chattanooga Police Department wanted to seek any information that would allow them to vilify the deceased and justify the suspected brutal actions of their officers. On January 3, Dr. Frank King, the chief medical examiner for Hamilton County, conducted the autopsy without any notice to family members about the impending procedure. We were told upon our arrival in Chattanooga on January 4 that police officials were present during the autopsy. I assume that it was at their request. Family members were neither involved nor consulted. We were not even given an opportunity to identify the body as actually being that of Leslie. We were told that information found in Leslie's car was used for identification purposes. People can have documents in their vehicle that may belong to someone else. Use of those documents could not represent an official positive identification. Why would they autopsy him before any family members could positively identify the body? This fact is especially troubling, considering that family members were at the hospital but were denied the request to see him.

As Leslie's family, we now feel confident that we know how Leslie died, regardless of the outcome of the Chattanooga Police Department's internal investigation. Two medical examiners, independent of each other, completed an extensive, detailed autopsy and provided a report to our attorneys, who forwarded the results to us. Dr. Frank King of the Office of the Hamilton County Medical Examiner, Chattanooga,

Tennessee, and Dr. Bruce Levy of the Forensic Medical Center for Forensic Medicine in Nashville, Tennessee, conducted the autopsies. At the time of Dr. Levy's examination of Leslie's body, he was the chief medical examiner for the State of Tennessee. Each pathologist concluded that homicide was the cause of death.

In the following summative discussions, I will provide more information from official reports, and results from interviewing eyewitnesses. A deposition summary from one of the officers involved in the physical confrontation that resulted in Leslie's death is also included. That deposition describes incidents leading up to Leslie's death. Mention of conflicting reports and other factors contributing to Leslie's homicide are also noted.

AUTOPSY REPORT OF DR. FRANK KING

In Dr. King's official report, dated March 24, 2004,[21] the summary page listed six possibilities as to the manner of death. The directions stated that only one possibility should be selected. The options were accident, suicide, homicide, natural, unknown, and pending. Based on the box that Dr. King checked, he concluded that Leslie's death was a homicide. As the probable cause of death, he wrote "positional asphyxia during physical restraint in the setting of acute ethanol intoxication, acute cocaine intoxication, catecholamine excess cardiomyopathy, and mild obesity." It was interesting that he did not include statements reporting that Leslie's body had multiple abrasions, multiple contusions, a dislocated and fractured shoulder, and multiple rib fractures—twenty-one, to be exact. The report specifically stated that the lower lateral rib fractures were unlikely to be caused by cardiopulmonary resuscitation. So, how did all of those injuries occur? Why were those items not included in the summary statement? Of course, I am aware that staff members of the Office of the Hamilton County Medical Examiner are employees of Hamilton County, in which the city of Chattanooga is located. Historically, the medical examiner's office works closely with the Chattanooga Police Department, and the medical examiner is one of the highest-paid county employees. At the time of Leslie's death, the salary of Dr. King was higher than that of Chattanooga's mayor, Bob Corker.

In the autopsy's detailed summary, there were no significant abnormalities found for the lungs, liver, kidneys, thyroid, spleen, adrenal glands, pancreas, stomach, or brain. Other than Leslie's injuries and the officer's subsequent actions, which prevented him from breathing, the autopsy report appeared to indicate that Leslie was relatively healthy. Leslie was seventy-one inches in height and, yes, overweight at 232 pounds, but this is hardly a condition that would cause one to stop breathing. I strongly agree with Dr. King that the death of my unarmed son was a homicide. Legally, there are various forms of homicide, but it is still the killing of a person by another.[22]

The reported conclusions specific to toxicology were conflicting. The urine tests from the Baroness Erlanger hospital emergency room reported an alcohol level above the legal limit, but no evidence of cocaine. Dr. King's investigation included a report from the Tennessee Bureau of Investigation (TBI), which reported blood and urine samples analyzed on January 25, 2004, and taken at different times. One blood sample detected ethyl alcohol, but no cocaine. Another detected no drugs in the urine sample. A third blood sample contained 0.07 ug/ml of cocaine. When the family met with Dr. King, he stated that, in his analysis of the fluid from Leslie's eyes, there was alcohol found, but no cocaine. He stated that he felt that the eye fluid might give a more accurate postmortem analysis. I asked him directly whether those TBI-reported combined levels of alcohol and cocaine would probably cause erratic behavior or death. He said, "No," and further stated that the reported cocaine level was considered only a trace. I will always wonder why there was no cocaine found in the tests conducted by the hospital and the local medical examiner.

During later conversations about Leslie's death, certain police officials and media personnel chose to highlight the fact that Dr. King reported traces of cocaine in Leslie's body. Often when people hear of the presence of cocaine the assumption is that death was caused by drugs. For example, one Chattanooga Times Free Press article subheading read, "Prater death resulted from drugs, suffocation during local police restraint." The headline was "Autopsy Reveals Struggle." Neither heading mentioned Leslie's extensive injuries.[23] Yet homicide by positional asphyxia—and in the presence of extensive injuries—was the cause of death.

The conclusion that it was homicide was arrived at by independent examinations from two medical examiners. Because I am not a medical examiner, I choose to believe the professional pathologists. Leslie's autopsy findings were later reviewed by Dr. Michael Baden, a nationally renowned and extremely experienced medical examiner. He concurred with the homicide conclusion. In fact, I was told that Dr. Baden, after reviewing autopsy documents, expressed that the condition of Leslie's body was one of the most brutal cases he had ever reviewed. This information was reported to me by Nick Brustin, one of our attorneys, who spoke directly with Dr. Baden.

Although the autopsy reports answered the medical question of how Leslie died, we still don't have the answer for the reason his life was taken. Why did those officers prevent Leslie from breathing? I suspect that we will never know the truth. Personally, I believe that there was malicious intent. If that was not the case, the level of incompetence on the part of those officers suggests that they should not be employed in a position of determining life or death.

According to Dr. King's report, injuries to Leslie's body were numerous. As previously stated, there were twenty-one rib fractures, with only some that may have been caused by cardiopulmonary resuscitation. His final diagnosis listed multiple abrasions on Leslie's lower back, right leg, knee, and wrists. There were also multiple contusions to the right upper and lower chest, right and left arms, left thigh, and both wrists. In addition, Leslie's left shoulder joint was dislocated, with a fracture of the left humeral head, which is the upper arm bone. The report further described that there was acute hemorrhage of the pubic and lower abdominal wall soft tissues and scrotal sac consistent with blunt trauma impact. According to an eyewitness to Leslie's homicide, we were told that a police officer kicked Leslie in the scrotum, which would be consistent with the reported injuries documented in the written autopsy report. One can easily imagine the pain he suffered.

The autopsy report further documented that emergency medical intervention included cardiopulmonary resuscitation with the use of EKG pads, a nasogastric tube, an endotracheal tube, an intravenous line, and a Foley catheter, used to drain urine. This intervention occurred at the hospital. Additional information, documented in the report, was that there was blood drainage from Leslie's nose and ears. His fingernails were short and contained no foreign material or any evidence of trauma. This account is consistent with the fact that Leslie was not a violent person and, from all accounts, did not attempt to even scratch or harm the officers in any way. His movements were to fight death. He wanted to breathe, so he could live. I was also told that there were particles of mud and grass in his nostrils, which is consistent with eyewitness reports that Leslie's head was pushed facedown into the dirt.

Because of our mistrust of the law enforcement system in Chattanooga, and based on suggestions from trusted community advocates, we felt that we needed an autopsy examination independent of Chattanooga. Our mistrust of their police department in dealing with police brutality allegations was based on perceptions developed over fifty years of residency in Chattanooga. We just knew too much about how the department operated. We were also influenced by the fact that there had been a controversial murder investigation in Chattanooga that had led to the victim's body being exhumed. I did not want to risk having to remove Leslie's body from his grave. So, we asked attorney John Wolfe to assist us in making arrangements for a second autopsy.

Payment of $2,000 was required for the second autopsy. We were fortunate that we could afford this expense. Some families have to forgo an independent autopsy because there is no time to raise the money. You either have it right then or you don't. Also, there was some urgency in getting this second autopsy completed because of the need to set a date for the funeral in Chattanooga. We were required to sign an autopsy permit form. On this permit form, which Dwight and I signed on January 7, five days after Leslie's death, there was a question asked: "What do you, as the next of kin, wish to learn from this autopsy?" Dwight's written response was "What caused our young son to die?"

SUMMARY OF AUTOPSY REPORT FROM
DR. BRUCE LEVY

On January 8, 2004, at 9:30 a.m., the second autopsy was conducted in Nashville by Dr. Levy. The official report, dated January 26, 2004, was received on April 7, 2004, by attorney Wolfe. In the summary of the case statement, the last notation written by Dr. Levy reported, "While the ruling as to manner of death is best left to the responsible medical examiner, in this case I agree with the ruling of Dr. King in classifying this death as a homicide."[24]

Dr. Levy's report was divided into three sections: the external, internal, and microscopic examinations. I won't overburden this recounting with all of the details of his findings, but I will provide some summaries to give a sense of the similarities between the two reports, as well as some statements unique to Dr. Levy's conclusions. In the first sentence of the report, Dr. Levy described Leslie as a well-developed, well-nourished black male, measuring seventy-one inches whose appearance is consistent with the reported age of thirty-seven years. He further documented that Leslie's body weight was 232½ pounds, which was far from the 300 pounds publicly reported by Police Chief Dotson.

Dr. Levy reported numerous injuries in the external examination. There were abrasions and contusions on the right side of the face, although there were no skull fractures. To avoid confusion, here are some definitions: an abrasion is an injury caused by a grinding or rubbing away by friction; a laceration is a torn or ragged wound; and a contusion is an injury to tissue, without laceration.[25] There was a contusion of 3 × 2 inches on the right side of the chest, beneath the right nipple. I was surprised by this level of detail in the measurement of injuries, never having had any reason to read an autopsy report before. But after Leslie's death, we faced many situations that were foreign to me. There were eight contusions on the left lateral aspect of the abdomen and multiple superficial abrasions and lacerations on Leslie's lower back. Dr. Levy reported multiple rib fractures involving the left ribs, numbers 1 through 10. There were also fractures to the right ribs involving numbers 2 through 7.

Included in Dr. Levy's external examination were details of blunt force injuries to the extremities. Beginning with the right side of Leslie's body, there were multiple superficial injuries of both arms and legs. Contusions were numerous, including those found on the right shoulder, right upper arm, right forearm, and the right wrist. On the right hand, there were abrasions on the third and fourth fingers. Further injuries of the right extremities included abrasions of the thigh, right knee, the mid-portion of the calf, and a linear abrasion near the ankle. The left extremities sustained injuries as well. There were contusions on the upper arm, forearm, elbow, and the wrist. There was a contusion on the left thigh, near the groin. There were three other contusions on the left thigh. Additionally, there were five abrasions near the knee, as well as another abrasion on the anterior aspect of the left knee. It is important to remember that, prior to Leslie's interaction with four Chattanooga police officers, there is no evidence that he had any of those injuries. I continue to maintain that he was brutally beaten, without cause.

Dr. Levy noted that Leslie's skull was without fracture and that there were no abrasions, contusions, or lacerations on the scalp. There were no injuries to the tongue. I thought it was interesting that the larynx and trachea, related to the respiratory system for breathing, were noted as absent, thus unavailable for Dr. Levy to examine. To my knowledge, the location of those missing parts remains a mystery. When Dr. Levy examined the lungs, he noted that there were slight black pigment deposits. This was of no surprise to me, because Leslie was a smoker. As for the cardiovascular system, there were no noted abnormalities, and the cardiac values were noted as normal. Dr. Levy did not state that Leslie had an enlarged heart.

Dr. Levy provided detailed descriptions of his findings of the various body systems. The cardiovascular and respiratory systems were examined thoroughly, as well as the digestive and endocrine systems. His conclusive findings in examining those systems were reported as unremarkable. He further reported that, aside from the injuries noted in the external evaluation, the musculoskeletal system was also unremarkable.

According to Dr. Levy, the cause of death was cardiorespiratory arrest during violent struggle in the setting of an acute combined cocaine and ethanol intoxication. Dr. Levy was unable to conduct an independent toxicology analysis, because certain organs were placed in fluid, which would have voided any accuracy of lab tests. I asked the funeral director about this and was told that those organs were placed in the fluid to decrease odor. I believe there was another motive, but I had no proof. Dr. Levy concluded his report with a section titled "Summary of Case." In that section he mentioned that, although the wording of the cause-of-death statements (i.e., his and Dr. King's) were somewhat different, the opinions and conclusions were essentially indistinguishable. He further stated that deaths under similar circumstances are classically referred to as "excited delirium."

"Excited delirium" is used more often by police departments and medical examiners in an attempt to explain why some people suddenly die in police custody. It is a controversial diagnosis. However, I have seen no evidence whereby excited delirium could explain the broken bones and bruises on Leslie's body. It is important to note that excited delirium is not recognized by the American Medical Association or the American Psychological Association as a medical or mental health condition. It is used by police as a means of whitewashing excessive force and inappropriate use of control techniques by officers during an arrest.[26] Furthermore, according to Theresa Di Maio, author of *Excited Delirium Syndrome: Cause of Death and Prevention*, delirium is characterized by disorientation, a disorganized thought process, and disturbances in speech. When that mental state involves violent behavior, it is called excited delirium.[27] There is no mention of excited delirium in the final sentence of Dr. Levy's report. His written conclusion from his report is as follows: "While the ruling as to manner of death is best left to the responsible medical examiner, in this case I agree with the ruling of Dr. King in classifying this death as a homicide."

SUMMARY OF AUTOPSY FOLLOW-UP MEETING WITH DR. KING AND THE FAMILY

Our church pastor, also a Hamilton County commissioner at that time, was instrumental in helping us to get a meeting with Dr. King. On February 16, 2004, Dr. King agreed to meet with the family to discuss the outcome of his preliminary autopsy report. I can easily remember that date, because it was my birthday. I guess fate can be cruel sometimes, because that meeting was not a welcome birthday gift, and it certainly was not happy. Dr. King's assistant was also present. Dwight and I were joined at the Forensic Center by my aunt Louise; her sons, Spencer and Ronald, and Ronald's wife, Dollie; Dwight's sister, Terry; his brothers, Herman and Michael; and Michael's wife, Kathy.

Dr. King began the meeting with some prepared statements, some of which I determined to be propaganda. He said that he was independent and did not deal with political pressure, and that his first responsibility was to be open and honest with the family. He continued his statements by saying that he did not favor any group, including the police. According to his remarks, the media sometimes stirs up controversy, and that we should not believe everything we hear.

Because I was aware that there had been police officials present at Leslie's autopsy, I asked if that was a customary practice. Dr. King stated that he allows them to attend for training purposes. But according to verbal feedback from police officials, the persons present were veteran police officials with years of tenure with the Chattanooga Police Department. These were not junior officers in training. I also asked whether other individuals were allowed to be present during an autopsy. Dr. King responded, "That is at my discretion."

In that meeting, Dr. King reviewed his findings, page by page and tissue by tissue. His descriptions were very thorough and graphic. Although I wanted to run from the room, I just sat there with tears streaming down my face. As Dr. King talked, I could visualize every injury inflicted upon Leslie's body, feel his pain, and hear his screams. It was as though I was an eyewitness to his homicide.

CONFLICTING INFORMATION, UNANSWERED DISCREPANCIES, AND REMAINING QUESTIONS

The report submitted by the Office of the Hamilton County Medical Examiner said that the decedent collapsed after a fight with the police. Based on eyewitness reports and police testimony, Leslie did not fight with the police. He was still breathing and trying to move his head to the side, while already facedown on the ground, with hands double-cuffed behind his back and police officers on his body. This description is clearly very different from his being involved in a fight and collapsing.

That same report from the county medical examiner stated that Leslie expired in the emergency room. Another document completed by Erlanger Hospital personnel reported that Leslie was dead on arrival (DOA), which would be consistent with eyewitness reports. People at the scene stated that Leslie was dead when his body was removed from Central Avenue. With a DOA assessment, why did the hospital medical providers hook him up to life support? Subsequently, why did they take him off life support without permission from family members? It was always my understanding that once a patient was put on life support, family members would be involved in the decision to remove that support. In a private meeting that Dwight and I had with two police detectives on January 12, 2004, the detective supervisor in charge of the investigation admitted that Leslie died at the scene. That admission was consistent with eyewitness reports.

MEETING WITH POLICE DETECTIVES IN CHARGE OF THE INVESTIGATION

I will refer to these detectives as Detectives One and Two, with Detective One being the supervisor. During the first week of Leslie's death, Detective Two requested to meet with us at the Police Services Center. We rejected his initial suggested day and time for the meeting because we were too busy. We had a son to bury. We were also not eager to participate in what we believed to be their cover-up activities. We did agree for a meeting at a later date.

Detective One facilitated the meeting. He began by stating that our first meeting with the police had turned out to be more of a public meeting than a family meeting, as they had requested. We told him that everyone in that first meeting was a family member except our pastor. We further explained that maybe he had a different concept of family. We reminded him that this meeting was requested by the department. Detective One then stated that the meeting with the family was a courtesy. As you might imagine, this angered us. I quickly responded that I disagreed, that it was not a courtesy; it was their responsibility to meet with the family. I think it is accurate to state that, beginning at that point, the meeting did not go well. There was no foul language, but it was certainly not cordial. We were angry and, in my opinion, Detective One was arrogant and rude.

After only a few minutes with the detectives, Dwight and I determined that it was a mistake to meet with them, and the discussion was definitely a waste of our valuable time. They started the conversation by telling us that they had talked to a number of people to try to determine what Leslie's day was like. It was interesting that they seemed to have no interest in talking with Leslie's brother and sister-in-law, who had been with him at the beginning of his day, prior to their leaving Chattanooga for their drive back to Chicago. Who did he see that day? Who did he talk to that day? Where did he go that day? Those were the type of questions for which they had been seeking answers. It was immediately clear to us that they were trying to build a case against Leslie.

Their investigation, as they called it, was a waste of taxpayer dollars and an insult to us. I was totally amazed, and I could not see how any of their actions or concerns addressed the fact that Leslie had died after their officers had manhandled him. All of the things they reported to us had no relationship to his death. The people they had talked to or who had talked to Leslie or seen him earlier on the Friday of his death were not the persons who killed him. His homicide was not caused by conversations. According to the detectives, they had talked to several people on Martin Luther King Boulevard, which was near where Leslie had died. None of those people had any connection to Leslie's death. There was no mention that they had spoken to the police officers who had been at the scene. In fact, I said to them, "You are acting as though there is some unknown killer on the loose, like Jack the Ripper or something. That is not the case. We know who killed Leslie." We wanted to know what they were doing to work toward justice for Leslie and mandate accountability of those responsible for his murder. Getting that answer was the only reason we had agreed to meet with the detectives that week, which was, obviously, still a very busy and stressful time for us.

Detective One started talking about the autopsy. We didn't mention any of the things that Dr. King had told us. We let him talk as much as he wanted. Because he was in the room when the autopsy was being done, we believed that he might give us some critical information that we had not already heard. Interestingly, he avoided mentioning the injuries that were very traumatic to the body. In fact, he made some false statements. Here are some of the statements he made: there was hemorrhaging in the right eye; abrasions to the body; no broken bones; minor abrasions were on the back; there were three to ten rib fractures on each side, but no hemorrhaging to the ribs; rib injuries could be caused by the fall; no neck compression; there was an enlarged heart, but no heart damage; he was diabetic; no external or internal damage to organs; and there was no trauma to the body. One would have to wonder how he would have described injuries to a body as a result of trauma.

For this meeting, Dwight and I had agreed that I would be the primary spokesperson and he would take the notes. The following summary is taken from his written documentation.

Loretta: I noticed that the newspaper reported that Leslie had ten DUI arrests. I believe this to be false. We would like to see those arrest reports.

Detective One: There weren't ten DUI arrests. We found records of only two. They can't be released until the investigation is complete.

Loretta: Why wasn't a Taser used instead of physical contact?

Detective One: The pepper spray did not affect him. There was no Taser available.

Loretta: Why are you interested in tracking his day? We are concerned about the time period of the incident and his death.

No reply.

Loretta: Why is there erroneous information about this incident put in the paper?

Detective One: I am working on my thirtieth year. I do not read the papers. So much is out there. I don't know what was put in the paper.

Loretta: Leslie did not weigh 300 pounds. He weighed approximately 232 pounds. Where did you get the 300 pounds?

Detective One: We made a mistake. We did not weigh him.
[Note: This was a strange answer because Detective One was at the autopsy. He had previously stated, during the meeting on January 5, 2004, that he knew Leslie's weight.]

Dwight: Did our son have a pulse after he stopped moving?

Detective One: He did not have a pulse.

Dwight: Are you saying that he was flat-lined at the scene?

Detective One: He was flat-lined at the scene.

Loretta: Is it customary for the mayor to show up on the scene of an incident?

Detective One: Yes, he often goes to the scene when arrests are made.

Loretta: How can this be, because if he did that with routine arrests, how would he have time to be the mayor? Arrests are happening all the time and all over the city simultaneously.

Detective One: I don't keep the mayor's schedule.
[Note: At that time, the mayor of Chattanooga was Bob Corker, who is a current US senator.]

Loretta: Are you concerned about how the police are perceived by the public with all of these deaths?

Detective One: I don' care about public relations or their perception of the police.

Loretta: It is open season on black men. Can we get a copy of the training curriculum at the Police Academy?

Detective One: I can't get that for you, but you can contact the training department, if you want to know more about the training.

Loretta: Why does it seem that police are judged at different standards than others?

Detective One: Police have killed men and they go to jail. There are many police in jail.

Loretta: I use to have a lot of respect for the police and was instrumental in getting the DARE (Drug Abuse Resistance Education) program started in Chattanooga. I wanted youth to have a positive interaction with police. That was when I directed the Drug Free Schools Program. Police are drunk with power.

Loretta: I question the strategy of the point system used in the Chattanooga Police Department. The system is only going to make things worse because police will lie on citizens just so they can get points to earn a day off. Killing citizens seems to be better than the point system, because they can immediately get a week's vacation with pay.
[Note: The point system allowed police officers to earn points based on the number of arrests made. When they reach a specified number of points, they can earn a paid day off.]

Dwight: Are the police officers back on the beat?

Detective One: I don't know.

Dwight and Loretta: What about the release of Leslie's property?

Detective Two: We have a list that has items on it that we are releasing.

Dwight: What is the situation with his cell phone? I thought you told us that you did not have his cell phone. We have asked about this several times.

Detective Two: They found it the other night wedged down under the emergency brake.

Detective One: Do you know why Leslie pulled his clothes off?

Loretta: No, if he had not been killed, he could tell us.
[Note: We did not prompt Detective One for his next statement, but he made it anyway. Notice what he says about drugs in Leslie's system (this was prior to any official toxicology report).]

Detective One: I think he had drugs in his system. My nephew, my sister's son in Memphis, died when he was sixteen. He was using drugs. Cocaine makes you feel real hot and he took off his clothes. Some friends were trying to restrain him and he ended up dying. So, I know how you feel.

Loretta: Have you had a son killed by the police?

Detective One: No.

Loretta: Then you don't know how we feel.

In retrospect, it was a very interesting meeting, with them mostly telling us what they found out about Leslie's day prior to his death and to deflect guilt from those police officers. Dwight and I both thought that this was strange because Leslie was not the victim of some unknown killer on the loose, as I stated previously. It seemed to me that they had no interest in conducting an impartial, objective investigation. From my knowledge of these types of situations, it is common practice for the police to re-victimize the victim. They spend time looking for anything bad that they can use to disqualify the victim as a human being, deserving of life. When Detective One talked about his nephew, I think he was trying to make us believe that his nephew's circumstances mirrored those of Leslie. Dwight immediately responded that he didn't see why Detective One was talking about his relative's death, because the circumstances had nothing to do with the investigation into Leslie's death that they were assigned to conduct. From Detective One's description of his nephew's death, I don't believe that his nephew had multiple broken bones and bruises. His nephew was not the victim of aggressive police tactics, including actions making it impossible for any human to breathe.

I also remember that Detective One tried to intimidate us, but Dwight didn't note what he said. Dwight was quickly angered and made it clear to both detectives that we were not intimidated by them. We believed that police officers were responsible for Leslie's death and they should be working from that premise, not that Leslie's death was due to some unknown occurrence, without explanation. In a further display of his arrogance, Detective One reiterated that they did not have to meet with us, as though they were doing us a favor. Our immediate response was that they asked for this meeting; we did not.

Based on the dynamics of that meeting, we were even more convinced that a cover-up was in progress. The meeting did not end cordially. Prior to leaving the room, I stated that they should not call us anymore that week, because we had a child to bury and would not return to the Police Services Center that week. After that meeting, we had a dreaded appointment at the cemetery. For me and Dwight, all of our energy from that point forward that week was consumed with Leslie's funeral and burial.

There were a few other interesting dynamics that occurred on that same day of meeting with those two detectives. Prior to meeting with them, I had a telephone conversation with Detective Two. I asked him, "When could we get Leslie's clothes?" He stated that they were holding his clothes as evidence that Leslie was nude when the police arrived. That didn't make any sense to me, and I told him so. I said, "We have never challenged the fact that Leslie was unclothed when the police arrived." I stressed that because his body was nude during two autopsies and his body was not clothed while being embalmed, I failed to see how their keeping his clothes would be necessary for their investigation. There was a pause; he seemed not to know how to respond. Finally, he said that he would have to discuss it with his supervisor. He called me back and told me that they would release the clothing to us when we came out to the Police Services Center later that day.

Then there was the matter of what to do with Leslie's car. Dwight and I had already discussed the car, which was a stick shift and an older model vehicle than either of us drove. We knew that Leslie had the car for only a short period and had not finished paying for it. Neither Dwight nor our younger son Stefan, nor I, had any use for the car. As you might imagine, the matter of the car was of little concern to us. Our major issue was dealing with our anger. Police department officers had killed Leslie and, in our opinion, the department was already showing signs of a cover-up. Also, we sensed no indication from any police officials that they were sympathetic or cared, in any way, about what we were experiencing or that Leslie was dead. Our feeling, in regard to the car, was that we did not authorize them to take the car, so we had no responsibility for it.

During the telephone conversation prior to the meeting, Detective Two had said, "You all will have to come and get the car. We have it on the back lot, but we need our space on the lot. If you don't get it, we will have it towed, and you will have to pay the towing fee and storage cost to get the car." His tone was very cold, rude, and arrogant, with no sensitivity to the fact that we were parents still in shock from the trauma of losing a son. My first statement to him was "We are not prepared to take the car today." Then I immediately reflected on his arrogant attitude and quickly followed up with a second statement. I said, "We don't need or want the car; you can give it back to the car dealer for all we care; we don't want it." I could tell that he was shocked by my response, because his first verbal reaction was "Uh, uh, uh." He then stated that he would have to check on that, because they had never had this type of situation before, in which a family refused to take possession of the car. I believe that incident was just one of many in which our family's interactions with them were different from prior experiences with other families in their numerous in-custody death cases. We were determined that we would not respond to the bullying practices that had probably worked so well for them in the past. Even today, thirteen years later, I have no idea what they did with the car. Even though Detective Two had threatened us, we have never been billed for any expenses related to the car.

To retrieve Leslie's belongings, we had to go to a location down the street from where the meeting was held. Detective Two met us there. When we arrived at that location, I noticed Leslie's car on the lot. I asked to examine the car. Detective Two said that he could take me to the car but that it was completely empty because they had removed everything. I insisted that I still wanted to go out to the car. I guess it was just an emotional thing. I knew that the driver's seat was the last place that Leslie had sat. In my mind, I felt that I would be able to somehow feel his presence. So, Dwight went into the building to get Leslie's other belongings and Detective Two and I went out to the car. To my amazement, there was a cassette tape placed on the driver's seat. The tape was from the music group the Police, titled "Every Breath You Take." At first, I was speechless when I picked up the tape and read the title. Then I showed it to Detective Two and said, "This is exactly how Leslie died. The police took his breath away." He made no comment.

I still have that cassette tape. I have two feelings about that incident. One is that police officers were mocking Leslie's death. It was as though they were saying to us, "Yes, we killed him and there is nothing you can do about it." The other thing I felt is that, somehow, Leslie was confirming how they killed him. Even after death, he was speaking to me to let me know how he died. I now understand when people say that chills ran through their body. That is what I experienced. Even Detective Two appeared to be shocked that the tape was left on the seat, in a position in which we could not have avoided seeing it. I think the detective actually believed the car was empty. The tape was left there for us to see, because no one knew that we would refuse to take possession of Leslie's car. That incident was just another example of the cruelty of some of "Chattanooga's finest."

After viewing the car, the detective and I joined Dwight inside the building, as he was waiting for Leslie's other belongings. The property staff brought out several bags to give us. We signed for them and left the building. From those bags, there was only one clothing item that we retrieved: a baseball cap that Stefan had given Leslie as a Christmas gift. Leslie loved baseball caps, and he wore this particular cap on the day of his death. The last memory that Stefan has of his brother is Leslie wearing this cap, as he was waving good-bye to him. Stefan wanted the cap buried with Leslie. We discussed this with the funeral director, who complied. Immediately before the final closing of the casket, that ball cap was placed inside.

The Chattanooga Police Department continued to regard Leslie's death as a mystery, even after two medical examiners, after completing detailed autopsies, independent of each other, concluded that Leslie's death was a homicide. Furthermore, in 2004, there were sixteen homicides in Chattanooga, and Leslie's death on January 2 was listed as the first for that year.[28] I feel that I am among countless numbers of mothers who are suffering because of the murder of an unarmed son or daughter.

SUMMARIES OF SELECTED OTHER ACCOUNTS OF HOW LESLIE VAUGHN PRATER DIED

There were eyewitnesses to Leslie's homicide. We have not spoken to everyone who saw Leslie take his last breath. I will share the accounts of two eyewitnesses who volunteered to speak with us. I will refer to them as Witness One and Witness Two. Many Chattanooga residents fear potential harassment, or even worse, from the police. People often supported us in secret ways, by sending cards of encouragement or telephoning us; approaching us with kind words at church, in a restaurant, or at the mall; or contributing money to help us fight for justice, but they would not come out publicly when we held a rally or a march. Unlike us, they still lived in Chattanooga and feared repercussions. In one instance, a former high school classmate told me that she thought it was awful what those officers had done to our son, but she couldn't come to our march because she worked for the city and feared the loss of her job. Unfortunately, gone are the days of courage like that of the people who participated in the Montgomery bus boycott. Most people don't get intimately involved in these controversial issues until it directly impacts them, or unless there is a dynamic leader who can inspire and motivate people to action, as the late Dr. Martin Luther King Jr. did. But after fifty-three years, there seems to be a resurgence of another civil rights movement, which began in 2014. The homicides of unarmed Michael Brown in Ferguson, Missouri, and Eric Garner in New York,[29] followed by release of the movie *Selma*,[30] ignited a new social justice call to action.

Witness One initiated the conversation with us. Weeks after Leslie's death, Dwight and I were walking around the crime scene. A woman called out to us and asked if we were Leslie's parents. Possibly she had seen us on television after his death. We affirmed that we were his parents. She asked if we would come up to her apartment, because she wanted to talk with us. She lived in an upstairs apartment in the building next to the alley where Leslie died. According to Witness One, she saw him drive into the area, get out of his vehicle, and take off his clothes. She called the police, because she felt the man needed help. She stated that she regretted calling them. She said, "I didn't know they would come and kill him." Also, she was surprised later to realize that she knew Leslie. She didn't recognize him that night, because it was dark.

When the first officer who interacted with Leslie arrived, Witness One noticed that the officer was talking to Leslie and the two of them started walking toward his car. When other officers arrived, Leslie was surrounded by them, and immediately the physical contact began. Leslie was taken to the ground. She was on her back porch at that time but went back into the house to attend to her crying baby. When she came back out on the porch, there were officers next to her building involved in a discussion. She said that they seemed nervous and were talking about what they were going to do. She overheard them state that the man was dead. She also noted that a lot of people had gathered to see what was happening. She suspected that many of them were probably from neighboring houses and apartments. Also, a funeral home across the street was hosting a viewing. She believed that some of the onlookers were funeral home staff and people attending the family hour. Witness One told us that the police had interviewed her. During that interview, they kept trying to get her to say that she feared for her life and that of her baby when she saw Leslie. She said that she refused to say that because she didn't feel threatened at all but only wanted to get help for Leslie.

Witness Two contacted us through a mutual friend. As fate would have it, I actually knew this person. According to our mutual friend, he wanted to tell us what he saw, but he didn't want people to know that he met with us. He also feared losing his job. He gave the friend a number for us to contact him. We followed up with that information. We met with him on the afternoon of February 16, 2004, in a Sunday School classroom of a local church. He witnessed the beating of Leslie and saw Leslie take his last breath. He saw an officer kicking him, while others were holding him down. I asked him if Leslie said anything. Witness Two was the one who told me that Leslie said, "It's not over."

Dwight took notes to document our discussion with Witness Two. The following are excerpts from those notes that include our questions and the response of the witness:

Question: What did you observe when you got on the scene that night? Where was our son at that time?

Response: When I arrived on the scene, I noticed that there were four officers who had him on the ground and he was groaning and moaning. There were two officers on each side of him. They were pinning him down with their knees. Your son was facedown and his hands were handcuffed behind his back. The black officer was down near his legs.

Question: What else did you observe on this night?

Response: The policemen kept their knees in his back until he stopped moving. I do believe your son would have been alive today if they had let him get up after they handcuffed him, but they kept him facedown on the ground. There was a fifth officer that walked up onto the scene and put his foot on the back of your son's neck or shoulder. After doing this, he then walked back toward the police cars.

Question: Do you know who he was or his rank? Did you see his car?

Response: No, I didn't know his name or rank. His car was parked farther down the road.

Question: Were there any police vehicles near our son?

Response: There were approximately nine cars in the area. An officer who works the Alton Park area drove one of the cars. There was a car, I believe #135, that was parked on the street. Another car that was driven by a police sergeant (car #303) was parked near the scene.

Question: What was the sergeant from car #303 doing?

Response: I noticed several things about this person. First of all, he went to his car and got a stun gun. He walked toward the scene

and he turned and went back to the car. He put the stun gun back in the vehicle.

Question: How do you know it was a stun gun?

Response: I knew what it was when he was walking toward your son. He was testing it and I could see the arc.

Question: We were told that no one had a Taser on the scene.

Response: I am telling you what I saw.

Question: Did you happen to see the name of this police sergeant?

Response: No, I didn't get a chance to see his name, but I remember car #303.

Question: You mentioned some other things you noticed about the sergeant. Please tell us the rest.

Response: After he had put the stun gun back into the vehicle, he went to the trunk of the car and pulled out something white. I don't know if this item was pants or a blanket. He closed the trunk and walked toward the scene; then he turned around and went back to the car and placed the item back into the trunk. This same sergeant later came over to the funeral home and asked if they had a sheet.

Question: Did this seem strange to you? Did it seem strange that he would put things back into the vehicle without using them?

Response: It did seem a bit odd.

Question: Was there anything else you noticed about the sergeant's actions?

Response: After he put the white item back into the trunk, he got a defibrillator out and walked toward your son. He then turned around and put it back into the vehicle. [Comment: One doesn't need to use a defibrillator on a dead person, further supporting statements that Leslie died at the scene.]

Question: Did these actions seem odd?

Response: They were unusual.

Question: We have asked the police if there were any cars on the scene that had police cameras. We were told that they were all older vehicles and didn't have such equipment. Can you describe the cars that you saw on the scene?

Response: The cars I saw looked like new vehicles, including car #303.

Question: Do you remember approximately the time frame between when you noticed my son on the ground and when the emergency vehicle arrived?

Response: It was approximately fifteen to twenty minutes before the emergency vehicle arrived.

The meeting with this witness further confirmed our belief that Leslie was not fighting with the police; that they could have allowed him to breathe, especially after they had handcuffed him; and that Leslie died at the scene. Once a person is handcuffed, he or she is considered in custody. When we later confronted police officials with having misled us in saying that all of the cars were older and without cameras, we were told that, yes, there was a car equipped with a camera, but there was no tape in the camera.

The last account I will share is a summary of the deposition given by one of the four officers involved in the physical altercation with Leslie. A deposition is a written testimony taken under oath. It is a public court record, made available through the Freedom of Information Act. I will refer to him as Officer One, because he was identified as the first officer to have direct contact with Leslie and the only one to give a deposition. There were plans to depose all four, but the case was settled prior to the scheduling of the other three officers.

Because Officer One completed a deposition, I am more aware of his personal profile than that of the others. I will share what has been documented in public files about the other three officers. All of the officers were white, except for one African American. One of the other officers was thirty-two years old and hired on March 22, 1996. He had a law enforcement background as a US Marine military police officer. The African American officer was a forty-three-year-old Chattanooga native. He had law enforcement experience with the Tennessee Department of Corrections. Previously, he had been charged with aggravated assault, after surprising a burglar. He was hired on February 2, 1998.

The youngest of the four officers was twenty-three years old and also a native of Chattanooga. He was hired on July 26, 2002, with no law enforcement experience.[31]

According to Officer One, the two youngest officers were friends and arrived on the scene together. They went through the police academy together and were hired by the Chattanooga Police Department on the same date. It is interesting that another white academy classmate of theirs, with no direct relationship to our case, was involved in a case in which he shot and killed an unarmed African American male. While going to get a sandwich during his lunch break, John Eric Henderson was stopped because of a malfunctioning muffler, a routine traffic stop. Officer Christopher Gaynor, a rookie police officer completing only four days of unsupervised patrol, asked Mr. Henderson to get his registration information from his glove compartment. Mr. Henderson complied but was killed anyway because the officer stated that he thought he saw a gun in the glove compartment. In addition to the registration, there was only a bottle of cologne in the glove compartment.[32] One has to wonder about the quality of the training received by that cohort of cadets.

Officer One was twenty-nine years old with no prior law enforcement experience. He joined the Chattanooga Police Department about eighteen months before Leslie's death in January 2004. This particular officer was selected to be the first of the four directly involved in Leslie's homicide to give a deposition. Attorney Nick Brustin, one of the New York attorneys, stated to us that he sensed that this particular officer would be most likely to tell the truth. Mr. Brustin had a lot of insight, wisdom, and experience from his involvement with some high-profile social justice cases, including the Abner Louima case in New York.[33]

The summary of the deposition from Officer One was from his statements taken on February 8, 2006, at the offices of the Wilson Reporting Agency. Dwight and I traveled to Chattanooga to sit in on the deposition. Others present were our attorneys (Chattanooga and New York representatives), the Chattanooga city attorneys, and a court reporter. Although Dwight and I were allowed to sit in on the proceedings, we were strictly instructed that we could not ask any questions or make any comments. We were told to remain silent. If we did not comply, we would be asked to leave the room.

The deposition of Officer One, the first he had ever given in his brief career, was recorded using machine shorthand and later produced in a typewritten document of 313 pages. I will only summarize excerpts from the document that are pertinent to this chapter in explaining how Leslie died, and related events of that night. In some instances, I added comments that I have put in bold print. The excerpts are in the order that the statements were given, but not necessarily in any other order, such as when certain actions occurred. In some instances, the same question was asked more than once, but in a different way. The session, led by our attorney Nick Brustin, began with general instructions to clarify the process. Also, based on a question asked by Mr. Brustin and Officer One's response, it was clear that the officer understood that the city would pay for any damages against him if he were found liable in this case. Nick Brustin asked all of the questions.

Officer One was a high school and community college graduate, with an associate's degree in aviation management. He expressed that he had started to pursue a degree in electrical engineering and would like to continue that in the future. He had completed the police academy training, which was his only law enforcement credential for his current position. It was interesting that he stated that he joined the police department because he had always been interested in that, although he chose to get his two-year degree in another discipline. I wondered why he did not choose to get an associate's degree in criminal justice, but I could not ask any questions. He admitted that his wife's sister was married to the son of a high-ranking official in the Chattanooga Police Department. Maybe that was a factor in his joining the force. I have the impression that, within the law enforcement and justice system communities, there is an unusual amount of nepotism.

Before joining the police force, his job experience included working in a grocery store seafood department; moving furniture for a moving company; working for an aviation company and training for airline refueling; working at the YMCA to spot for those lifting weights and signing out cardio equipment in the fitness center; and working as a student engineer for the Tennessee Valley Authority. He stated that, within the department, he is known as someone who is into physical conditioning. He was six feet, four inches, and weighed 261 pounds in 2006, which was larger in size than Leslie. At the time of Leslie's death, he stated that he believed he weighed in the range of 240–250 pounds, which was still larger than Leslie.

I'm addressing the matter of education, training, and work experience because lack of appropriate training is often an issue in physical interactions between police officers and the public. Also, research has reported that the more education an officer has in criminal justice courses, the less likely he or she is to resort to needless aggressive behavior when dealing with confrontation. According to researchers Rydberg and Terrill, higher education carries no influence over the probability of an arrest or search occurring in an interaction with police and suspects, but does significantly reduce the occurrence of force.[34] It seems likely that reducing the occurrence of force would also reduce the occurrence of death when unarmed citizens are confronted by the police.

During the early phase of the deposition, Mr. Brustin asked a question to clarify a policy in regard to the use of Tasers. Officer One stated that Tasers were not only to be used by sergeants. His response would lead one to conclude that other officers could use Tasers as well. This was different from what police administrators said to us in a prior conversation, just another of the many contradictory statements from Chattanooga Police Department personnel.

Following is a summary of the testimony from the deposition of Officer One while under oath. For the following items 1–32, statements in bold print represent comments I added for further clarification or as reactions to statements:

1. When Leslie was taken away from the scene, he was not breathing.
2. When the use-of-force report was filled out, the four officers involved were in a conference room, without anyone else present. Officer One filled out the report, after they had all discussed what they wanted to put on it. This was the first use-of-force report that he had ever filled out, although there were two other officers there with many more years of experience as police officers. Officer One admitted that he was concerned about this being his first report in a case in which a civilian had died.
3. When they went to the Police Services Center to discuss and fill out the report, they knew that Leslie was dead. Before he signed the report, each of the other officers read it. After there was agreement from all, he signed the report.

4. It was the understanding of Officer One that they were following departmental policy when only one use-of-force report was filled out, rather than four separate reports completed independently and without collaboration among the officers. No supervisor had told the officers that they should not meet together and no supervisor was in the room when the use-of-force report was being completed.

5. Because Leslie had died, Officer One knew that there would be a full Internal Affairs investigation and that he could be seriously disciplined if the investigation outcome reported that excessive force was used. He admitted that he knew he could potentially be fired or criminally prosecuted, or both.

6. Officer One admitted to using the word "nigger" in a joke and had also heard another officer using a racial epithet like "nigger."

7. Officer One admitted knowing that all of the officers involved in Leslie's death had been exonerated, based on a memo from the deputy chief. The memo further stated that the officers were to be commended on their personal restraint and obvious compassion when dealing with the suspect. **I am still unsure which of the officers' actions were displays of compassion. Maybe it was because they did not leave Leslie's body on the pavement for hours, as the police officers did with the body of Michael Brown in Ferguson, Missouri.[35] I wish they had shown compassion by not killing him.**

8. Officer One admitted that no officer suffered any injury in connection with the interaction with Leslie, not even any bruises. **This admission is consistent with eyewitness testimonies; statements from the medical examiner, Dr. King; and my belief that Leslie caused no harm to the officers. I believe Leslie's movements were made in an effort to breathe.**

9. Officer One admitted that his father had sent an e-mail to us. **I received that e-mail, which I consider to have been very nasty and was meant to cause us even more emotional pain. The e-mail labeled me as a terrible mother.**

10. When the first two officers arrived on the scene, Leslie was standing, not running and screaming, as some had reported in error. When Leslie was taken to the ground, the struggle occurred in one location. **Leslie was taken to the ground after the two**

older officers arrived, with the thirty-two-year-old officer leading the charge.

11. **According to the police report, Leslie was handcuffed at 18:58.30 (6:58 p.m.). At the moment he was handcuffed (double-handcuffed and tight enough to cause bruising), he was considered officially in custody.** Officer One stated that Leslie could not be officially in custody until he was handcuffed, although he wasn't sure if they were planning to arrest him or just contain him until the ambulance arrived.

12. At 18:57.09 Officer One called in a fight. He made the call because he was the only one with hands free, as two other officers were taking Leslie to the ground. At 18:58.37, after Leslie was handcuffed, Officer One canceled the call for anybody else en route. He felt that he didn't need any additional assistance. At 18:59, Officer One stated that the party was in custody. **My question is "Why didn't they put Leslie on his feet at that time, or at least turn him over or turn his head to the side?"**

13. When Officer One was dealing with Leslie, he knew he could have charged Leslie with the misdemeanor of indecent exposure. It was clearly evident that Leslie was naked. After reports later identified Leslie as intoxicated, he could have also been guilty of the misdemeanor of public intoxication. **In my opinion, these misdemeanors do not warrant a death penalty sentence.**

14. Officer One stated that during his twenty-six weeks of the police academy, he did not recall any training that restraints and take downs were high-risk tasks. He also admitted that, to his knowledge, there were no policies in the Chattanooga Police Department that dealt with how to handle emotionally disturbed or potentially emotionally disturbed persons.

15. **Nick Brustin pressed him on this training issue.** Officer One stated that if someone is in an emotional state, you handcuff the person and make sure that there is no danger to the officers, the citizen, and the general public. He did admit that he had no idea of what the policy actually said.

16. Attorney Brustin asked Officer One if the written policy was going to state that you restrain emotionally disturbed persons

as soon as possible. The officer responded, "I told you I don't know."

17. Officer One described Leslie as acting disoriented and said that he was naked, but he did not know if Leslie was under the influence of drugs and alcohol that might affect their interaction. He did say that Leslie told him that he was diabetic.

18. Officer One stated that if there was any training or guidance on how to communicate with someone who may be emotionally disturbed, he could not remember any such training. He also stated that he did not recall any departmental policies that specifically discussed interacting with emotionally disturbed persons. **I might mention that this obvious training deficiency is scary, especially considering that one in sixty-eight children is diagnosed with autism. According to the Center for Disease Control (CDC), this number is increasing.**[36] **I'm not suggesting that Leslie was autistic, but there is a potentially tragic outcome for an individual diagnosed with autism spectrum disorder when confronted with an ill-prepared police officer. That is simply a dangerous combination. As an example, the person may be unable to cognitively process an order, such as "put up your hands." Not obeying an officer's command can lead to death, even for unarmed citizens.**

19. Officer One was unaware of any training that stated that when someone is disoriented, it is important that only one person speak to that person.

20. Officer One had begun to establish rapport with Leslie and, based on directions from the officer, he and Leslie were walking toward Leslie's car to retrieve his clothes. As they began to walk toward the car, Leslie asked for a light to see how to avoid some glass that was in the area, because he had cut his foot on some glass in the gravel. This seemed reasonable to Officer One, according to his statement. During the time of their dialogue, he had not made a decision as to whether he was going to arrest Leslie. Officer One also stated that he felt safe with Leslie.

21. While Leslie and Officer One were talking with each other, there was nothing that prohibited his partner from going to Leslie's car

to secure the vehicle, since Leslie did not have his car keys on his person. **This is an important point because one of the later excuses given for "taking Leslie down" was that they were afraid that he was going to get in his car and drive away.** However, Officer One admitted that Leslie never said anything about driving the car.

22. While Leslie was walking toward the car voluntarily, the thirty-two-year-old officer arrived. Officer One was still assessing the situation and, as stated previously, had not made the decision to arrest Leslie. At that point, he stated that he was trying to help Leslie. Leslie was cooperating with Officer One and following his directions. Leslie was voluntarily walking with Officer One toward his car to retrieve and put on his clothes.

23. Based on Officer One's testimony, the dynamics of the situation immediately changed upon the arrival of the thirty-two-year-old officer. Without asking any questions of the first officers on the scene regarding the assessment of the situation, the first words spoken by the thirty-two-year-old officer to Leslie and from a distance were "Put your hands behind your back." When he made that statement, Officer One understood that to mean that they were going to handcuff Leslie, although he had not decided to even arrest Leslie and Leslie was cooperating. **I stress this point of cooperation because people often state that citizens should do exactly as they are told by the police. In Leslie's situation, even when there is compliance of an unarmed citizen, death could still be the result. Leslie had been told to accompany Officer One to his car to get his clothes to put on, which he was in the process of doing. Now, this other officer was saying "Put your hands behind your back," which was a statement in conflict with following the order of Officer One.**

24. Officer One admitted that up to the point when the other officer asked Leslie to put his hands behind his back, there was no specific training that Officer One had received in how to handle that situation. He did not recall having received any specific training on how to deal with someone who is disoriented, whether they were emotionally disturbed or under the influence of drugs or

alcohol. Prior to the arrival of the thirty-two-year-old officer, Officer One stated that he was talking to Leslie in a calm manner to de-escalate the situation and gain compliance. **That strategy was working, before the thirty-two-year-old officer, with the military background, arrived.**

25. When the officer shouted to Leslie to put his hands behind his back, Leslie was still walking voluntarily toward his car with Officer One, as he had been instructed. At that point, the thirty-two-year-old officer led the charge to take Leslie "down," using an arm bar technique, because Leslie had not put his hands behind his back. This was at 18:46, or 6:46 p.m. EST. **This "take down" was the first step that led to Leslie's death from positional asphyxiation.**[37]

26. Movements by Leslie were in an effort to try to pull himself up and away from the officers, while being held facedown. This was stated by Officer One, who also admitted that Leslie made no aggressive movements toward the officers. **It was documented in the deposition that none of the officers sustained any injuries.**

27. While Leslie was cuffed and facedown, Officer One put his weight on the back of Leslie's legs and shot mace in Leslie's face, although he admitted to not remembering, from his training, the appropriate timing of a shot of mace. In addition to him, two other officers were applying pressure to Leslie's body, using their arms and knees. They were joined by the African American officer. The manner in which they held Leslie down resulted in pressure on his back, shoulder, chest, and arms. According to Officer One, Leslie was trying to roll over and was yelling and screaming at that time. His yelling began at the point of being sprayed with mace. **One could only imagine the physical pain he must have been experiencing. When our family met with the medical examiner, Dr. King, he told us that, because of the injuries to Leslie's body, he suffered a lot of pain prior to his death. This knowledge still haunts me, as it would most parents. As previously stated, it is as though I can still feel his pain, even thirteen years after his death.**

28. The African American officer joined the restraint sequence and, along with the thirty-two-year-old officer, they crossed Leslie's

ankles and pushed his legs towards his buttocks and held him in that position for a period of time. **This is the deadly and illegal hog-tie restraint technique that is even against the policy of the Chattanooga Police Department. So, they went against their own department's policy.** While they were using the hog-tie restraint, Officer One was putting pressure on the right side of Leslie's body and his partner was on the left side. **Leslie had already been handcuffed and maced once at that time, and was still lying facedown. During the deposition session, Officer One admitted that he had never heard of the "hog tie" restraint. It wasn't taught at the academy.** After Nick Brustin described the hog-tie position, Officer One stated that he had only associated the description of the position with techniques used at a rodeo, but not with police work. He didn't know that the use of the hog-tie could lead to somebody dying. Officer One stated that if he had been trained, he would not have done that.

29. According to Officer One, Leslie had exhibited no active resistance until he was facedown in the grass, on his stomach and chest. According to documentation and Officer One's testimony, Leslie was maced and handcuffed at 6:58.30 p.m. Later, he was maced again by Officer One and once by his partner, for a total of three times, **which further compromised Leslie's ability to breathe.** Officer One couldn't remember if he received training that it was appropriate for two people to use mace against one individual, or if it was appropriate to do three half-second to second shots of mace into one person's face in a short period of time. He stated that the only thing he could remember from training is that if the person was still noncompliant, you could continue to use the mace if needed. **I must mention here that during our first conversation, with the police chief, he told us that there was no pepper spray used. That was just another one of the many lies, or alternative facts, communicated to us by police officials in this case.**

30. Leslie was held down for about eleven minutes, until the officers decided that Leslie was, in the words of Officer One, compliant. When Leslie was turned over at 7:08.47, it was noticed that he

wasn't breathing. **In this case, the word "compliant" was the same as "deceased." The manner in which Leslie's body was positioned and held is consistent with the conclusion by two medical examiners that positional asphyxia was the cause of death.**

31. **Of note is that Officer One admitted that he had never received any training about positional asphyxia. In fact, prior to our case, he had never heard of it.** He did not recall any training that there was a particular danger of someone dying from positional asphyxia when they were maintained in a face-down position, while rear handcuffed and after being maced. According to Officer One, if he had known about positional asphyxia, he would not have employed a practice that could lead to someone dying. **During the session, Nick Brustin showed the video *Positional Asphyxia, NYPD Training Division*. The video clearly demonstrated that as soon as persons are handcuffed, officers are supposed to get them off of their stomach.** Officer One stated that he had never seen the video.

32. Attorney Brustin asked Officer One a series of questions related to the injuries to Leslie's body, in which Officer One constantly replied, "I don't know." He didn't know how Leslie got twenty-one fractures on sixteen of his ribs. He didn't know why there was severe bruising to Leslie's scrotum, **although an eyewitness reported seeing an officer kick Leslie in the scrotum.** Officer One stated that he didn't know how Leslie got contusions on his lower back, his right upper chest, his right lower chest, his right arm and forearm, his left shoulder, his left arm and forearm, his left thigh, or his wrist. Officer One also stated that he didn't know how Leslie got abrasions on his lower back, on his legs and knees, and on his wrists. He finally agreed that the injuries described by Mr. Brustin could be considered the result of a somewhat violent struggle.

The deposition lasted six hours and forty-five minutes. During that time, there was a moment when my eyes locked with those of Officer One. His body language seemed to say, "I'm sorry," although he has never spoke those words to us. There was a brief lunch and bathroom break. In good faith, there were documents requested for the deposition that were not provided. Mr. Brustin stated, "If we receive new documents that relate to this witness, our position will be . . . and hopefully we can negotiate a resolution . . . would be that he may need to come in for some questioning on those documents." I received a copy of the deposition from attorney John Wolfe on June 15, 2007.

I will repeat my original question: "How did Leslie Vaughn Prater die?" Leslie's death was officially identified as a homicide on two autopsy reports and the death certificate. His death was one of many that occurred in the United States after physical contact with police officers. Yet justice is commonly denied in these cases. I am amazed by the zeal with which the United States government selectively goes to other countries to fight for human rights, while human rights are violated right here in this country, right here in our own neighborhoods. Police officers can violate human rights of Americans, even kill unarmed Americans, and it seems as though the majority of US citizens and elected officials look the other way or make excuses for the actions of abusive officers. In these situations, the country refuses to admit the possibility that police misconduct is real and rampant, potentially reaching crisis proportions. People are in denial. Yes, there are honorable people who choose to become police officers, and we need those public servants. However, many people feel that anyone who puts on a police uniform and badge can do no wrong. There would be a lot fewer graves in the cemetery if that were true.

②

POLICE BRUTALITY

Myth or Reality?

A myth is a concept that some believe to be true but is not documented with facts; reality, on the other hand, has a foundation in actual experience. Of course, there are always philosophical gray areas and subjective perceptions. In this chapter, I am proposing that police brutality is reality. After reading the chapter, you may or may not alter your opinion. I recall the old adage that "a man convinced against his will is of the same opinion still." I cannot imagine any words or circumstances that could convince me that police brutality is nonexistent.

After viewing a Cable News Network (CNN) report on Tuesday, April 6, 2015, my immediate thoughts were focused on another grieving family. The startling report featured a video of a black man running from a white police officer in North Charleston, South Carolina. Fifty-year-old Walter Scott was shot in the back and killed by Officer Michael Slager. Fortunately, Mayor Keith Summey of North Charleston spoke on behalf of justice. He said, "It doesn't matter if you are behind the shield or just a citizen; when you are wrong, you have to take responsibility for your actions." Officer Slager was arrested, charged with murder, and held without bond.[1] Initially, the officer denied any wrongdoing. On May 2, 2017, he entered a plea deal admitting to using excessive force in the shooting death of Mr. Scott.[2]

Did the murder of unarmed Walter Scott cause you to pause and wonder if Officer Slager was a terrorist? I would expect a response of "no." If nothing else, I imagine that I just got your attention. Let me further get your attention by continuing with some more strong language. *Terror, terrorist,* and *terrorism* are words commonly used in the media. Most of the time, the focus is on acts of terrorism in other countries or preventing terrorists from infiltrating the United States. You may question why I am introducing terrorism into this discussion. How is terrorism connected to police brutality? Here is my response: I view terrorism as the use of violence to intimidate another. If reports are accurate, in neighborhoods all over the United States, police are intimidating people and denying citizens the right to life, liberty, and the pursuit of happiness. Certainly, Mr. Scott was denied his right to life after a routine traffic stop. This common injustice is evidenced through assaults and homicides perpetrated by law enforcement officers. Collectively, these incidents are often referred to as police brutality, a civil rights violation that occurs when a police officer uses excessive force with regard to a civilian.[3]

I pose the question, "Should the Centers for Disease Control declare a health crisis in urban America because of deaths resulting from the social disease of police brutality?" Has this disease, which can impair one's ability to continue breathing, reached epidemic proportions? I think so, because an epidemic is a rapid proliferation of a condition, and a disease impairs a vital health function. I learned in elementary school that breathing is a necessary function of being alive.

Reported incidents of police brutality have been continually increasing at a rapid pace, which would qualify as an epidemic. Can you imagine the number of incidents that are never reported? You may say, "But that doesn't mean that even the reported allegations are true," and you would be correct. In America, the increase in police brutality is a frightening reality. According to those reports, in the decade from 2003 to 2013, the number of people murdered by police reached five thousand. This is in contrast to the 4,489 soldiers killed since the inception of the Iraq war until December 2013. Police presence is being turned into a military, with the enemy being anyone who would dare question their authority.[4]

In the December 18, 2007, edition of *USA Today*, the Department of Justice reported that police brutality cases have increased by 25 percent from 2001 to 2007 over the previous seven years.[5] This report represents reality. You may feel that police brutality is a myth and doesn't actually occur. The fact that it hasn't happened to you or someone in your family is not proof that it doesn't happen to others. If you are not a person of color, it is more likely that you have not been a victim of police brutality, although police violence cuts across racial lines. If you are African American, you are far more likely to die at the hands of a police officer than if you are white.[6]

There are others of the opinion that police brutality is a reality. Consider the following from Amnesty International, in which the group cites a previous report:

> While only a minority of the many thousands of law enforcement officers in America engage in deliberate and wanton brutality, Amnesty International found that too little was done to monitor and check persistent abusers, or to ensure that police tactics in certain common situations minimized the risk of unnecessary force and injury. The report also highlighted evidence that racial and ethnic minorities were disproportionately the victims of police misconduct, including false arrest and harassment, as well as verbal and physical abuse.[7]

Unfortunately, in prior years, few of these incidents were documented on videotape. In more recent times, advances in cell phone and camera technologies have resulted in an increased number of recorded altercations between police officers and citizens. In the case of Mr. Scott's murder, a citizen was walking to work and saw the altercation, which he recorded using a cell phone. In 2014, a movement began to require all police officers to wear body cameras. If this occurs, these recordings can be helpful, although recorded evidence of police wrongdoing doesn't guarantee that citizens will receive justice. Regardless of the circumstances or evidence, overwhelmingly, police officers are not held accountable for behavior resulting in the injury or death of citizens. For example, the outcomes of cases in Los Angeles document that officers there receive few indictments or convictions.[8] Furthermore, even twenty-three years after the Rodney King videotaped incident, victims of police violence get even less justice.[9]

Consider the case of the unmerciful beating of Adam Tatum, a thirty-seven-year-old African American male in Chattanooga, Tennessee, on

June 14, 2012. Police were called to the scene at the Salvation Army because of a disturbance involving two persons arguing, one being Mr. Tatum, who was kicking a door. In response to the call, two white officers arrived and struck Mr. Tatum repeatedly with batons and fists, shocked him with a stun gun, and maced him. According to the results of the investigation, Mr. Tatum was hit forty-four times with a metal police baton and choked. He suffered six fractures to his right leg and two to his left leg, including a compound fracture. The chief of police released those officers from duty. He stated that this case was one of the worst cases of excessive force he had seen in his twenty-five-year career, and that he would not subject the citizens of Chattanooga to these two officers.[10]

A video of this violent beating shows the bloody victim on the floor begging for his life and for them to stop beating him. A Hamilton County grand jury declined to indict the officers on criminal charges. A six-month federal investigation also yielded no charges. The outcome of this situation was that the police officers hired attorneys, and an administrative law judge granted their appeal to get their jobs back. After their reinstatement, they sued the city for $500,000. The lawsuit was settled. The officers received back pay, pension contributions, and an additional $15,000 for a total of $88,000 between them. They agreed to resign, with no negative documents in their file. Mr. Tatum also sued the city and received a $125,000 settlement.[11]

I traveled to Chattanooga to sit in on some of the Tatum hearings because of my personal interest in this type of case. I watched the video, which was shown during the hearing, although it was available on the internet and was featured in a number of televised news reports. Mr. Tatum's mother had to leave the courtroom, because she could not bear to watch the video. The video clearly was a demonstration of the use of excessive force. Because their files documented a clean employment record, the officers probably sought employment in another police department, where they now can continue their street justice behavior. In Chattanooga, even fired police officers rarely lose their certification, which allows them to maintain eligibility to work for other police departments. For example, between 2011 and April 2015, no fired officers from Chattanooga were decertified, which was not the case in other major cities in Tennessee, according to the Tennessee Peace Officers

Training Standards Commission.[12] From that report, one might surmise that the best place in Tennessee for a "bad cop" to work is in Chattanooga, although Chattanooga also has good police officers.

The structure that protects police officers from accountability in police brutality accusations is collectively referred to as the "Blue Wall of Silence." It is interesting that the "Blue Wall" is not as effective if an officer is accused of theft or selling drugs or weapons. Those criminal offenses can result in suspensions, dismissals, indictments, and convictions resulting in incarceration. Officers can receive more punishment for stealing than for using excessive force, even if it leads to death.[13] They are even disciplined for insubordination or for other actions unbecoming of an officer. In 2005, a ten-year veteran officer in the Chattanooga Police Department was dismissed for "touching himself" behind a grocery store and downloading pornography on his city computer.[14] Many years ago, there was an incident of an off-duty police officer stealing steaks from a store where he was working as a part-time security guard. He was fired. I mention that case because I personally knew this person, who had been a respected officer in the community. However, if an officer assaults or kills an unarmed citizen, the resources of the "Blue Wall" are immediately activated. All the officer has to do is repeat the phrase "I thought my life was in danger," or "I felt threatened," even if there are no rational circumstances to support such accusations. The wall is strong, it is built very high, and it is supported by a system that is in blind denial.

One might think that the "Blue Wall" would be weakened after numerous claims of abuse against particular officers, but that doesn't seem to make a difference either. Those complaints are often dismissed. As an example, in the July 8, 2001, edition of the Cincinnati Enquirer, it was reported that out of the hundreds of complaints against the police in Cincinnati, more than 90 percent were dismissed. The complaints were rarely forwarded to Internal Affairs or to the city's independent investigatory agency. Those complaints were considered minor.[15] Because even complaints that have been videotaped and resulted in death have been dismissed, I must ask, "What represents a major complaint?"

When lay citizens are charged with offenses, such as assault, manslaughter, or murder, the outcome is different, in comparison to accusations against police officers. In one case in Chattanooga, the district attorney charged three men with first-degree murder after they beat sixty-four-year-old James Sanders to death.[16] No one questioned that arrest or conviction. It was viewed as a criminal act deserving of punishment. All things being equal, if the perpetrators had been police officers, they might well have been rewarded with a week off with pay and full exoneration. That was our experience, one of receiving no support from the district attorney, a former police officer. I saw little difference between the death of Mr. Sanders and that of Leslie Prater, except there were four perpetrators in our case and those responsible were police officers, who were not arrested, indicted, or convicted. Is that a double standard, or what?

Anyone, regardless of race, economic status, or any other demographic variable, can be a victim of cruel, violent, and inhuman acts of terrorism, resulting in death. Consider the domestic terrorist attacks in the Oklahoma City bombing or the infamous September 11, 2001, attacks. Unfortunately, terrorism is not new to Americans, especially African Americans. Our experiences with terrorism predate Americans' experiences with al Qaida and other terrorist groups. Black people have experienced terrorism in America for decades, even within their own neighborhoods.[17] When persons bombed a church in Birmingham, Alabama, on September 15, 1963, and killed four children in Sunday School, that was terrorism. During that time in our country's history, bombings were so common that Birmingham became known as Bombingham.[18] When Klan members burned crosses in the yards of African Americans, those were terrorist acts. When police released vicious dogs on people and used water hoses to spray unarmed people to prevent them from participating in peaceful protests in Alabama, those were acts of terrorism, used to intimidate a group of people. Some of these terrorist acts were featured in the book *The Butler*[19] and subsequently in the film *Lee Daniels' The Butler*, released in the summer of 2013. Furthermore, Medgar Evers was a victim of a terrorist act when he was gunned down in his driveway in Jackson, Mississippi, on June 12, 1963.[20] Did you know that the Evers's home was the only one on their street in which the main entrance was on the side of the house? That design was deliberate, because the family feared that a front door might attract snipers.

When black men were routinely lynched from the nearest tree, persons committing those crimes were terrorists. As reported in the previous chapter, thousands of black men have been lynched.[21] Unfortunately, lynching is alive and well today, because there is more than one way to lynch: There are burnings, beatings, shootings, and dragging people behind cars. Again, I stress that among the common features of lynching is group participation in the killing, which is motivated by twisted notions of justice or racial hatred.[22] From that perspective, death from brutality by a group of police officers is indeed an example of a modern-day lynching.

Amnesty International, as reported by researcher Budimir Babovic, defined police brutality as the use of excessive force, or any type of unwarranted physical force used by police officers in a given incident, that can be deadly or non-deadly. Often the physical force greatly exceeds the threat encountered. Sometimes force is used when there is no threat. Instances of such excessive force include the following: fatal and non-fatal shootings, use of electro-shock weapons, beatings, misuse of batons and chemical sprays, dangerous restraint holds that sometimes lead to death, positional asphyxia, and ill-treatment within prisons. More simply stated, police brutality is inhuman, cruel, and violent behavior.[23]

The American Civil Liberties Union (ACLU) has joined this discussion, publishing *Fighting Police Abuse: A Community Action Manual.* An operating assumption in the manual is that police abuse is a serious problem with a long history and seems to defy all attempts at eradication. The problem is national, considering that the nineteen thousand law enforcement agencies across the nation are essentially independent. No police department in the country is known to be completely free of misconduct. According to the manual, the Department of Justice has been insufficiently aggressive in prosecuting cases of police abuse.[24] This perceived lack of support from the Justice Department could be a contributing factor in violent community responses to this injustice, such as the case in Baltimore after the questionable circumstances surrounding the death of Freddie Gray.[25] Simply stated, people are getting tired of the unjustified murders of their family members and neighbors by persons who are paid to serve and protect them. The community wants justice and accountability.

Victims of these brutal acts are from all races and ethnic backgrounds. However, it appears that a disproportionate number of victims are men of color, and white police officers are the perpetrators. This seems to be a fact that cannot be denied. It is not a myth. A letter in the *St. Louis Post-Dispatch* questioned why no one talks about black police officers who kill unarmed young white men.[26] Maybe it is because those situations are rare or not reported as often. Until a friend sent me information about a case that she discovered, I had not seen one report of that scenario. It was an account of a black police officer who shot an unarmed white teenager in Mobile, Alabama, in 2014. According to the Mobile county grand jury, the officer acted in self-defense.[27] That outcome is similar to other cases when unarmed citizens are killed by police officers, regardless of skin color. The color of significance is blue, as in the "Blue Wall of Silence."

Because I am an African American mother and my personal experience is with my son, an African American male victim, more of my discussion is focused on African Americans. I hasten to say that I realize that non–African Americans have also been victims of police brutality, and their families have suffered as much as we have. I am sensitive to those families dealing with their tragedies. I personally know some of these families, especially the mothers. We have a common bond that transcends race.

There are attitudes that serve to excuse police when their behavior is inappropriate. Acts of police brutality are often camouflaged as police doing their jobs to serve and protect. Such behavior is unconstitutional and controversial, as in the often-debated Stop-and-Frisk policy in New York City, which overwhelmingly negatively impacted persons of color, because a disproportionate number of those individuals were stopped.[28] Stop and Frisk, identified as a crime prevention tactic, allows a police officer to stop a person based on "reasonable suspicion" of criminal activity and frisk based on reasonable suspicion that the person is armed and dangerous. This practice was first approved by the Supreme Court in 1968. From the available empirical data, the practice is growing and has clearly targeted minorities. Data from New York City demonstrate the best landmark examples of the problems with Stop and Frisk. In 2008, there were three hundred fourteen thousand stops. By 2011, the number had grown to six hundred eighty-six thousand stops, which represented 8 percent of New York's population. Of that number of stops, 83 percent involved African American and Hispanic individuals, compared to 10 percent of whites. Eighty-eight percent of the stops resulted in no further law enforcement actions, which would cause one to believe that possibly those individuals were not dangerous or involved in criminal activity. In frisking for weapons, only 1.5 percent of those incidents found weapons, with more weapons found among white individuals stopped.[29] In the Stop-and-Frisk situations, minorities can certainly identify with the cartoon character Charlie Brown, as featured in the song by the Coasters, an African American pop group. In their "Charlie Brown" song, the repeated refrain is "Why's everybody always picking on me?" Considering immigration policies proposed in 2017, I fear "Stop and Frisk" practices will expand.

There are explanations offered that police work is stressful, a particular officer was having a bad day, or the adrenaline started to flow, which caused the officers to resort to mob behavior. Researchers have proposed other views to explain police brutality, especially in communities with low income. One research study reported, "When the perceived threat of underclass violence is great, all that is required for political explanations for police killings is for the powerful to be less willing to interfere with police methods, which seems to be a common occurrence."[30] Another concluded that police officers have long-standing negative attitudes toward black males stereotyped as criminals, pimps, drug dealers, and "gangsta-thugs."[31] I might also mention that the word "thugs" is now being identified as the new "N" word. These attitudes can serve to justify aggressive behavior in urban communities in particular. In general, it appears that it is only when there is a well-publicized incident of police brutality, with video and numerous television reports, that the attitudes of the general population are influenced.[32] Otherwise, the assumption is that police officers are the good guys and black men are the bad guys.[33] In the unfortunate and tragic situation in which police officers are killed by citizens, those citizens have rarely been black men.[34] More recently, passive acceptance is changing and there are visible social justice movements in urban communities, often described as "taking it to the streets" through protest marches. Sadly, some individuals have also used these opportunities to riot and burn neighborhood businesses. I don't deny that police work can be difficult, dangerous, and challenging, but that is no excuse for police officers to commit un-warranted criminal acts of assault and homicide as part of their duty to serve and protect.

One might question whether police misconduct is learned behavior, as proposed by researchers Allison Chappell and Alex Piquero. Their premise is that police officers are encouraged to be abusive in response to internal peer pressure.[35] Their theory is supported by Thomas Barker in his belief that officers indulge in corrupt behavior as a way of gaining peer approval and acceptance.[36] It's true that police work requires personal risks that are an inseparable part of the job. These risks allow officers an excuse to use violence, even when it is not warranted. In the presence of African American men, even unarmed and law-abiding African American men, it appears that police officers have an unusual and unwarranted fear for their personal safety. In deaths from officers using firearms, one would think that white officers are trained to shoot black men on sight and ask questions later, even when the black male is a twelve-year-old child on the playground with a toy gun.[37] Then there was the case of the North Miami Beach Police using images of black men for target practice. This was discovered by a woman who recognized her brother's picture at a shooting range where police snipers had been practicing. When confronted with this information, the police chief told NBC news, "The decision to use the mug shots of black men was ill-considered, but that no rules were broken."[38]

These shootings can occur when a black male victim is unarmed and clearly committing no crime. There are numerous examples of these incidents, such as the case of John Henderson, previously mentioned. His homicide occurred approximately eight months before Leslie was killed. The situation, leading up to Mr. Henderson's death, is an example of what can still happen to an innocent unarmed black man when he precisely follows the commands of the officer. The Henderson case was just one of many in which a police officer received no sentence resulting in incarceration for killing an unarmed black man or youth. Patrolman Gaynor, who killed Mr. Henderson, was fired from the Chattanooga Police Department on September 22, 2003, after the grand jury returned an indictment.[39] Gaynor was charged with criminally negligent homicide, which resulted in two trials. The first trial ended in a mistrial[40] and the second acquitted Officer Gaynor.[41] Subsequently, Gaynor was hired by the Hamilton County Sheriff's Department. On May 8, 2009, Gaynor received an award as the "Communications Officer of the Year."[42]

What is the root of this irrational fear that white police officers appear to have of black men? In the research literature, Jerome Skolnick identified the stereotype of the "symbolic assailant" as a contributing factor. According to Skolnick, the symbolic assailant is someone who by their dress, language, and manner of walking is perceived by the police as posing a threat.[43] In policing literature, the symbolic assailant is a young, African American male living in an economically deprived community. This stereotyping is very dangerous and can easily result in the abuse or killing of innocent black men and in unfairly blaming black men for society's crime problems.[44]

The reality is that many innocent black men have spent years in prison for crimes they did not commit. This fact has been documented by the Innocence Project, a national litigation and public policy initiative dedicated to exonerating wrongfully convicted individuals through DNA testing and reforming the criminal justice system, to prevent future injustices.[45] Coincidentally, The Innocence Project was founded by Barry Scheck and Peter Neufeld, attorneys from the New York law firm who were part of our legal team.

According to the Death Penalty Information Center, 159 persons in the United States have been exonerated and released from death row since 1973. The most recent at this writing was Ralph Daniel Wright Jr., released on May 11, 2017.[46] Anthony Ray Hinton, another innocent man, was one of those "lucky" death row inmates. He managed to escape "Yellow Mama," the name given to Alabama's electric chair. He was released on April 3, 2015, after spending twenty-eight years in a prison cell. Attorney Bryan Stevenson, director of the Alabama-based Equal Justice Initiative, referred to Hinton's situation as a case study in how poverty and racial bias can lead to a wrongful conviction. Mr. Hinton was twenty-nine years old when he was arrested. In June 2015, he was fifty-nine years old. Stevenson fought for sixteen years for the case to be reopened. Mr. Hinton was innocent of the 1985 conviction of two murders in two separate robberies in Birmingham, Alabama. New ballistics tests contradicted the only evidence used to convict him. At the time the crimes were committed, Mr. Hinton was working at a grocery store warehouse, located fifteen miles from the scene of the killings.

The fact that he wasn't near the location of the murders didn't seem to matter. The prosecution's case was upheld because "they" said bullet casings, matching those from a gun belonging to Mr. Hinton's mother, were found at the scene.[47] Obviously, someone lied.

When a black man is a suspect, he is characterized as a potential menace to society who can legitimately be stopped and frisked, harassed, intimidated, and brutalized or killed, if necessary, in the interest of maintaining public safety.[48] A comparison of racial victimization rates clearly documents that the rate of police killings is much greater for blacks than for non-Hispanic whites.[49] Thus, there is a disproportionate probability that blacks, and especially black men, will be killed by the police, in comparison to other racial and gender groups. Based on the outcome of the interactions between law enforcement officers and African American males, I think that black men have many more reasons to fear police officers than for police officers to fear them. Researchers support this premise and report that, in the unfortunate situations in which police are killed by citizens, those citizens are usually not black men.[50]

Black men, whether incarcerated or free, innocent or guilty, must carry the stigma of "suspect." Other members of society are aware of this stereotyped profile and use it to their advantage. Consider the case of Charles Stuart, a Boston resident who murdered his pregnant wife in 1989 and fabricated a story that a black male assailant killed his spouse. The Boston police immediately invaded black neighborhoods to threaten and interrogate black males who vaguely resembled the phantom suspect's description. I would imagine that many black males were profiled, because some people feel that all blacks look alike. Then there was the lie told by Susan Smith of South Carolina. She killed her two children in 1994 by drowning them in a car. Initially, she told police that she had been carjacked by a black man who took her car and kidnapped her children. Again, without any investigation or critical thinking, the police immediately initiated a manhunt for another phantom African American man.[51] There was also the case of Jesse Michael Anderson, who killed his wife by stabbing her five times in the head and face, and slightly cutting himself. He told the authorities that two African American men had attacked the couple. This was another "racial hoax," a term used to fabricate a crime and use race when blaming another person.

After Anderson's conviction and imprisonment, he was a fellow inmate of serial killer Jeffrey Dahmer. Ironically, both Anderson and Dahmer were killed by inmate Christopher Scarver.[52] In my opinion, these are extreme examples of racial profiling. Black men have a high probability of being stopped and harassed by the police. This appears to be true whether they are driving while black, walking while black, running while black, standing while black, sitting while black, bicycling while black, or just being black.[53]

Overall, neighborhoods in which there is a high concentration of black families tend to have less social capital and resources. In residential areas where people have more money and influence, police treatment of citizens is better. Police tend to use less aggression, regardless of the criminal actions of persons living in those neighborhoods. Unlike in "inner-city" neighborhoods, these residents are given the benefit of the doubt. In contrast, the focus is more on control through force in neighborhoods where residents are economically disenfranchised.[54] Overall, the powerless residents are vulnerable and the powerful law enforcement officers maintain domination through surveillance, manipulation, coercion, or physical force.[55]

When black people complain about white officers' use of force against them, often people ask, "What about black-on-black crime?" I would not deny that black-on-black crime is a concern, but what about white-on-white crime? White-on-white crime exceeds black-on-black crime. Seventy percent of arrests in cities and rural areas are of whites, but the penal institutions are overcrowded with black men.[56] Consider the report that in 2011, there were more cases of whites killing whites than blacks killing blacks.[57] I know this situation would surprise most people. The mainstream media obsesses over black-on-black violence, in comparison to white-on-white violence. Furthermore, violent crimes committed by whites are explained as the result of deviant behavior, but when black men commit violent crimes, their behavior is attributed to race. When James Holmes killed twelve people and injured seventy in the Aurora, Colorado, theater shooting in July 2012, no one blamed all young white males. I believe that discussing black-on-black crime within the same context of police brutality only helps to reinforce the unfair stereotype that most black men are violent criminals.

Attorney General Janet Reno addressed the problem of police brutality, especially against men of color. She gave a speech at the National Press Club Luncheon on Thursday, April 15, 1999, in which she stated:

> The issue is national in scope and reaches people all across the country. For too many people, especially in minority communities, the trust that is so essential to effective policing does not exist, because residents believe that police have used excessive force, law enforcement is too aggressive, and that law enforcement is biased, disrespectful, and unfair.[58]

In my opinion, reports from research, documented personal accounts from victims, televised accounts, eyewitness video recordings, and viral web postings confirm that police brutality is a reality. There are also enough reports of deaths of unarmed citizens while in police custody to indicate that accusations of police brutality are true. Police officers may never admit to any wrongdoing, but that doesn't mean that the accusations are false. Many families are left with their loved one's body to bury and a grave to visit, which serves as more tangible evidence of this injustice. Those unarmed citizens were among the living, immediately prior to the physical encounter with police officers.

In the informational brochure *The Body Count: Let None Live in Fear*, members of the Concerned Citizens for Justice (CCJ), a social advocacy organization in Chattanooga, used the brochure as the mechanism to report the results of their extensive research. The group's findings reported deaths occurring after an interaction with law enforcement officers in Chattanooga and the surrounding area, beginning in 1981. These deaths were of both black and white citizens. The list was updated in 2004 to include Leslie's death as number 48. Since then, there have been other deaths added to *The Body Count*. According to CCJ members, compiling information for *The Body Count* was an attempt to record the number of people who have been killed by members of the Chattanooga–Hamilton County Police Departments over a number of years. The listing for Leslie is as follows:

> 48. Leslie Vaughn Prater, 37, Black. Killed January 2, 2004. Residents called police after noticing Mr. Prater naked in an alley near Central Avenue. When police arrived, they were unsure of Mr. Prater's physical or mental condition, but could clearly ascertain that he was unarmed. Police

immediately took actions resulting in Mr. Prater's dying from positional asphyxiation, in combination with a severe beating by 4 police officers. Mr. Prater's body sustained injuries including 21 rib fractures, a broken arm, a dislocated shoulder, blunt trauma to the scrotum, and a large number of abrasions and bruises.

Even before 1981, there were incidences of alleged police misconduct in Chattanooga. The book *Both Sides of the Fence* unveiled corruption in the Chattanooga Police Department in the 1940s through the 1980s.[59] It was revealed that there were police officers as active members of the Ku Klux Klan. That was interesting, but not surprising. On October 11, 2004, while remodeling a popular downtown building in Chattanooga, a brick wall mural was discovered. The four paintings, which had been covered with Sheetrock, showed a hooded Klan member astride a horse. It is believed that Klan meetings, including attendance by prominent Chattanooga families, were held in that building.[60]

Both Sides of the Fence was written in 2006 by Bob Martin, a retired officer from the Chattanooga Police Department. The book documented his actual experiences and observations of corrupt activities. He admits to being a part of the corruption as a "bad cop" at one point. He reported that he later became a Christian and converted to being a "good cop"—hence the book's title. During the time span discussed in his book, Chattanooga is described as a town protected by a corrupt and self-serving local government; the powerful and privileged had their hands on all of the strings; and there was innocence accused and guilt unpunished.[61]

When I think of innocence accused in Chattanooga, my mind immediately recalls the historical account of Ed Johnson, a black man lynched in 1906. Johnson was falsely accused and convicted of raping a white woman. He was held in jail, where his safety was not protected and a lynch mob was allowed to "break in" and take him to the Walnut Street Bridge for the hanging. I have marched across that bridge to protest Leslie's death. On the top of Johnson's tombstone are his final words: "God Bless You All. I am A Innocent Man." At the bottom is written "Blessed are the dead that die in the Lord."[62] Almost one hundred years later, on February, 26, 2000, Mr. Johnson was cleared of the rape conviction. The request to clear his name was brought forward by a local black minister and former county commissioner, the Rev. Paul McDaniel.[63] You may be thinking, "How is the Johnson lynching connected to police brutality?" I mention the case of Ed Johnson because I believe that the lives of black men don't matter to some people, the past is being repeated, but disguised by some police officers as dutifully serving and protecting. We need to know our past so as not to repeat the horrors of the past. In so many ways, it feels like our past is catching up with us.[64]

Because of the numerous deaths of African American males while in police custody, it appears that police departments are ideal places of employment for persons who endorse ideas held by Klan members. Ideally, one could abuse and kill black people and get paid for it. One wouldn't need to hide behind a sheet and hood but merely put on a police uniform and badge. Based on the experience of many families, we have the answer to the question posed by the ABC television series *How to Get Away with Murder*. One answer may be to first join a police department.

I stress again that the majority of police officers are hardworking, fair-minded, conscientious individuals. Research reports that 50–70 percent of the brutality complaints are lodged against only 5–15 percent of police officers.[65] One police officer volunteered to tell me, however, that when he was employed in a police department in Illinois, he observed that at least 25 percent was a more accurate percentage of abusers. He resigned because he was uncomfortable in that environment. It's understandable why some people experience fear when alone and approached by an officer. There is no way of initially knowing if this officer is among the 5–15 percent or the 85–95 percent.

Most African Americans are law-abiding citizens and may never have been in a confrontation with police officers. Yet, from persons with whom I have spoken and from my own personal experience, some African Americans believe their skin color attracts unwarranted attention from law enforcement or security officers. I recall a round-trip airline experience while traveling with a white colleague from Illinois to New York soon after the 9/11 tragedy. On that particular trip, at every checkpoint, I was always pulled aside for an additional security check from a Transportation Security Administration (TSA) staff member. My friend asked, "Why do they keep stopping you?" I replied, "I guess it is because I have the face of a criminal." So, African Americans are potential suspects merely because of their skin color. This could explain author Marvin Free's theory of why there will likely be numerous interactions between African Americans and the criminal justice system.[66] Feelings of anxiety when African Americans are stopped by police officers, especially if alone, are understandable, regardless of the racial profile of the officer. In fact, black people may be at an additional disadvantage if stopped by a black officer when a white officer is present. According to research, there is a tendency for the black officer to be more aggressive with a black suspect when on duty with a white partner. The black officer may want to avoid the appearance of showing favoritism, which results in the black citizen being treated worse than if he had first been approached by a white officer.[67] In our case of Leslie's death, the original report was that three white officers were involved. Oddly, a few days later, a black officer's name was added. Also, there was a black police chief in charge when Leslie was killed. Based on his behavior and decisions, there may as well have been a white Klansman in charge.

I can't speak for all African Americans, but I do believe that many law-abiding African Americans, when stopped by the police, don't initially assume that the officer is stopping them to assist them or to secure their safety, even when that may be the case. When a black male is approached by a police officer, his blood pressure automatically begins to rise, because he doesn't know if he is being approached by a "good cop" or a "bad cop," to put it simply. He is more likely to expect the enforcement approach, which is different from the serve-and-protect approach, used in predominately white neighborhoods.[68] Most white citizens may be accustomed to the serve-and-protect scenario, while black citizens may be more accustomed to the enforcement approach, which is often accompanied with hostile, disrespectful language.

The racial integration of neighborhoods can have a negative impact on men of color residing in those communities. Actually, population demographics are changing the face of suburban neighborhoods. There are several factors contributing to this shifting paradigm, including the slow white population growth, new minority populations, and increased residential freedom for a new generation of blacks with economic stability. According to the 2010 census, half of metropolitan blacks became suburban residents, creating "black flight." A growing number of these communities are achieving the "melting pot," with

35 percent minority representation.[69] I feel that this information is significant. I wonder how many police academies are informing future officers of these social dynamics. This information is important because persons of color are stopped in these neighborhoods while traveling to and from their homes, or while merely visiting friends and relatives. Police officers are asking, "Why are you in this community?" Officers may immediately assume that minorities in "white neighborhoods" are there for criminal activity, without any reason for such a conclusion except that the individual is a black male. Consider the case of unarmed black teenager Trayvon Martin. He was merely walking with a beverage and snack in his hand, but because of his race he was profiled and killed.[70]

This racial profiling of innocent black men also happens to African American celebrities and upper-middle-class citizens. T. J. Holmes, a television journalist, was followed closely by a police cruiser and stopped as he was approximately a mile from his home in Atlanta. The officer told him that he was stopped because he wanted to know if he had automobile insurance. Mr. Holmes was also asked to show the officer a bill of sale for the car he was driving.[71] Dr. Henry Louis Gates, a prominent scholar of African American history and Harvard professor, was arrested on the porch of his Cambridge, Massachusetts, home. A person had called the police after seeing two black men on the porch trying to enter the home. It seems it never occurred to the caller, or the police sergeant, that this black man could actually be the homeowner.[72] Dr. Gates's example is one that Georgetown University Professor Michael Eric Dyson refers to as "housing while black."[73] The attempt to address the Gates matter resulted in a meeting infamously referred to as the "Beer Summit." President Obama hosted the meeting at the White House that included Dr. Gates, Sergeant Crowley, and Vice President Biden, with beer serving as the mediator.[74]

Some people are programmed to quickly associate brown skin with criminal activity and act accordingly. On February 6, 2015, the police in Madison, Alabama, received a call from a woman stating that a skinny black guy, whom she had not seen before, was walking in her neighborhood. According to the *Huntsville Times*, the woman stated that the man looked suspicious and was peering into garages. When police arrived and approached the man, he did not follow their orders and repeated "no English." The outcome of the confrontation was that un-armed Sureshbhal Patel was brutalized. He was non-English-speaking and unable to decipher the officer's directions. He received severe neck injuries as he was forced to the ground. He is partially paralyzed and may never walk again. The fifty-seven-year-old Mr. Patel, from India, had only been in the United States for a few days to visit his son, who is a homeowner in that neighborhood. It appears that there was noth-ing suspicious about Mr. Patel, other than that he was strolling in the neighborhood clothed in brown skin. The police officer was arrested and a lawsuit is pending.[75]

The concept of "to serve and protect" may not apply to African American men, even when they are harming no one and are only in need of help themselves. Consider the tragic case of unarmed, twenty-four-year-old Jonathan Ferrell. He was seeking assistance after he was involved in an automobile accident, which occurred after dark on September 14, 2013. He managed to walk from the accident scene to a house and knocked on the door to seek help. The home was located in Northeast Mecklenburg near Charlotte, North Carolina. The resident called the police, as she was alarmed by a black man knocking at her door and thought he was trying to break into her house. When the police arrived, Mr. Ferrell probably was happy to see them and thought they were there to serve and protect him. Unfortunately, Officer Randall Kerrick did not give Mr. Ferrell a chance to explain his circumstances. As he ran toward the police for help, Officer Kerrick fired twelve times at Ferrell. Ten of those bullets hit Mr. Ferrell and killed him. Jonathan's mother, Georgia Ferrell, clearly expressed my feelings in these matters and those of other mothers. She said, "You took a piece of my heart that I can never get back."[76] Similar to Leslie's situation, Jonathan Ferrell's cry for help was met with death. This tragedy added to the mounting incidents of a white police officer killing an unarmed young black man. Unarmed Ferrell was running toward the police and was shot to death. Unarmed Walter Scott was running from a police officer but was still shot to death.[77] Unarmed twenty-three-year-old Sean Bell was shot and killed by police officers on his wedding day in Queens, New York.[78] For young black males, it seems to be a miracle to survive an encounter with aggressive police officers, especially if those officers are poorly trained and/or have a negative attitude toward black males.

Racial profiling can be a precursor leading to the wrongful death of unarmed citizens. One might ask, "So what usually happens to the police in these situations?" What I have discovered is that when police are accused of these murders, there is often little or no accountability. They are innocent until proven innocent. An excellent example is the fatal shooting of unarmed eighteen-year-old Michael Brown by Officer Darren Wilson on August 9, 2014, in Ferguson, Missouri. Although there were eyewitnesses to the shooting of Mr. Brown, who some witnesses said held his hands up in surrender, Wilson killed him anyway. There was no disputing the fact that Michael Brown was unarmed. Officer Wilson was never arrested, but he was put on an extended paid leave, which I still identify as an extended vacation. Wilson was cleared of any civil rights violations but eventually resigned from the police department in November 2014.[79] The Ferguson situation is talked about worldwide and appears to be a lightning rod for the beginning of what may be the next significant civil rights movement. Many are questioning, "What is the incentive for abusive officers to stop this behavior?" There is no one conclusive response. Possibly the lack of indictments and imprisonment of these officers in most of these cases is one reason the practice of using excessive force is growing instead of decreasing.[80]

In addition to accountability, resulting in loss of freedom, another possible incentive for police to avoid the use of excessive force is the loss of income. If more of these cases ended in officers losing their jobs, there would be less aggressive behavior used against residents. Also, if the guilty officers were responsible for paying their own attorneys, court fees, and lawsuit judgments against them, they might think twice before shooting unarmed citizens and using other forms of unnecessary force to end a person's life. Who are the fiscal losers? All of us, as taxpayers, are the fiscal losers. According to Nick Wing of the *Huffington Post*, we pay a shocking amount in lawsuit judgments for police misconduct. Here are merely a few examples from his investigative report. Chicago spent $521 million from 2004 to 2014; New York City spent $348 million from 2006 to 2011; Los Angeles spent $101 million from 2002 to 2011; and Oakland, California, spent $74 million from 1990 to 2014.[81] That money could have been applied toward addressing quality-of-life issues, such as enhancements in education, health, economic development, and affordable housing.

We often hear the sentiment expressed that no one is above the law. Often, police officers are provided a status that is above the law, especially in matters involving assaults and the deaths of citizens. The role of an officer is a powerful one, which can easily be abused. For the percentage of officers who are dishonest, there seems to be little limits to their abuse. They have the power to manipulate the reports, including the creation of false reports in which there was actually no crime. They can easily lie, and their accounts of the incidents are more likely to be upheld by the justice system than the words of lay citizens. They can plant drugs and weapons on people and in their vehicles to increase the likelihood of felony convictions. Police officers have a lot of autonomy and discretion in how they choose to apply the law. For example, there are a number of alternatives an officer has when engaging in traffic law enforcement. The officer can take an offender into custody by making an arrest, issue a traffic citation, issue a written warning, issue a verbal warning, or take no action.[82] Also, an officer can choose to kill an unarmed person during a routine traffic stop.

I support the sentiment expressed by the 1968 Kerner Commission that police misconduct, whether described as brutality, harassment, verbal abuse, or discourtesy, cannot be tolerated, even if it is infrequent.[83] From the 2009 and 2010 annual and quarterly statistics in Cato Institute's work titled *National Police Misconduct Reporting Project*, it was reported that more police misconduct was for excessive force than any other category, representing 25 percent. From those cases, 58 percent involved fist strikes, throws, choke holds, baton strikes, and other physical attacks; 145 involved firearms; and 10 percent involved Tasers. When there were deaths involved, 70 percent involved firearms.[84]

In part, this book was written as a warning that any one of us or a member of our family can become a victim of police brutality. We could merely be at the wrong place at the wrong time or encounter the wrong police officer, especially if we are alone. No matter your status, income, or accomplishments, you could be at risk of harassment, arrest, injury, or death by those employed to protect the public peace. We must not continue to blindly accept what David Feige refers to as "The Myth of the Hero Cop." Feige states that police unions have created a perception that all police officers are heroic public figures, valiantly trying to protect us. According to Feige, since September 11, the story of the hero cop has become so powerful and pervasive that even questioning police behavior is decried as disloyal, un-American, and dangerous.[85]

Yes, I do believe that Leslie's death resulted from police brutality. This is a theme that you will find throughout this book. My feelings on the matter of police maltreatment are clearly summarized. No one should have to wonder what I think. We are either victims or silent partners in the brutal and racist acts of some police officers. We all pay in some way when even one of us is denied his or her constitutional rights. Silence is not a friend; silence is the enemy. We do not live in a post-racial society, and there is work to do. As Leslie stated in his last words, "It's not over."

3

PROFILING
Reported Research and Personal Experiences

The purpose of this chapter is to explore a suspected relationship between racial profiling and police brutality. Profiling is complex and multidimensional and involves using specific characteristics as a guide to perceptions and actions. These perceptions and actions advantage some and disadvantage others. Profiling is not a simple concept, which might explain why there are so many social dynamics related to this discriminate behavior. We all engage in profiling on some level; all profiling is not bad. A "Handicapped Only" sign in a parking lot is a kind of profiling, but one that is positive for persons with special needs. One would doubt that anyone using a wheelchair would complain about having reserved parking near a building's entrance.

Individuals have complained of profiling while shopping. If you have seen the movie *Pretty Woman*, you may recall the experience of the character played by Julia Roberts. Because she was initially profiled as a non-desirable who could not afford clothing in a high-end boutique, she was treated badly in that store. When she later returned and was profiled as a woman with obvious financial means, she was treated much differently and with respect. My African American friends and I have been followed and profiled in stores, as though the salesclerk expected us to steal merchandise. We have also been ignored by clerks, who assumed that we could not afford anything in their upscale store.

From among many personal examples of profiling while shopping, I will share one that is still memorable. More than twenty years ago, my friend Phyllis and I were shopping in a boutique mall in the exclusive Buckhead area of Atlanta. We were dressed casually and were not carrying signs that said, "We are college professors and can afford to shop here." Phyllis, a professor of fashion design and merchandising, was shopping for a comforter for her bed. We went into a store that sold comforters made with fabrics imported from various countries. As a professor of merchandising, Phyllis was familiar with the characteristics of quality linens. At first, the white male clerk ignored us, as we looked at almost every comforter in the store. Finally, Phyllis saw a comforter that interested her, but it was on a high shelf and enclosed in a plastic bag. When she motioned for the clerk to assist us, he came over but appeared to be annoyed. She asked him to retrieve the comforter from the high shelf and take it out of the packaging. She wanted the entire design exposed. His first response was "Why should I take it down?" Phyllis asked, "Why shouldn't you take it down?" He replied, "Because I will just have to put it back, because you're not going to buy it anyway," He further stated, "I'm not going to take the comforter out of the packaging, because that would mean that I would have to refold it to put it back in the bag." He then immediately left the store for his lunch break.

This was a small store and there was only one other person working there, who was behind the counter. Phyllis went over to this gentleman and found out that he was the owner. She told him what happened, and he appeared shocked and angry. He apologized and said he would be happy to show her the comforter and any other item in the store, plus give her a 20 percent discount. He was very helpful and accommodating in every way. Because of his behavior, and the fact that Phyllis really liked the comforter, she purchased it and the coordinating pillows and dust ruffle. He was able to complete the $900 sale. I remember Phyllis saying to me later, "If possible, it is always better to deal directly with the owner." Unless a salesperson is working on commission, it doesn't matter to them if they make the sale. I could not help but wonder if that salesclerk treated white women shoppers the way we were treated.

As an African American, I know that profiling occurs in restaurants. I have experienced many of those incidents. One that was the most amazing was in Savannah, Georgia. While there attending a national conference, several other participants and I decided to go to dinner at a nationally known Savannah restaurant. The group consisted of about nine African American women and one white participant, a friend traveling with me. When we arrived, the staff person at the podium, near the outside entrance, put us on the wait list. That was the procedure, because they didn't take reservations. We noticed that there were several groups ahead of us and we were okay with that. What alarmed us was that even after waiting for more than an hour, several groupings of white people who came after us gave their information and were seated. This happened more than once. When we questioned the staff member, she would simply say that we were next, but she lied. We were finally seated.

The most significant outcome of that experience was the "eye-opening" realization and subsequent reaction from my white friend. She was amazed and incensed when she stated, "I don't know how you all can deal with this; I just couldn't be black in America." Of course, we don't have a choice, and we have dealt with a lot of unfairness and disparities over the years. One might wonder, "Why didn't you all just leave?" The reason we didn't leave was because we were too weak from hunger to start all over with a long wait at another restaurant. This was the same friend with me when I was continuously stopped for additional scanning at airport checkpoints, mentioned previously.

Profiling, whether intentional or unintentional, is quite common in relation to employment outcomes. If you have ever attended an interview skills workshop, you are probably aware of situations that could potentially disadvantage an applicant. The way you dress, wear your hair, walk, and talk are some variables to consider.

Males who insist on wearing sagging pants, revealing their underwear, have a more difficult time gaining employment than others who dress more conservatively. I recall a situation in which my husband placed an order at a fast-food drive-through restaurant. When we got to the window, he noticed that the person preparing the sandwiches wore sagging pants. He canceled our order. That was profiling, because he equated the display of the worker's underwear with being unsanitary.

There have been studies that suggest that persons perceived as physically attractive have a better chance of employment, in comparison to those perceived as less physically attractive, by whatever measure one uses. For example, very few Fortune 500 male CEOs have beards.[1] Years ago, an airline stewardess was required to be of a certain age and weight to be considered for initial and continued employment. The cliché that "blonds have more fun" is a stereotype meant to imply that female blonds may be less serious or intelligent than brunettes. In stereotyping, there is a standardized mental representation of people. The subtype of the "blond bombshell" is often associated with attractive blond-haired women. In some media presentations, blonds are portrayed in images that undermine the power of women.[2] As with most profiling and stereotyping, the characterization of these women is unfair and prejudicial. An excellent example of the attitude is portrayed in the movie *Legally Blonde*. Reese Witherspoon's character is portrayed as a joke for enrolling in law school at Harvard University.

Profiling is applied to the way we speak and write. In the United States, Standard English is preferable to Ebonics, and especially during job interviews. The term *Ebonics* was originally coined in 1973 to refer to a colloquial dialect, or variation of Standard English, spoken by some African Americans.[3] It was outrageous that there were some educators, working primarily with black children in inner-city schools, who endorsed the teaching and use of Ebonics. In 1996, the Oakland California Unified School District passed a resolution declaring Ebonics the primary language of the African American students in its schools.[4] Although there has been a national Ebonics debate, the use of Ebonics in "the real world" could limit future professional opportunities. Fortunately, the Oakland Ebonics resolution was later retracted. Overall, the way we speak is transferred to our writing. Persons are stigmatized if their written expressions are at variance with traditional or Standard English.

There are other terms closely related to profiling. Discrimination is a more structured term for describing collective situations and attitudes of profiling, which is a less overt term. We may have our own unique idea of what should be classified as discrimination. When I think of that word, I think of isolating differences. A formal definition is that discrimination is the process by which two stimuli differing in some aspect are responded to differently. This difference in response is identified as prejudice when there is a different treatment or favor on a basis other than individual merit.[5] Much has been written about the concepts of racism, prejudice, and discrimination; they have been talked about extensively within popular media and social science circles; and numerous laws have been designed to address these issues. Yet it is easy to confuse racism and prejudice. I favor the distinction proposed by researcher Wornie Reed. She reports that racial prejudice and racism both refer to ways in which people devalue, demean, and disadvantage others. She further proposes that racial prejudice is a negative attitude, judgment, or feeling about a person and is generalized from beliefs about the group to which the person belongs. Racism is the behavioral manifestation of that racial prejudice.[6] A related conclusion, proposed by Pat Bido, is that power plus prejudice equals racism.[7]

If I detailed descriptions of all of the laws aimed at voiding society of discrimination based on race, I would need to produce volumes of books. In this chapter, I will discuss those situations related to police brutality in opposition to the Fourteenth Amendment of the Constitution of the United States, adopted on July 9, 1868. This amendment addressed citizenship rights and equal protection of the laws, in response to the treatment of former slaves after the American Civil War.[8] This amendment, which has generated more lawsuits than any other, is fascinating to me. *Brown v. Board of Education* is one such lawsuit that claimed a violation of citizenship rights. In that decision, the Supreme Court ruled that segregated public schools for blacks and whites were "inherently unequal" and that African Americans were denied "equal protection under the laws." Section 1 of the Fourteenth Amendment is especially relevant to this discussion: It reads as follows:

> All persons born or naturalized in the United States, and subject to the jurisdiction thereof, are citizens of the United States and of the State wherein they reside. No State shall make or enforce any law which shall abridge the privileges or immunities of citizens of the United States; nor shall any State deprive any person of life, liberty, or property, without due process of law; nor deny to any person within its jurisdiction the equal protection of the laws.[9]

Can you imagine the positive social environment that would exist if all persons and organizations abided by Section One of that amendment? Society would not have needed the controversial and misunderstood law of affirmative action, established as an attempt to mandate fairness. Also, the collective "isms" of sexism, racism, ageism, and classism, some of the more visible signs of discrimination, would be nonexistent. But the law is ignored too often, resulting in a seemingly endless number of lawsuits.

Affirmative action refers to various government policies aimed to increase the proportion of African Americans, women, and other minorities in jobs and educational institutions historically dominated by white men.[10] I hasten to add that many think that affirmative action is designed to hire unqualified persons to "colorize" the office. My personal attitude is that intelligence and talent are distributed among all categories of people. When we discriminate solely based on skin color, we may eliminate the one person who has the cure for cancer, for instance. I have heard some people, even women, say, "I would never vote for a woman to become president of the United States." That is a clear example of sexism. A female candidate could be the most qualified potential leader. So far in America, unlike in some other countries, this theory has not been tested. Many believe that African Americans have been overwhelmingly advantaged by affirmative action. The fact is that the persons most advantaged by affirmative action are white females.[11]

Based on the intent of the Fourteenth Amendment, the government required that all persons be treated with equal concern and respect. Throughout the years, there have been actions to circumvent the law. After the Civil War, the Southern states began enacting the Black Codes in 1865 and 1866 to deprive African Americans of many basic rights afforded to white Americans. The laws were specifically designed to replace the social controls of slavery and ensure continuance of white supremacy.[12] Essentially, these laws would trump the provisions of the Emancipation Proclamation and the Thirteenth Amendment, which abolished slavery. The Black Codes authorized more severe punishments for African Americans than would be imposed on white persons for committing the same criminal offense. African Americans continue to complain about that practice because it still exists. The label "Black Codes" has gone away. Today, it is called "justice" and sometimes feels like "just us." According to Nkechi Taifa, during the past fifty years, the United States has moved from overt racist lynchings and blatant discrimination to mass incarceration as its punishment of choice.[13]

Black prisoners are given nearly 20 percent longer sentences than whites for the same crime. The research confirms that the racial divide in sentencing has even widened since the US Supreme Court struck down the Booker ruling in 1984, a law requiring judges to impose sentences within the predetermined sentencing guidelines. After that ruling, judges were allowed personal discretion in determining the length of sentences. That change has resulted in a resurgence of the Black Codes, because blacks, on average, received longer sentences than whites did for similar offenses.[14] Overall, black males were treated differently by the criminal justice system, in comparison to white males.

At this juncture, the discussion of profiling, prejudice, and racial inequities may not necessarily imply behavior that leads to death. However, my review of some historical events in America has caused me to pause and ponder certain questions that continue to haunt me. Did Leslie's race precipitate the outcome of his interaction with police officers? Could he have been a victim of behaviors guided by a modern-day version of the Black Codes? I suspect the fact that Leslie was a young, African American male contributed to his death. Attitudes are deeply ingrained and can be difficult to change, including attitudes of police officers. These attitudes, whether positive or negative, can impact one's behavior in the workplace, regardless of the chosen profession. Decisions and behaviors are influenced by attitudes.

Unlike in some other professions, the decisions and actions of law enforcement officials can directly and instantly affect matters of life or death. A police officer's attitudes comprise a serious component of that officer's effectiveness. More precisely, negative attitudes by some police officers toward certain populations impact their selection of strategies to maintain law and order. Attitudes formed by police officers in the treatment or maltreatment of black men, especially, are the result of years of input and complexity of experiences.[15] Those who have internalized these negative attitudes are prone to actions commonly labeled as racial profiling, which can lead to police brutality.

As a social scientist and an African American mother of two African American sons, I had long been aware of the general stereotype of racial profiling, the concept of attributing negative attitudes toward persons of color. According to the American Civil Liberties Union, racial profiling refers to the discriminatory practice by law enforcement officials of targeting individuals for suspicion of crime based on the individual's race, ethnicity, religion, or national origin.[16] This suspicion is often used as an excuse to assume that an individual is engaging in criminal behavior or preparing to participate in criminal activities. Some may even applaud racial profiling as a proactive strategy in decreasing possible criminal acts.

It is unfortunate that people make assumptions about others merely because of skin pigmentation. Beginning with my childhood years, I had always been socialized to not worry about what people thought about me because of the color of my skin. I was raised in Tennessee by strong grandparents, originally from rural Alabama, who provided a foundation for me to develop a positive self-concept that did not allow others to define me. In many instances, including within my subsequent professional experiences, I determined that their advice was good to follow. It served me well throughout the years, and allowed me to thrive within environments in which there were few, if any, other persons of color.

In parenting my own children, I would not have been so concerned about prejudicial feelings of specific individuals, except that I believed those attitudes could result in negative and violent behaviors toward my sons. These attitudes, identified collectively as hatred, could prompt actions that actually lead to the harming or death of targeted individuals. On July 17, 2015, a white, twenty-one-year-old male entered the historic Emanuel African Methodist Episcopal Church in Charleston, South Carolina, with the pretense of participating in a weekly prayer service and Bible study. After an hour of engaging with the black people in attendance, he rose and announced that he was there to kill black people. His actions resulted in the shooting deaths of nine innocent people. One of the massacred was Rev. Clementa C. Pinckney, the forty-one-year-old pastor and a state senator of South Carolina. These actions sparked a renewed call for the Confederate flag to be removed from South Carolina's state capital mall. Numerous retailers, including Walmart, voluntarily removed items from their stores that featured the flag. Besides the 45-caliber gun used in those killings, hatred was the biggest factor that resulted in the demise of those innocent citizens, ranging in ages from twenty-six to eighty-three.[17] Subsequently, a jury convicted the killer and he was sentenced to death.[18]

One only has to recall documented actions of Ku Klux Klan (KKK) members as examples of other tragic outcomes of racial profiling.[19] Persons born since 1965 may have little or no knowledge of these past injustices. They may be unaware of the hatred spewed by that organization or how racial attitudes can influence laws and policy.

Some may not realize that interracial marriage was once a crime. If blacks and whites married, they were subject to arrest for a felony and subsequently punished in prison for one to five years. This antimiscegenation law existed in some states until as late as 1967.[20] It ended with the landmark Supreme Court decision of the *Loving v. Virginia* case, in support of the marriage between Richard Loving, a twenty-three-year-old white male, and Mildred Jeter, a seventeen-year-old black female. They had married legally in Washington, D.C., in 1958 but were arrested when they returned to their Virginia home. Their one-year prison sentence was suspended if they agreed to leave the state for twenty-five years. Ethiopian-Irish actress Ruth Negga was nominated in 2017 for an Academy Award for her performance in the film *Loving*.[21]

Unfortunately, the KKK is not in the past and is very present today. The group's attitudes resonate even among law enforcers. The KKK provides a convenient framework for hatred and is known for its intolerance and violence. The organization was first formed as the Invisible Empire of the South in 1866 in Pulaski, Tennessee, my home state. Its first leader, or Grand Wizard, was Nathan Bedford Forrest, a former Confederate general. Although the group claims to be a Christian organization, it has been labeled as the oldest among American hate groups. Its secret membership is nonexclusive in regard to occupations. Originally, African Americans had been the group's target, but the KKK's intolerance has been extended to other persons of color, Jews, and persons who prefer same-sex partners.[22] Basically, members focus on any group that is different from them.

I consider the KKK a terrorist group, because they use intimidation in the form of violence, such as lynchings, burnings, bombings, shootings, and other acts that sometimes lead to the death or injury of innocent people. Often, they are not held accountable for these deadly deeds. Over the years, Klan membership has fluctuated, but the organization still has an estimated five to eight thousand self-reported members.[23] One deeply disturbing act was the September 15, 1963, bombing of the Sixteenth Street Baptist Church that killed four young girls in a Sunday School classroom in Birmingham, Alabama.[24] In my opinion, that was an act of domestic terrorism. As recently as March 2013, the KKK planned a rally in Memphis, Tennessee, to protest the city's decision to remove the name of Nathan Bedford Forrest from one of its parks.[25] It has also been reported that the group raised money in support of Darren Wilson, the police officer who shot and killed unarmed Michael Brown in Ferguson, Missouri, on August 9, 2014.[26]

From a social science research perspective, I will admit that it is challenging to prove "cause and effect." Do I believe that the KKK was directly involved in Leslie's death? Absolutely not, but I do feel that sentiments common among KKK members are comparable to beliefs held by some law enforcement officers. When there are unfounded negative assumptions applied to one group, especially young African American males, that is a basis for concern. From visual observations, there is no denying that Leslie was a young African American male. Certainly, there is no way for me to prove that Leslie would be alive today if he had been an unarmed Caucasian thirty-seven-year-old male in obvious need of assistance.

From personal observations, readings, historical accounts, and other media sources, I felt that our two African American sons would need to be educated about the potential dangers of being an African American male in America. Their mere combined gender and racial status could attract negative attitudes toward them and, subsequently, cause them undue harm. The reality of this fear was evidenced early in their lives. During most of their childhood, we lived in what society describes as a predominantly white neighborhood. In fact, our family was the first black family to move into a particular subdivision of Hamilton County in Chattanooga, Tennessee. No, we were not exclusively seeking to move into a "white" neighborhood. At that time in the mid- to late 1970s, in the eastern part of the county, most of the new residential housing was in the communities of East Brainerd. Even today, that region is still a popular area for single-family housing, although the neighborhoods are much more diverse now than when we moved there in 1976.

When we moved to East Brainerd, Leslie was in the fourth grade, and Stefan was in kindergarten. The public schools in East Brainerd had a good reputation for excellence, which appealed to us. During that time in Hamilton County, there was no mandated kindergarten in the public schools. So, Stefan attended a private Catholic school kindergarten in downtown Chattanooga, and Leslie attended a public elementary school in East Brainerd. Dwight and I have always supported public education. From our experience, we received an outstanding elementary and secondary school education in public schools, and I was teaching in a public school.

As a young couple, with very young boys, we were initially not focused on overt racial issues. So, I will admit, we were naive about the potential impact of our young sons being racially isolated in predominantly white school settings. Prior to our move to East Brainerd, Leslie had been in an urban school setting with mostly other African American students. Stefan was in a private-home preschool setting, with other African American children. Moving into the county, I later realized, precipitated a culture shock to their social system. This realization was especially glaring when, years later and after they were young adults, I was looking through some of their elementary school pictures. In most of those pictures, my sons were the only African Americans in the picture. While examining those pictures, I only had to shake my head and ask myself, "How could we have missed that?" We were concerned with giving our sons a better physical neighborhood environment and opportunities to attend schools with a good reputation for educating students.

There is an opportunity cost to such decisions that impacts African American children and their parents. I should have been sensitive to the fact that we were still living in the South, with prevailing attitudes that racial segregation was preferred to integration. Those attitudes prevailed in other parts of the United States as well. However, like other parents, we still wanted our children to have the best possible education. Within a few years, I will admit that I had to question whether moving into the county at that time was the best decision for our sons' overall emotional health and well-being.

Interestingly, Stefan encountered a racial incident when he was in the private Catholic kindergarten. Considering he was only five years old, I didn't think we needed to talk to him about racial attitudes. I thought

Dwight and I had more time to prepare for "the talk." I soon realized that I was wrong. I recall the day when Stefan, as an innocent kindergarten child, came home and announced that he knew what he wanted to be when he grew up. My mind immediately pictured him in some well-meaning profession. With anticipation, I was excited to hear of his choice. He continued by saying, "When I grow up, I want to be a white man." I was shocked and saddened, but I tried to hide my horror from him. I knew that pursuing such a goal would engender some serious self-esteem issues and maybe even black self-hatred, a concept that has been researched by numerous scholars.[27] I gained my composure and calmly asked him, "Why do you want to grow up and be a white man?" He responded, "Mary Kathryn and I want to get married when we grow up, and she said that her mother said that she could not marry me, because I was black and she was white." I must admit that I was relieved by the simplicity of his motive. So, I calmly responded, "You and Mary Kathryn don't have to be of the same skin color to get married, but if her mother wants you all to be the same, go back to school tomorrow and tell Mary Kathryn to tell her mother that she wants to grow up to be a black woman." Assuming that Stefan relayed this message to his "girlfriend" and that Mary Kathryn obeyed, I wish I could have seen her mother's facial expression after hearing of Mary Kathryn's plans. Interestingly, when Stefan did marry, he married a white woman.

In early childhood, the prominent groups in Stefan's world of understanding were boys and girls, men and women, mothers and fathers, brothers and sisters, and teachers. He did not identify persons according to membership within racial or ethnic groupings. That realization would come later. I am reminded of a question posed in an Undoing Racism workshop I attended years ago, with black and white participants. The presenter asked, "When did you know you were black or when did you know you were white?" The only people in the room who immediately responded were black people. We all could recall the incident or circumstances that clearly identified us as being black. The white participants had no response and appeared confused by the question.

The white participants might have been less confused if they had read *Black Like Me*. The book is a case study of John Howard Griffin's research. He was a southern white man who wanted to know what it was like to be a black man. With the assistance of a physician, he used medication to darken his skin. He wrote about how the same people responded to him differently as a white man than they did when they thought he was a black man. Basically, feedback was positive as a white man and negative when he masqueraded as black. He wrote about his revelation and new understanding of white privilege, the existence of which many still deny.[28] Because of the benefits of white privilege, people cannot understand why Rachel Dolezal, a white woman, would pretend to be a black woman during her employment with the NAACP.[29] It is far more common for interracial fair-skinned black people to "pass" as white, such as portrayed in the 1959 movie *Imitation of Life*, starring Lana Turner. The original 1934 film of the same name starred Claudette Colbert. *Imitation of Life* has been named as one of the twenty-five most important films on race.[30] In America, if one examines statistics of employment, education, housing, bank accounts, health status, or any measure chosen, it appears that there are benefits to being white.

When Stefan completed kindergarten, he was enrolled in Westview Elementary School, a public school in the county. This was the same school Leslie attended. Both boys soon confronted negative racial attitudes. When Stefan was in the first grade, he came home one day and reported to me that he was washing his hands in the bathroom and one of his classmates said to him, "Why are you washing your hands? You are black and you will always be dirty." Stefan was hurt and confused because he didn't understand why his classmate referred to him as being black. He had heard the term from Mary Kathryn, which he had probably forgotten, but still didn't understand the social construct applied to racial identity. By another societal label, Stefan is described as fair skinned or "bright," a term used by many to refer to African Americans with light complexions. As a young elementary school student, he identified the color of black as being the color of his black crayon, for example, which caused him to be further confused as to why his classmate would call him black. His skin was not the color of his black crayon or his black shoes. Imagine our struggle, as parents of a six-year-old, trying to explain racism in America. Again, we had thought we would have more time to prepare for those discussions. For the second time, we were so wrong. I had to wonder, "When did the parents of the white child in the bathroom incident socialize their son to hate?" I firmly believe that babies are born without these negative attitudes.

Leslie also experienced childhood racial profiling incidents. To my knowledge, the most memorable problem he faced was on the school bus as a middle school student. Because our family was the only African American family in the subdivision, he was the only black child on the bus that picked up students in our neighborhood. To further complicate matters, middle school and high school students rode the same bus. He was a sixth grader, but he was harassed by students who were juniors and seniors in high school. This was also during the time that the mini-series *Roots* was first aired on television. The high school bullies used a lot of the terms from *Roots*, which gave them an enormous amount of hostile material in their efforts to humiliate and intimidate Leslie.

When Leslie reported these incidents to us, I immediately scheduled a meeting with school system administrators to voice a complaint. After the discussion at the meeting, their ineffective solution was to reserve a seat for Leslie behind the driver, rather than holding the guilty students accountable for their actions. Of course, their ridiculous attempt at a solution did not work because other students expressed resentment of this special treatment. The bus was overcrowded and some students were forced to stand. Yes, I know that safety is compromised in that daily dangerous practice, but that is what happened. Even if some students entered the school bus prior to Leslie's arrival, no one else could sit in his seat behind the driver. That seat was reserved for "the black kid." This special treatment infuriated students even more, especially the high school students.

As a parent, when your child is hurting, you are hurting. So, we had to resort to a desperate measure. The school officials may have had good intentions, considering their limited ability to problem solve, but their solution was not working for us. They made no plans to punish the bullies or to contact the parents of those few high school students. I always felt that the bullies should have been suspended from riding the bus, at least until their behavior changed. I discussed the matter with the mother of one bully, with the anticipation that she would reprimand her son. After I explained her son's actions to her, she replied that I should have thought about potential consequences before I moved into a "white" neighborhood.

After that discussion, I knew for certain that I needed to resolve this problem and could expect no help from school officials or the parents of the bullies. My desperate, but effective, solution was that I voluntarily removed Leslie from that bus route. We had an African American friend who lived in another county subdivision. I would take Leslie to their house and he caught the bus with other African American children. On my way home from work in the afternoon, I would pick him up from their home. He experienced no bullying on that bus route. Dwight was working out of town, so I was the lone parent with this responsibility.

Stefan didn't have the bus problem because only elementary school children rode that bus. Thus, he continued to travel on a different bus that picked him up and returned him in front of our house. Recently, there is much talk and attention given to the topic of children being bullied in school or en route to school. Believe me, this is nothing new. In the 1970s, we didn't have the use of social media to more easily communicate these horrors. However, advanced technology has facilitated the unfortunate horrible incidents of cyberbullying.[31] This action is the latest destructive mechanism used by cowardly bullies.

Leslie experienced more racial profiling as a teenager. He had no interactions with officers from the Chattanooga City Police Department or the Hamilton County Sheriff's Department prior to his adolescent years. If research reports that African American males are more likely to be confronted by police officers than other people are true,[32] then I suppose Leslie was likely to have a confrontation with police officers at some point in his life.

When Leslie began to drive, he was stopped and followed numerous times by police officers near our residence for merely attempting to get home. These stops were especially frequent when he returned home after dark. Like most teenagers, he had a part-time job and attended school and social activities, which meant that he sometimes arrived home after sunset, especially during the winter months, when darkness came early. He became aware that police perceived him as threatening because of his skin color and that his white friends in our neighborhood were not stopped by police officers when they returned home after dark. Sometimes he would be a passenger in their vehicles and witnessed that there were no incidents with the police. Because police officers stopped him for no apparent reason, he knew that our fears for his safety were valid. His experiences support research findings that black men have the highest probability of being stopped and harassed by the police.[33]

Racial profiling is exactly what Leslie experienced as he drove to and from his home. Without any of us realizing it at the time, he was a victim of what has been previously described as the "symbolic assailant." This person is someone who, because of skin color, dress, language, or possibly manner of walking, is perceived by the police as posing a threat.[34] Leslie was impeccable in his dress, usually wearing the most popular name-brand clothes at that time, such as Izod shirts. He spoke proper English and did not walk with the stereotypical bounce. I recall that he had even been accused by some African American youth of "talking white" because he used Standard English. However, he was still a black teenager. He was visibly a minority male.

Racial profiling has remained active throughout the decades. The "symbolic assailant" label is still used. Consider the case of Trayvon Martin, a seventeen-year-old unarmed African American teenager killed in February 2012 in Sanford, Florida, by a neighborhood watch volunteer.[35] In policing literature, as further described by Skolnick in 1994, the symbolic assailant is a young African American male, most likely perceived to be from a family of low income.[36] Of course, this stereotyping is very dangerous and can easily result in the abuse or killing of innocent black men and youth. When police officers observed Leslie entering our neighborhood, they assumed all residents were white families. Thus, only white teenagers had the privilege of unlimited access to that subdivision, in which Leslie actually lived. In fact, we lived in Shenandoah for five years before another black family moved into the neighborhood. I recall that every time I told my grandmother that we had a new neighbor, she would always ask, "Are they black people?" I think she believed that we would return home one day and discover a burning cross in our yard, our house on fire, or a brick or bomb thrown through our window. She had reasons to be nervous, because some of those incidents were occurring in neighborhoods across America. Fortunately, we didn't experience any of those overt hateful incidents. Our experiences with hatred were more passive, until Leslie's death.

If reported statistics are true, a significant variable contributing to Leslie's death is the fact that he was a black male. Among some police officers, the assumption is that most black men are criminals, pimps, drug dealers, and "gangsta-thugs."[37] When police officers internalize these attitudes, and their actions, based on these views, are supported by the double standard of justice for officers, which will not hold them accountable for their actions, even if a death occurs, then we have a volatile combination that fosters and perpetuates abuse. To avoid prosecution, officers only have to say, "I felt threatened." Those three words tend to eliminate the possibility of their being punished.

Although Leslie had experienced racial profiling in the past, clearly on January 2, 2004, he was not profiled in the sense of being deliberately targeted and harassed as an African American man. Leslie was not stopped by police officers because of the color of his skin. Citizens called the police because they saw another citizen in need. This is what was told to us by a resident who called the police. Racial profiling was not what brought police officers to Leslie on that fatal night. After they arrived, however, I still firmly believe that police brutality was used to resolve an encounter that should have had a peaceful, non-life-threatening outcome.

There is no way that I can substantiate my feelings that, as a young African American male, Leslie's life held no value to those officers. I could be totally wrong, and I sincerely hope to God that I am. But I will always believe that, if Leslie had been an unarmed, helpless white young man in need of assistance, with everything else being equal, he would have been helped. Instead, he was the first homicide victim in Chattanooga, Tennessee, in 2004. I will always believe that his right to life was ignored. He was helpless, obviously unarmed, and no threat to the officers who answered the call on the early evening of Friday, January 2, 2004. In fact, someone told me that there was a similar report of an unarmed, nude white young man on the same weekend of Leslie's death. The outcome was that this young man was helped, rather than killed. Because it was New Year's weekend, I would imagine that the police received several calls resulting from intoxication. I asked the police chief about the report of an intoxicated nude white male that weekend but got no response from him. However, I remain tormented by the belief that Leslie's skin color contributed to his death. One often hears the accusation that people of color "play the race card" to excuse their actions. For African Americans in the United States, however, the suspicion is that the race card is comparable to the joker in a deck of cards. It could surface at any time to wreak havoc in your life. I believe that there was no reason for Leslie's body to have received the injuries and inhumane treatment from those officers. No one will ever be able to convince me otherwise.[38]

In 1992, in an effort to bring calm during the Los Angeles riots, Rodney King made a simple plea. He passionately asked, "Can we all get along?"[39] Why can't we, as members of a civilized society, respond "yes" to that question? In 2017, we are still struggling with this plague of destructive divisions. Years ago, the blueprint of "The Birmingham Pledge" provided guidance on the issue of racism. In January 2000, a joint resolution of Congress was passed to recognize the Birmingham Pledge. In 2001, President George W. Bush proclaimed September 14–21 as National Birmingham Pledge Week and encouraged all citizens to join him in renewing their commitment to fight racism and uphold equal justice and opportunity. Most people are not even aware of this pledge. Until recently, I had not heard of it. I am so pleased that Carolyn McKinstry shared the pledge in her book *While the World Watched*.[40] The pledge is as follows:

- I believe that every person has worth as an individual.
- I believe that every person is entitled to dignity and respect, regardless of race or color.
- I believe that every thought and every act of racial prejudice is harmful; if it is in my thought or act, then it is harmful to me as well as to others.
- Therefore, from this day forward, I will strive daily to eliminate racial prejudice from my thoughts and actions.
- I will discourage racial prejudice by others at every opportunity.
- I will treat all people with dignity and respect; and I will strive daily to honor this pledge, knowing that the world will be a better place because of my effort.

4

REVIEW OF POLICE DEPARTMENTAL RESPONSES TO IN-CUSTODY DEATHS

"I am sorry for your loss." "Remain calm and allow us to do our investigation." "We will conduct a transparent investigation and keep you informed." From watching the evening news, our own experience, and experiences of others with whom I have interacted, those words, spoken by a police chief to family members after an in-custody death of a loved one, are now quite familiar. Usually, the media and community advocacy groups are told that a fair investigation will occur. "We will get to the bottom of this" are often words spoken into the microphone. How often have we heard a televised report in which the representative of a police department or a mayor's office said, "There will be a thorough investigation conducted by Internal Affairs"? Are those words merely rehearsed sounds coming from their mouths, without any degree of sensitivity that a life has been taken? Can families have hope that those sounds represent more than empty promises?

Bearing news of a loved one's death to the family is undoubtedly a tough part of a cop's job. In deaths caused by police officers, however, police administrators may avoid immediate direct contact with families of the deceased. They may choose to delegate that responsibility to others or merely assume that the family will eventually find out about the death. In some situations, it may even be a television reporter who delivers the news, a health care worker at the hospital, or an extended family member. The immediate family may be among the last ones to know. I can speak factually about this, because that is what happened in our situation.

Dwight and I were visiting relatives Dot and Alvin in St. Louis, Missouri, for the New Year's weekend. After going out for dinner and social activities on January 2, we returned to their home near midnight CST. There was a message on their answering machine from a 423 area code. I immediately recognized it as being a number from Chattanooga but initially could not identify to whom the number belonged. I felt my blood pressure immediately rising. My closest extended family in Chattanooga knew that I was in St. Louis. The call had come in near 11:00 p.m. (or midnight in Chattanooga, which is on EST), so I didn't think they would call me just to chat. I returned the call, and my cousin Spencer answered. He said, "It is Leslie." We both paused, which seemed like forever, but it was probably only a fraction of a second. I said, "What is it, what has happened?" Then I heard the words that forever changed our lives: "Leslie is dead." I just remember shouting a series of "No, No, No . . ."

Dot took the phone and got more information. According to Spencer, near midnight, a nurse came into the hospital's waiting room and told family members that Leslie was dead. We were later told that police officials were at the hospital, but none sought contact with the family. Leslie's aunt and cousins asked the nurse if they could see Leslie, but their request was refused. She told them that no one could see him because his body was considered a crime scene. Based on information revealed to us later, we believe we know why family members were not allowed to see Leslie. Could it be that police officials did not want the family to see the condition of his body, with bruises and other indications of physical abuse and trauma?

While still at the hospital, family members began to telephone other relatives and friends in Chattanooga. Everyone they called already knew that Leslie was dead because they had seen a report on Chattanooga's local 11:00 news: Leslie's name had been released to the news media, even prior to the notification of the next of kin. Leslie was not married and had no children, which meant that Dwight and I were clearly the closest relatives. Even more shocking is that the news media knew

Leslie had died before any family members, including those who were still at the hospital, anxiously awaiting information on Leslie's condition. After police department officials, followed by the mayor and hospital employees, the television-viewing audience was the next to be notified about Leslie's death. Of course, the very first persons to know that Leslie was dead were those who witnessed him take his last breath at the scene.

At the hospital, the nurse gave extended family members a piece of paper containing a name and number to call for more information. Spen shared that information with Dot. She telephoned that contact, who happened to be a police department official, and told him that she was representing Leslie's parents. Dot said that the officer seemed surprised that Dwight and I had a representative. Maybe he initially thought that we already had an attorney. But it was just that we were at Dot's home and unable to talk. The officer said, "I need to talk to the parents so that information can be released to the public." We later discovered that information had already been released to the public, including Leslie's name. Although we literally could not talk to the officer at that moment, it should not have mattered. Anyone with common sense could anticipate that we were in shock and distressed. I still don't understand their rush to disclose Leslie's name to the media before any family member had been informed of his death or identified his body. Depending on the circumstances, sometimes it is days before a name is released, either to allow adequate time to locate and inform the next of kin or for other reasons. Journalists commonly report deaths on television and in newspapers without identifying the name of the victim. They usually say, "The name of the victim is being withheld until notification of the next of kin." That courtesy was not provided to us, as Leslie's parents, or his extended family members.

When we returned home the next day after Leslie was killed, I thought it was unusual that there were no answering machine messages from the Chattanooga Police Department. We did not have a private telephone number and could have easily been contacted on our land line connection. Surely the department had enough investigative expertise to easily locate a telephone number. Also, there was no indication that the Chattanooga Police Department had contacted the Cape Girardeau Police Department to seek a representative to go to our home to deliver the news. I know that this does happen in some instances, but probably not when police officers are responsible for the death. I concluded that there was clearly no attempt by the Chattanooga Police Department to contact us. This perceived lack of sensitivity, compounded by later actions of the police department, sent a message of caution that screamed loudly at me, "Something is very wrong with this situation."

As I emotionally prepared to telephone the police chief, I remained perplexed as to why there was not a message from him on our answering machine. When I called the chief and introduced myself as Dr. Loretta Prater, the mother of Leslie Vaughn Prater, he was quick to express the common phrase: "I'm sorry for your loss." He immediately followed with the promise of a thorough investigation, because they didn't have all of the facts to know what happened to cause Leslie's death. "We will get to the bottom of this," he said, as though Leslie's death was some big mystery. There was one statement he made to me that I will never forget, because it seemed very odd, so inappropriate, and so outrageous. He said, "I'm just glad that they didn't shoot him." I was extremely upset by his remark. Without even having to think, my reactive and angry response was "What do you mean, you are glad that they didn't shoot him? He's still dead; regardless of whether he was shot or not, dead is dead." Prior to ending the conversation, he told me that Leslie's body was at the county's forensic center, and we could go there to identify the body when we arrived in Chattanooga the next day. After the identification, they would release the body to our chosen funeral director. That promise turned out to be a lie, among the many lies told to us, because we were denied entrance into the forensic center to identify Leslie.

During the six-hour drive to Chattanooga, I just kept wondering how I could live without Leslie. How could I possibly face all of the tomorrows that were ahead of me? Could it really be true that Leslie was dead? There was hope that there was some mistake. Relatives had already told us of the first newspaper report that Leslie was more than six feet tall and weighed more than three hundred pounds. Could someone else be in the morgue? Rationally, I knew that I was immediately in Kübler-Ross's stage of denial,[1] as previously mentioned. Maybe focusing on denial helps one to avoid shock.

Prior to realizing the authority of the chief was compromised, I contacted the forensic center upon arrival in Chattanooga. The purpose of my call was to schedule a time to identify Leslie's body. However, the response received was opposite of the chief's directives to us. We were informed that the center was closed. It didn't seem to matter when I told them what the police chief had said. Obviously, there was a communication dissonance between the center personnel and the chief, and we were caught in the middle. The chief's directives were totally dismissed.

We were asked to provide the name of the funeral home we wanted to use. It seemed odd that the forensic staff assumed that the body was Leslie's, prior to any family member making a positive identification. There was identification in his car removed from the scene of the death, but there had not been a positive identification. Maybe I had watched too many detective stories on television, but it seemed to me that paperwork found in a car was not the same as a positive identification of a body. The forensic center staff told us that we would have to wait until Monday to see the body but would have to see it at the funeral home. This conflict of guidelines was an indication that, at least in Chattanooga, procedures in these matters were random.

With ongoing reporting of in-custody deaths, it appears that police departments create procedures at the moment the death occurs, as if there is no anticipation that their department could face such a tragedy. Many police departments have a Special Weapons and Tactics team, more commonly known as SWAT. How many departments have an established public relations' crisis intervention team? Because of the numerous mistakes department officials make after an in-custody death, it appears that special training is needed in effective strategies of public relations to oversee a constructive response to these situations.

In the absence of such a plan, the erratic behavior of police administrators causes confusion among the public, serves to ignite a pattern of mistrust, and makes it difficult to expect predetermined actions from departmental personnel. There are a few exceptions of inconsistency. The public can expect that the police officer or officers involved will be placed on paid administrative leave, the department will seek to protect the identity of officers, and that initially, pertinent information will be held in secret. While the department is busy ignoring the victim's family members and consuming time developing defensive strategies to deflect any guilt from officers, families may be unaware of the death of their loved one. Also, I would be remiss if I failed to mention that department personnel invest a lot of energy in immediately seeking anything "bad" about the deceased to report to the public. A profile of a horrible person, underserving of life, is quickly developed as a characteristic of the victim. At least that seems to be the case of unarmed forty-year-old Terence Crutcher, among others. Terence was shot in Tulsa, Oklahoma, on September 16, 2016, by police officer Betty Shelby. She claimed fear for her life, although video footage clearly showed the victim was walking away from her. Moments prior to his death, a police officer, in a helicopter above the altercation, identified Terence as looking like a "bad dude." After Terence was killed, details of his prior involvement with police officers were quickly investigated and exposed.[2]

Compared to our experience, the notification of next of kin can be even worse when the in-custody death occurs after incarceration. Unfortunately, there is no national standard regarding family notification in jail deaths. The American Correctional Association recommends that there is a process by which individuals are notified in case of serious illness, serious injury, or death. The recommendation is from their International Core Standards document, presented at their Standards Committee meeting on January 25, 2013, in Houston, Texas, and communicated on the American Correctional Association website.

Although jailors and prison guards are not labeled as police officers, they are equally responsible for those in their custody, and the behavior of some jail and prison officials, appears to be inhumane and totally insensitive toward family members. Just because people are incarcerated doesn't mean that they have been forgotten. Why are innocent family members subjected to needless pain and suffering? In the majority of cases with problems of notifications, I sense that people would like to know if their relative has died while serving time in a penal institution. There are too many of these unfortunate situations of families not being notified of their loved one's death. Actually, one is too many. I am going to share a mere two of these cases with you.

Forty-year-old Willie Lee was incarcerated on March 15, 2014, in the Orleans Parish Prison. He was being held in lieu of a $20,500 bond.

Nine days later, he was dead. There were conflicting reports of what caused his death. The sheriff's office reported that Lee had extensive heart problems and died from cardiac arrest. An inmate later reported to Lee's former girlfriend that the "sudden heart problem" was caused by a beating by inmates, followed by excessive force and lack of medical attention by prison guards. Lee was taken to Interim Louisiana State University Hospital at 10:35 p.m. on March 23, 2014, and pronounced dead at 12:17 a.m. on March 24, 2014. Family members were totally unaware that he had even been injured and taken to the hospital.

In the meantime, Lee's mother, Margie Lee Hulitt, was busy still raising bail money and trying to contact her son by telephone. Her repeated attempts to reach Willie failed. With every attempt, she would receive the same recorded message that her son had been released. She was confused by that response, because she knew that the family had not yet paid the bond. Ms. Hulitt asked her daughter, a deputy at the prison, to try to contact her brother. His sister looked through the prison computer system for information and received the same notice as her mother—that Willie Lee had been released. As previously mentioned, the notification of her son's death came indirectly through an inmate contacting Lee's former girlfriend, who then contacted Ms. Hulitt with the sad news. All that time, officials never bothered to contact the family, who assumed that he was still in custody. Orleans Parish Prison had been under federal investigation related to numerous in-custody deaths. Within a nine-year period after Hurricane Katrina, forty-four inmates suffering from an illness or injury died at Orleans Parish Prison or died at a hospital after being sent there from Orleans Parish Prison.[3]

In another disgraceful situation, twenty-two-year-old Lonnie Hamilton was incarcerated at Marcy Correctional Facility in New York. After his January 2016 incarceration, Lonnie's family tried to telephone him for several weeks before seeking his address to write him a letter. On May 6, 2016, they looked on the state's correctional website to find his address and were shocked to see that he was listed as deceased. Further inquiries revealed that Lonnie Hamilton died on March 18, 2016, and was already buried in a cemetery near the prison. Prison officials told family members that he committed suicide while in solitary confinement and that they were unable to reach family members.[4] In this case, New York State's Department of Corrections and Community Supervision Directive #4013, for administrative responsibility after an inmate's death, was not followed. An excerpt from the six-page policy, dated November 26, 2013, is as follows:

> The prison's chaplain or Supervising Offender Rehabilitation Coordinator must notify the next of kin or another pre-designated individual of the inmate's death. If a working telephone number can't be found, the facility is required to send two certified letters to at least two next of kin or pre-designated individuals. If that proves unsuccessful, it is "recommended" that the facility reach out to local law enforcement officials for help.[5]

Family members were further horrified by the fact that Lonnie was not embalmed. His body was just put in a box and placed in the prison's cemetery. There was no opportunity for the family to say good-bye. The chaplain reported trying to contact the father twice, but the cell phone number was not working. The father's address was still the same one that officials used when they arrested Lonnie at the father's home, but no certified letter was sent.[6]

It is interesting that between 2001 and 2014 there was a fourteen-year high of 50,785 prisoner deaths in state and federal prisons, with 45,640 of those prisoner deaths occurring in state prisons. Furthermore, in state institutions, suicide is reported as the leading cause of death. This alarming information was reported by CBS News on August 4, 2015, with the title "Inmate deaths on the rise in United States prisons and jails, says Bureau of Justice Statistics." I wonder how many families of those persons received timely notifications of the deaths. I venture to caution that a facility's report of suicide as the cause of death may not necessarily be accurate.

Let's consider the case of Sandra Bland. I met Geneva Reed-Veal, Sandra's mother, in St. Louis in 2016. We and several other grieving mothers attended a memorial event hosted by Lezley McSpadden, the mother of Michael Brown. Ms. Reed-Veal spoke of the circumstances surrounding Sandra's death. She vehemently expressed her belief that her daughter's death in a Texas jail on July 13, 2015, was a homicide, not a suicide. I share in her belief that there are reasons to be suspicious of the jailor's report on the cause of her daughter's death. In fact, one might question why Waller County, Texas, settled a wrongful death lawsuit with the family for $1.9 million if jailors were absolved of responsibility in Sandra's death. As in most in-custody cases that are eventually settled, there was no admission of wrongdoing.[7]

The deaths of many other incarcerated individuals are reported as natural causes. In 2011, a United States Department of Justice report cited cancer and heart disease, followed by respiratory disease and AIDS-related deaths, as significant causes of death in local jails and prisons.[8] In a different research report, liver disease was reported as the third leading cause of death in these institutions.[9] As with any group of statistics, teasing out the facts can be challenging, considering that there can be missing information, conflicting reports, and questions focused on the legitimacy of self-reporting of institutions. People die from natural causes without being incarcerated, so I am not suggesting that all of these deaths are questionable. However, considering the alarming numbers that are reported, one might question the reliability of reasons reported as the cause of death.

As in our case, and the experience of many others, Leslie was not incarcerated at the time of his death. According to data collected between 2003 and 2009, and reported in 2011 from the Bureau of Justice Statistics, 4,813 persons died during or shortly after law enforcement personnel attempted to arrest or restrain them. Also, about 60 percent of those arrest-related deaths, or 2,931, were classified as homicides by law enforcement personnel.[10] I can only assume that Leslie's death was among those numbers.

One would think that police departments would have anticipated that allegations of police brutality could occur and would have developed written proactive strategies to deal with these matters. Of course, even if a written policy is in place, there is no guarantee that behavior will match policy expectations. Because no two situations are identical, it is expected that there could be some variance in the responses. However, especially departments that have experienced in-custody deaths should be prepared with a constructive, consistent response, rather than a reactive one.

Consider the case of Freddie Gray, who died in custody in Baltimore on April 19, 2015. I realize that no two situations are exactly the same, but I must question, "Was there a policy in place in Baltimore to address in-custody death procedures?" On October 3, 2014, the *Baltimore Sun* reported that over the past four years, more than one hundred people won court judgments or settlements related to allegations of police brutality and civil rights violations.[11] Those payments totaled about $5.7 million. From that report alone, it appears that Baltimore should be quite familiar with matters of police misconduct, although not all allegations resulted in deaths.

Jerriell Lyles was a victim of police misconduct. Fortunately, he lived to tell his story. He had just purchased a carry-out box of chicken. A plainclothes Baltimore officer stopped him, frisked him, and ordered him to get down on the floor. He refused. Lyles later testified that the officer hit him hard. He said, "The blow was so heavy, my eyes swelled up. Blood was dripping down my nose and out my eye." The officer objected to Lyles's version but could not explain why he had stopped Lyles or how Lyles got hurt. The result was the city of Baltimore paid Lyles $200,000 in damages. In addition to the $5.7 million previously mentioned, the city paid $5.8 million to law firms. Since 2011, Baltimore has lost or settled more than one hundred cases related to police brutality.[12] The Lyles incident, and at least ninety-nine others, preceded Freddie Gray, who died after a neck injury while in police custody. Baltimore reached a $6.4 million settlement with Freddie Gray's family.[13] All six of the officers charged in Gray's death pleaded not guilty. Three were acquitted at trial, and charges were dropped against the remaining three.[14]

Procedures in response to in-custody deaths should be clearly stated and included in a written policy manual. There is no excuse for police department personnel to behave as though they are surprised by these occurrences and have no clue of how to respond. The departmental decision makers should not be "running around like a chicken with its head cut off," an expression used often by my late grandfather. Was there a written policy in Ferguson, Missouri, directing the police department to bring out armored military tanks and assault rifles after an announcement of a planned community march?[15] I doubt it.

One might expect that some departments, especially those located in large metropolitan areas, would be well experienced with in-custody deaths. In addition to Baltimore, other cities have had numerous occurrences of police misconduct, including killings of unarmed citizens, in which there is no apparent threat to the lives of officers. Although those cities have a history of these deaths, it appears that they still make the same mistakes over and over again in dealing with these matters. Maybe some of their officers are not making mistakes but are executing intentional actions. Trends of misconduct related to in-custody deaths have prompted investigations from the Department of Justice. Sadly, whether the federal government gets involved seems to be more dependent on the person serving as attorney general, rather than the legitimacy of the claims of police brutality.

Departments may not have any written policies of what to do or who will be responsible for specified actions when an in-custody death occurs. Could it be possible that there are police departments that have never experienced an in-custody death? Even if that is the case, does this mean that they cannot fathom an in-custody death happening in their jurisdiction? Do they perceive their officers to be better trained in avoiding in-custody deaths? When there is no obvious physical danger to officers, why don't they use critical thinking in the place of deadly force? In so many of those situations, in which officers are not threatened, why does their "split-second" decision end in a citizen's loss of life? I am merely asking questions predicated upon the mystery of how unarmed citizens posing no threat to the life of an officer can be a victim of these homicides. I don't need to hear the speech again that officers make split-second decisions. Everyone understands that lives of officers should be protected. I understand that as well, and I support continued life for everyone. Circumstances questioned by many are outside of the scenario in which police officers act in self-defense. Many question instances in which an unarmed citizen is running away from a police officer and is shot multiple times in the back, as in the case of unarmed African American Walter Scott, who was shot and killed while running away from Michael Slager, a white police officer. The fatality occurred on April 4, 2015, in North Charleston, South Carolina.[16] What could possibly be the rationale for that homicide? I have pondered that question but still have no answers. Do you?

According to the Bureau of Justice Statistics, there are approximately twelve thousand local police departments. The bureau defines a police department as a general purpose law enforcement agency, other than a sheriff's office, that is operated by a unit of local government, such as a town, city, township, or county.[17] I have no idea how many of these local police departments in the United States have embedded procedures in their policy manuals that deal with in-custody deaths and in-custody injuries. I applaud police departments that have taken these matters seriously, as indicated by their inclusion of directives in their policy manuals. For example, the police department in Urbana, Illinois, is among those that wisely established a policy to address officer-involved deaths of citizens. Its Policy 305, Serious Uses of Force and In-Custody Deaths, was adopted December 30, 2015. The five-page policy provides details for procedures applied to the death or injury of a person by their police officers. This is at least a first step, although there is no guarantee that the directives are followed. The purpose and scope of the Urbana policy states:

> The purpose of this policy is to establish policy and procedures for the investigation of an incident in which a person is injured or dies as the result of an officer-involved shooting or dies as a result of other action of an officer.[18]

In-custody death investigations are one-sided from the beginning. In many cases, there is more than one officer involved. So, the police officers can give their account of what happened, whether factual or not. Even if there is only one officer who made physical contact with the victim, often other officers may have witnessed the altercation. If there is a recording of the incident, the perception of officers may differ from that of others after reviewing the evidence. Unfortunately, the person who had the most accurate knowledge of what happened cannot contribute to the investigation. The voice of the deceased has been silenced. Who will tell that side of what actually occurred?

Will newspaper and television reporters give an accurate accounting of what happened? To answer this question, one first has to examine the source of the information reported by the media. Obviously, reporters are not expected to be everywhere when newsworthy incidents occur, and most of the information the public receives is secondary. In comparison to other situations, we would dismiss such content as "hearsay."

When an in-custody death occurs, where do newspaper and television reporters go for their information? It is not unusual for news agencies to assign reporters to work exclusively on crime-related stories, or the "police beat." A typical beat will include cops, courts, and the city council. That assignment can be stressful, challenging, and rewarding. Because of the content, these "beat" newspaper reporters are in a position to write many of the front-page stories.[19] For televised breaking news, we usually anticipate that the top anchor person will read the story.

What is the source of the content describing an in-custody death? There is not just one source. However, it is well known how powerful and lasting first impressions are. Those first interviews are critical for establishing the public's perception of the event and impression of the victim.

More often than not, police department officials are the first to give information to reporters about an in-custody death. Some departments have identified public relations officers for that role. Depending on the anticipated local and national public outcry, the mayor may also speak on behalf of the city and the police department. With larger public protests, the governor may get involved, as in the aftermath of demonstrations in Ferguson, Missouri, and Charlotte, North Carolina.

It would be helpful to have a policy in place and followed to determine which persons are to speak as police department representatives. If there are a number of people with this responsibility, the message should be consistent. In the event that a reporter quickly arrives on the scene, there may be an opportunity to speak to eyewitnesses even prior to receiving a statement from the official department representative. However, some people will absolutely refuse to get involved; others will not speak on camera or be quoted by name in a newspaper article. Some eyewitnesses may be fearful for their safety, anticipating repercussions from police officers. After witnessing the police kill one citizen, they may wonder who will protect them from the same fate. Did the body of Michael Brown lying in the street for hours serve as an effective vehicle of intimidation?

Accuracy is so important in reporting, and especially in crime reporting, but it may be considered less of a priority than being first to get the exclusive "breaking news" story. Moreover, it is in reporters' professional best interest to have a good relationship with police officers and officials, and to have fostered a platform of mutual trust. Sometimes that trust can be unconditional. They may accept the accounts of police officers as facts and quickly communicate those "facts" to the public.

The foundation of trust in reporters and police administrators is challenged when their reports are contradicted by video and audio from the scene. In the case of unarmed Walter Scott, for example, the police officer used the common defense that he felt his life was threatened, but the video showed the officer chasing Scott and shooting him five times in the back.[20] Yes, there are honest police officers with the highest degree of integrity, but they are probably not the same officers who would shoot an unarmed man in the back.

Like most families, prior to Leslie's death, we had not been directly involved in an in-custody wrongful death situation. However, Chattanooga was our hometown. During my fifty years of residency there, I had read of experiences with others in dealing with the city's police department and had developed a sense of caution. I already felt that I should not accept everything Chattanooga police officials said as factual. Like many African Americans in Chattanooga, I was familiar with the negative reputation of its police department. With that background, I approached contact with the police chief with suspicions. Chief Jimmie Dotson was from Texas and had only been in Chattanooga for a short time. I think he was unaware of my long history there and underestimated me as being one who would not question statements he gave to the press. The first newspaper report of Leslie's death was based on the interview the chief provided.

During my initial telephone discussion with the chief, my very uncharacteristic behavior was to say very little and mostly listen. The chief later reported on our conversation to the local media. He told them that he had spoken to the family and that we were very calm. Actually, he had only spoken to me. I think that he must have confused calmness with compliance, which is very different. I believe that he may have thought that we would be a family who had ultimate trust and faith in the police and would not question anything that he or his executive team said to us. He later learned that his initial impression of the family was very wrong. When I first talked to him, I was calm, because I was still in shock and in ultimate disbelief.

On January 3, 2004, the same Saturday that the chief had his first conversation with me, he held a press conference. The chief's statements were reported in a newspaper article written by Mike O'Neal and titled "Chief Pledges Death Probe to Be Open." The *Chattanooga*

Times Free Press featured this article on Sunday, January 4, 2004. This title was misleading, because our experience was that the probe was more closed than open. In fact, the behavior of departmental personnel indicated that they were actually focused on being as closed as possible, even to the extent of lying. Regarding media reports, the police department is advantaged and the victim and family members are disadvantaged. People tend to believe the initial reports of the police, especially if it is stated by the chief and there is no video recording to the contrary.

Even though the truth may come out later, there are people who still believe the initial words of the chief and feel that police can do no wrong. After reading portions of the first news account of Leslie's death, you may understand why the family developed a lack of trust in the Chattanooga Police Department, a feeling that still remains. In my opinion, the content of Chief Dotson's interview amounted to fake news. The following excerpts are exact statements as quoted from the previously mentioned January 4, 2004, article.

Excerpt #1: *"Our desire is to be as transparent as possible in all cases, especially when someone's resisting arrest ends in their death."*

Rather than resisting arrest, Leslie was cooperating, according to the deposition later given by one of the police officers named in the lawsuit. Instead of arresting Leslie for the misdemeanor of public nudity, Leslie received the capital punishment of death. I continue to maintain strongly that Leslie's movements, in an attempt to breathe, were his resistance to death. Also, the police investigation was as closed as possible, not transparent. As an example, the department was not forthcoming with some public documents requested by the family until we employed an attorney to secure those items.

Excerpt #2: *"Mr. Prater collapsed while officers were trying to restrain him and efforts to save his life were unsuccessful."*

Officers already had Leslie restrained. He was already on the ground with his hands cuffed tightly behind his back, while they were on top of him. In fact, there were two sets of handcuffs used. At least one of the officers weighed more than two hundred pounds. Leslie's face was pushed into the ground, his legs were placed in the unlawful hog-tie position, and he was pepper sprayed by two different officers at two different times, all of which would compromise anyone's ability to breathe. There were no actions indicative of trying to save Leslie's life. No one should be held in a prone position, with face and chest down, hands cuffed behind their back, and pressure placed on them. That position causes one to have trouble breathing, and one's automatic action is to move in an attempt to breathe.[21] In fact, Leslie's life was not in danger prior to those officers' abusive, unmerciful, and horrible actions. After Leslie died at the scene, another officer arrived with a defibrillator. Of course, it was never used.

Excerpt #3: *"The three white officers who were first on the scene have been placed on paid administrative leave while the investigation is under way."*

Leslie was an African American male. Because it was mentioned that the three officers were white, it was likely that racial overtones would surface. There was a picture of four officers, with their faces blurred, released on *Chattanoogan.com* on January 5, 2004. The caption read, "Chattanooga Police did not release photos of four officers placed on paid administrative leave in the death of Leslie Prater." The release of that particular picture was another deliberate misrepresentation of the facts, because the officers involved with our case did not want their pictures released. The file photo was actually of four white police officers who were not connected to Leslie's death. Later, the department revealed that there was a discovery that a fourth officer was involved. Conveniently, that officer was African American. My question is "How could the police chief make such a significant mistake in a matter resulting in the death of a citizen?"

Excerpt #4: *"Chief Dotson said he had been told Mr. Prater was more than 6 feet tall and weighed more than 300 pounds and the two officers' use of pepper spray did not subdue him."*

Leslie was five feet, nine inches tall and weighed 232.5 pounds, as previously noted. Chief Dotson reported this information as fact, rather than checking the validity of what he had been told. When I first talked to Chief Dotson on the telephone, he told me that no pepper spray was used. Since the chief was not on the scene when Leslie died, I suppose he also received that information from the liars on his staff.

> Excerpt #5: *"An ambulance was called while officers scuffled with Mr. Prater, but before he lost consciousness. The decision to call the ambulance was due to the fact that something was obviously wrong with Mr. Prater, from either a medical or mental standpoint. Also, because of his size, it was going to be difficult to transport him in the back of a patrol car."*

It was a blatant lie that an ambulance was called because he was too large to travel in a patrol car. According to eyewitnesses and the deposition from one of the officers, when Leslie stopped moving at the scene, he was dead. The ambulance was called because, as a dead person, he could not walk to the patrol car. It is also interesting that there are probably numerous police officers in Chattanooga who are much larger than Leslie was, but they manage to ride in patrol cars. In the deposition given by one of the officers holding Leslie facedown, he admitted to having a weight and height that exceeded Leslie's size. Does anyone know of a policy dictating a size or weight threshold for riding in the back of a police cruiser? In Chattanooga, are ambulances part of the police department fleet of vehicles, designated to transport in-custody persons weighing 232.5 pounds or more? I never heard of such a ridiculous rationale for calling an ambulance. Why not use their "paddy wagon," which is an enclosed van used to transport prisoners? Certainly, using the "paddy wagon" would be more logical than the valuable resource of an ambulance for transporting very large citizens after an arrest.

> Excerpt #6: *"When Mr. Prater passed out, an officer took an automatic defibrillator from his patrol car and was preparing to use it when paramedics arrived and began performing CPR."*

Mr. Prater did not pass out. Mr. Prater died. The misinformation fed to the media did not stop with the chief's initial interview. With every news item that we read, there were false statements. Family and friends provided us with copies of all of the local Chattanooga newspaper stories and some recordings of the local television news reports about Leslie's death. Dwight and I read everything and watched the recordings.

After we arrived in Chattanooga, we saw some of the television news stories in real time. After viewing those reports, I was convinced that someone needed to speak on Leslie's behalf. The family would have to let the public know that there were lies being reported about Leslie and how he died. I recalled from a communications class I took that when something is repeated at least three times, it can be perceived as fact. A year after Leslie's death, one of his classmates contacted me because she heard a rumor that he had died. I confirmed that his death was a fact and explained the circumstances. She had heard about that situation of a man being killed by the police but felt the reports were of someone else. She said, "The description of the man didn't fit Leslie."

Television reporters wanted to talk to the family. It seemed that they all wanted to get the first "exclusive" interview. Initially, they didn't realize that Leslie's parents were no longer residents of Chattanooga, especially since we still owned a home there. In trying to contact us, the reporters had merely looked in the telephone book and began calling people with the last name of Prater and asking if they were Leslie's parents. We know this to be true from the Prater relatives who were contacted. This was during the time when, in addition to cell phones, most households still had a land line, with the telephone number published in the local telephone book.

All of the national television networks—ABC, CBS, and NBC—have local affiliates in Chattanooga. Their reports were very one-sided, featuring the information that was being fed to them by the police. Only one station, in my opinion, attempted to present Leslie as a human being, rather than as some inanimate menace to society. I began to realize that, in addition to reaching out to the media, we would be subjected to unwanted media attention. In situations like this, families cannot avoid media attention.

I walked through that week as though I was acting in a play, because this could not possibly be happening to us. This only happens to people you read about in the newspaper or see on the evening news. Could all of this be real? I was sick of hearing the television reports with all of the misinformation received from the police department. I felt I had to discredit some of that and fight back. I agreed to talk to a reporter at one specific station, because that reporter seemed more humane than others at the competing networks.

In my opinion, the ABC affiliate station was the only local news station that did not report Leslie as a villain. There seemed to have been sensitivity in its reports. Because I wanted the community to know that Leslie was a human being, with a family who loved him, I contacted the ABC affiliate and agreed to talk with its reporter. That reporter had been the most genuine and fair in reporting Leslie's death. Also, talking on camera would allow me the opportunity to stress the fact that Leslie was nonviolent and unarmed when he was brutally killed by police officers. He was not a monster and posed no threat to the health and safety of those police officers or any other citizens.

Both Dwight and I went to meet the reporter, but we had already decided that I would speak on behalf of the family. Because of my years of teaching and public speaking engagements, including giving television interviews, I had more experience with reporters. Of the utmost importance to us was that the public should have the opportunity to be made aware that Leslie was a real person, and not just the object of a news story. I took pictures of him to share with the reporter. I described the activities featured in each picture and the relationship of Leslie to others in those photographs. In all of the pictures I shared with her, Leslie was flashing his signature smile.

I appreciated the professional manner in which the interview was conducted. From my observation of the reporter's body language, she seemed sensitive to our situation. I didn't sense any judgmental attitudes, as I had sensed from some of the other reporters' accounts viewed on competing networks. She was objective and open to my expressions. I got the feeling that she sincerely wanted to know how we had been affected by the sudden death of our son, as well as the reactions of others who loved Leslie. Reporters are different too. Yes, they are in professional positions, but they also have biases. This is not an indictment of that profession or any other; it is just that we all have internal biases that can cloud our judgment. The difference is that some people are in critical positions of influence, while others are not.

Most of us have witnessed several breaking news stories where the loved ones of a victim, especially mothers, appear to be very emotional and totally in shock. The mother may be the only parent present, surrounded by other relatives, friends, and neighbors. She may be screaming, unable to speak coherently, disoriented, or barely able to stand without assistance. Perhaps her child's body is stretched out on the pavement. That is when a reporter puts a microphone in her face, with the cameras rolling, and asks, "How do you feel?" How can family members coherently respond to that question?

I understand that journalists have a job to do. They are people too, with varying degrees of compassion. Like everyone else, their behavior may be impacted by their own personal experiences and attitudes. When they get home after those reports involving sudden death, are they distressed? In those in-custody death situations, we are talking about the end of a person's life. Unfortunately, it is beginning to seem that in-custody sudden deaths and other homicides, especially from firearms, are the "new normal." Even when natural disasters cause one to lose a home, without any loss of life, the homeowner interviewed may state, "We can rebuild; at least we have our lives." It is a very different story when death occurs. Is sensitivity training a part of the orientation for a career in broadcast journalism? If not, it should be. We were fortunate in being able to avoid immediate interviews. That time lapse provided the time to absorb some of the emotional shock before arriving in Chattanooga. Many families don't have that option.

The best thing a family can do is to schedule a rebuttal press conference or take the lead in the interview to combat the negative newsfeed provided by police personnel. If no family member feels comfortable doing this, recruit someone else for that role. The longer the police version is the only one spread across the airwaves, the more difficult it is to reverse the attitudes created. Families must protect their interests. Otherwise, there is an attempt to portray the deceased as a villain or as someone not deserving to remain on earth. I want you to think about this.

Notice that when police officers kill an unarmed citizen, there seems to be an immediate follow-up story of the victim's arrest record, if one exists. Police departments also express that police officers have to make split-second decisions. At the time of that split-second decision, officers likely know nothing about a person's past. They don't have a toxicology report at their immediate disposal. My question is, why does the past of the victim matter? In that split-second decision, in situations where the lives of police officers or others are clearly not in danger, what was the rush to use force? Why is it necessary to bring up the person's past?

What does that person's background have to do with that particular incident at that point in time? In situations in which the same officers seem to be involved in these in-custody deaths and injuries, why is the background of those officers not investigated and immediately reported? The questionable background of Officer Betty Shelby, with a past history of illegal drug offenses and assaults, was not reported immediately, in contrast to negative reports about Terence Crutcher, the unarmed citizen she killed. Both sides of the case were reported by Bill Whitaker on the April 2, 2017, segment of *60 Minutes*.[22]

Drug tests are a common a part of the investigation for the deceased, but not for the officers involved in the deaths. Why are there not drug tests for all involved? Police officers are not immune from the disease of addiction. These are questions that should be asked. We, as citizens, need to resist the manipulation of the facts that are focused on dehumanizing the deceased. Demand the facts and a fair process in investigating these in-custody deaths, especially those of the unarmed. Question the standard process of the police investigating themselves.

5

FUELING A LEGAL BATTLE

After a wrongful death tragedy, the one overriding thing that can fuel a legal battle is anger. It is an emotion that occurs over the lifespan and is part of the grief process. With anger, one may not realize what is beneath the surface, such as feelings of grief, helplessness, frustration, and feelings of being attacked or overwhelmed. We can receive instruction on alternatives to responding with anger, such as the choices taught in anger management classes. But it appears that such negative responses are natural, passively waiting stimuli to arouse those feeling.

The Albert Ellis Institute in New York is the host for the Anger Disorders Treatment and Research Center that provides assessment and treatment for people with anger and aggression problems.[1] Dr. Raymond DiGiuseppe, the institute's leader, is considered one of the outstanding experts on anger in the world. The late Albert Ellis, an American psychologist, developed Rational Emotive Behavior Therapy in 1955. He proposed that people's beliefs strongly affected their emotional functioning. The therapy is based on the assumption that human beings are born with a potential for both rational and irrational thinking.[2]

Homicide is not an event that is easy to accept. When the death of an unarmed citizen occurs at the hands of one charged to serve and protect, it is even more abhorrent. The anger of family members is fueled to such a degree that a legal battle becomes their only rational recourse. Beyond that, there is only the irrational: an eye for an eye, or using more violence to match the violence, such as in gang wars, when one member is killed and the reaction from that gang is to kill a member from the opposing gang.

All too often, we hear news reports of people, probably motivated by irrational anger, killing strangers for no apparent reasons. Sadly, on July 8, 2016, twelve Dallas police officers were ambushed, resulting in the deaths of five officers from gunshot wounds. Those officers had devoted their lives to serving and protecting. They had families who loved them. They were complete strangers to the killer, with no prior contact with their assailant or his family. The killer told police negotiators that he wanted to kill white people, especially white officers. The killer was upset about nationwide police shootings of black men, although he had no personal connection to any of the black male victims.[3]

Our family members were angry, very angry at the time of the killing, as family members of other wrongful death victims have been. But in no situation, of which I am aware, has there been a desire for physical retaliation against police officers. I have heard relatives say that the officers should be fired or that they should be behind bars. Those are sentiments shared by my family as well. Numerous times, I have stated that I want everyone to live, including police officers who kill unarmed citizens. There are alternative methods of punishment that preserve life. Anger, sometimes escalating to rage, can surface when there is no accountability for such a death. Even persons indirectly affected by those wrongful homicides display anger. This is evidenced by the thousands of people who come out and march against these horrendous acts, such as in the protests in New York City, Baltimore, Los Angeles, Ferguson, or in Washington, D.C. The deceased were strangers to most of the protestors. The participants were marching for justice.

Unfortunately, some marches like these begin peacefully and end differently. I agree that it is amazing that persons would destroy their own neighborhood as a demonstration of anger. The Los Angeles riots that began on April 29, 1992, occurred after the acquittal of four white police officers of assault and three of the four of using excessive force in the videotaped beating of unarmed African American Rodney King.[4] Mr.

King's plea of "Can't we all just get along?" is still a question for 2017. A documentary on the History Channel included interviews of some of the riot participants.[5] One man talked about just "getting caught up in the moment." When viewing some of the tapes from the riots, he expressed shame for his involvement of looting stores. In explaining why people would burn business establishments in their own neighborhood, it was said that people did not feel ownership of the neighborhood or compassion for the business owners. Some were still angry, because on March 16, 1991, a female Korean store owner shot and killed Latasha Harlins, a fifteen-year-old unarmed African American girl. Although Latasha's killer was convicted of voluntary manslaughter, she served no prison time. For shooting Latasha in the head, the killer was fined $500 and sentenced to five years of probation and four hundred hours of community service. The beating of Rodney King occurred on March 7, 1991. The beating of King, closely followed by Latasha's homicide, served to compound the anger of persons living in South Central Los Angeles. It seemed that the escalation of anger overshadowed the rational thought process of how they and their neighbors would be negatively impacted. The rioting destroyed or damaged more than one thousand buildings in the Los Angeles area. Many of those establishments were gone forever from that community.[6]

But in the United States there is legal recourse and a rational alternative to violence. In this chapter, I will give the details of the personal experiences of our family in the legal process. Details of our situation will vary from those of other families, but some experiences are common. The overall experience of how families of victims of police brutality are treated is not unique to us. It appears that police officials often deliberately try to anger family members. I was angry before arriving in Chattanooga because I was aware of the lies being circulated from the department; I was also still angry about what the police chief had said to me: "I'm glad they didn't shoot him."

As mentioned previously, days passed after Leslie was killed before family members were allowed to see the body. I couldn't understand why the police wanted to "hide" the body from family members. Dwight and I were finally allowed to identify the body on Monday morning, January 5, at the funeral home. Secretly, I kept hoping that there had been some mistake. Because we did not know what to expect or what

our reactions might be, Dwight and I decided it was best to go to the
funeral home without other family members. Our son Stefan had not
arrived back in Chattanooga from Chicago. He was still in shock and
emotionally and physically unable to travel.

Upon our arrival at the funeral home, the owner greeted us. He then
said, "I can't let you all see the body." His words ignited more anger.
He explained that Leslie's body was still split open from the autopsy,
and it was unwise for us to see the body in that condition. I immediately
responded that we needed to see the body that was supposed to be our
son Leslie. I stressed that no family member had seen the body. Family
members were not allowed to see the body at the hospital. We were not
allowed at the forensic center to identify the body. Now the funeral director was telling us that we couldn't see the body at the funeral home.
Three days had passed, and no family member had seen the body. We
were further frustrated and confused by the news reports that described
the physical attributes of the deceased as more than six feet tall and
more than three hundred pounds. That description did not fit Leslie.

The funeral director sensed my urgency, anger, grief, and other emotions even I could not identify. With his years of experience, he must
have known that we were not leaving the funeral home without seeing
the body stored in the basement. He immediately proposed a solution.
He suggested that we give him and his staff some time to prepare the
body for us to view. They would wrap the head and cover the body
with sheets, but we would be able to see the face. We agreed to that
compromise. He left the room and we remained in his office, anxiously
awaiting his return.

Within an hour, he appeared in the doorway and told us that the body
was ready. We were ushered down a narrow stairway into a small, dimly
lit room. The body was on a gurney. I walked over to the body and immediately knew that it was Leslie, although only the space between his
chin and forehead was exposed. Dwight was holding me up, but I think
that I was steady, because nothing seemed real. I just stared at the body.
I noticed that Leslie's beautiful eyes were partially opened. It looked
like he was resting, but he was very still. I just kept standing there, star-
ing at him. My passive and unemotional demeanor was interrupted by
a question posed to us from a staff member, a high school classmate,
and the only other person in the room. He had the responsibility of

embalming Leslie's body. He asked, "Did you know that his shoulder was broken?" We responded, "No." We were further angered by this news and could now understand why officials did not want any family members to see the body. Surely, if family members had been allowed to see Leslie's body at the hospital, they would have noticed the bruises and other injuries.

A police department representative had given an interview reported in the metro section of the *Chattanooga Times Free Press* under the heading "Autopsy finds no excessive force used." There were other misleading and false statements reported in that article, including "Hamilton County Medical Examiner Dr. Frank King examined Mr. Prater's body Saturday and could find no obvious cause of death." Because of the limitations imposed upon us by the funeral home director, we could not see any other body parts to determine the extent of Leslie's other injuries. Weeks later, we were provided with the autopsy reports, which detailed the numerous injuries to his body. The article also included a false statement from Chief Jimmie Dotson, who said, "While officers were scuffling with Mr. Prater, he lost consciousness and later died at Erlanger hospital."

The Chattanooga Police Department requested and scheduled a meeting with the family on January 5, 2004, the Monday evening after Leslie was killed. The meeting was held at the Police Services Center. This was another stressful event on that day, but I sensed that it was more dreaded by police officials than by family members. This meeting also occasioned a series of statements from police officials to further intensify our anger. It was an enlightening experience. We were looking forward to their facing us with an explanation of Leslie's death, because we were still quite perplexed.

We informed our family members in Chattanooga about the arrangements for the meeting. Twelve family members attended. The only exception was the attendance of the pastor of the local Second Missionary Baptist Church, in which our immediate family still held memberships, including Leslie. The pastor, a former Hamilton County commissioner, was there to extend spiritual and emotional support to the family. Otherwise, he was primarily an observer. If he had not been known and respected community-wide, because of his religious and political affiliations, I'm not certain the police chief would have allowed his attendance. The pastor only asked one question, which was in regard to the dispatching of the ambulance. He stated that the timing of dispatching the ambulance seemed odd if early accounts given by the police officers were true. As you recall, police claimed that Leslie was too large to fit into a patrol car and that an ambulance was needed in order to arrest and transport him.

I think the police officials expected that only Dwight and I would meet with them, because the meeting was initially scheduled to occur in a rather small conference room. But in many black families, ours included, when one requests the presence of family, it includes extended family as well. There were approximately a dozen police officials there. Among those in attendance were the police chief, selected detectives, the deputy chief of Uniformed Services, the deputy chief of the Investigative Division, and a department public relations person. When family members began to enter the room, it became obvious that the conference room was too small. Chief Dotson immediately announced that the meeting would be moved to a larger room. If the meeting had remained in that room, it would have been standing room only, with barely enough floor space for people to stand.

The alternate location was more of a modest theater setting, but large enough for everyone to be seated comfortably. There was an elevated platform facing rows of auditorium-style seating. The police officials all sat on the platform, towering over the lower section, allowing them, I suppose, a sense of power, since they were perched above us. Family members were seated in the lower front sections, facing police officials. Chief Dotson facilitated the meeting and began with introductions of those sitting with him. Dwight interrupted him by asking if the officers who had killed Leslie were on the platform; otherwise the introductions were of little relevance to him. Chief Dotson's response was "No." Dwight said, "Then introductions are not necessary."

That verbal exchange was followed by Dotson's "speech," which seemed very rehearsed and phony to me. He expressed a canned statement about being sorry for our loss and that he was committed to a full investigation into what happened on that night. I don't think he expected some of our responses. We were not swayed by his empty words of compassion and empty promises, perceived by me to be insincere. Although he had a reputation as the "Bible-carrying" chief, I was not impressed. His words added fuel to the "fire" of our anger. The following is Chief Dotson's statement:

Thank you for coming this afternoon. I would like to make a few statements, then will entertain questions. The investigation into the death of 37-year-old Leslie Vaughn Prater is still in the early stages. I would like to extend my sympathies to Mr. Prater's family. The Chattanooga Police Department certainly wishes this incident had ended differently. As is always our procedure in incidents such as this, complete and thorough investigations are being conducted by the Chattanooga Police Department's Major Crimes Division, the Internal Affairs Division, and by the Tennessee Bureau of Investigation. When those investigations are completed, the results will be shared with you, as has been our practice.

Investigations have so far not determined what might have motivated Mr. Prater to take off his clothes and create a disturbance in the 800 block of Central Avenue. It is hoped that an autopsy underway at this time might shed light on that, as well as determining the cause of Mr. Prater's death.

Although those issues are still unknown, there are several things known at this point:

- *Police were first called around 6:47 by someone complaining of a naked man in the streets. According to the caller, Mr. Prater parked his car, got out, stripped, and began running around the area, yelling.*
- *Less than 10 minutes later, officers arrived and made contact with Mr. Prater, then attempted to take him into custody for further investigation.*
- *Officers retrieved Mr. Prater's pants and asked him to put them on. He refused to be cooperative and resisted being taken into custody.*
- *Two officers did use pepper spray on Mr. Prater, but to no effect.*
- *During the scuffle, officers made the decision to call for an ambulance to respond to the scene. This was before Mr. Prater lost consciousness. I commend the officers for their foresight.*
- *The decision to call the ambulance was due to the fact that something was obviously wrong with Mr. Prater, from either a medical or mental standpoint.*
- *Also, because of his size, it was going to be difficult to transport him in the back of a patrol car; an ambulance is much larger and would make transport much easier.*

- *Thirdly, officers recognized that given all the factors in this incident, having medical personnel on the scene would be prudent.*
- *When Mr. Prater lost consciousness, one of the officers on the scene got an AED, an Automatic External Defibrillator, out of his patrol car, but before it could be used, paramedics were on the scene. They treated him there, then transported him the few blocks to Erlanger a short time later. He was pronounced dead at 10:05.*

As I stated earlier, the investigations into this incident are just beginning. Our desire is to be as transparent as possible in all cases, especially when someone resisting arrest ends in their death. We will provide you with additional information when we can.

We later discovered that there were several inaccuracies in the chief's initial statement. Chapter 1, "How Did Leslie Vaughn Prater Die?" identifies some of the false statements. Several statements in the officer's deposition also refute the account given by Dotson. Leslie's movements, with four officers pinning his body to the ground, were to resist death, and not arrest. I apologize for repeating myself, but it is difficult to avoid. Their lies were so obvious, consistent, and outrageous that I feel a need to expose them whenever they recur.

The following are a few opposing views to challenge the legitimacy of statements from Chief Dotson that evening:

- *When the first two officers arrived, they were trying to assess the situation and were not attempting to take Leslie into custody. In one officer's deposition, he stated that he had not even made a decision to arrest Leslie.*
- *Officers did not retrieve Leslie's pants and request him to put them on. Officer Chambers and Leslie were walking to his car to get his clothes when backup arrived and took Leslie to the ground, where he died. Leslie was cooperating with Chambers, as documented in a deposition.*
- *Leslie was not too large to get into a patrol car.*
- *Leslie was cooperative and did not resist the directions of officers on the scene. His later struggling was after he was double hand-cuffed, pepper sprayed, and placed facedown on the ground, with his breathing compromised by the officers' actions. While facedown,*

he was held in the "hog-tie" position. At no time did he exhibit any aggressive movements toward the officers. He was just trying to breathe.

- *Although officially later pronounced dead at the hospital, Leslie died at the scene. The initial document from the hospital emergency room reported that Leslie was dead on arrival. This was also confirmed by eyewitnesses and at another meeting with two police detectives.*

- *The police department was not transparent, but rather was more focused on covering the truth. Officials were uncooperative in providing additional information when requested.*

Dwight continued his questioning by asking Dotson for more explanation as to why an emergency vehicle was called to the scene, because there were conflicting reports in regard to that action. The chief gave no clear response to that specific question. Initially, the chief stated that upon approaching Leslie, the officers did not know whether they were dealing with a medical or mental case. Interestingly, their own departmental policy stated that when first approaching someone who they think could be experiencing a mental health episode, they should not touch the person unless that person is in imminent danger or posing an immediate threat to someone else. Neither of these options was applicable in Leslie's case. He was no threat to anyone. Therefore, they violated their own policy. They did have other options. For example, the Chattanooga Police Department does have a Special Weapons and Tactics (SWAT) team. Why wasn't the SWAT team contacted? There was time to make that request and wait for the response from the SWAT team. The officers answering the call were obviously ill trained for an interaction with a person suspected of a physical or mental condition. There was no life-or-death situation that required a split-second "lifesaving" decision from them.

Angry family members asked other questions. "When would we receive the autopsy report?" They said that no official reports would be forthcoming for a few months. "Was a Taser used?" We were told, "No, only sergeants carry Tasers, and no one on-site had a Taser." We found out later that this, too, was false. If they had used a Taser instead of excessive physical force, Leslie might not have died. On the other hand, the use of such devices is controversial. In the interest of the safety of citizens, some police departments have banned them. In a 2013 *Dallas Observer* article, Amnesty International reported that, over the past dozen years, 540 mostly unarmed people had died after police use of a conducted electrical weapon.[7] Unfortunately, the Chattanooga Police Department is not one of those law enforcement agencies. One month and four days after Leslie's death, the department purchased sixty new conducted electrical weapons. Also, in 2012, the American Heart Association published a peer-reviewed study reporting that the device can cause heart attacks and death.[8] Twenty-seven-year-old Nicholas Cody of Marianna, Florida, died after a sheriff's deputy used a Taser on him during a traffic stop.[9] Another case is that of twenty-one-year-old Patrick Lee of Nashville, Tennessee, who died two days after being shocked nineteen times by a Taser.[10] In both cases, police officers were cleared of any wrongdoing. It was determined that those young men died from excited delirium. I have to ask: Why is it that excited delirium is only fatal when excessive force from police officers is claimed? Do you think the families of those young men were angry over the death of their unarmed love ones? Wrongful death lawsuits were filed in both cases.

During the meeting, Dwight accused Chief Dotson of being a liar. He confronted the chief with the fact that he had lied about Leslie's weight and height. Dwight insisted on a retraction and asked the chief, "Where did you get that information?" Chief Dotson stated that police officials had given him that information. To our amazement, the chief had merely accepted their statements as factual, without confirming their reports. This was an unfortunate tendency we found to be very common between the chief and his officials. Dwight said to Dotson, "As the chief, it is your duty to know the facts before you disseminate information about individuals." The chief said, "We will issue a public retraction to my statement about Leslie's weight and height." That may have happened, but we never saw it. It seems that retractions are often found in obscure places in newspapers, if at all. Fewer than 2 percent of factually flawed articles in daily newspapers are actually followed by a correction.[11]

Detective Angel, a senior detective official, stated that he knew Leslie did not weigh more than three hundred pounds and was not more than six feet tall. In fact, Angel had been in the room when the autopsy was being completed. Dwight said to Angel, "It seems strange that you knew the facts, but the chief was not privy to the same information." Angel had allowed the chief to report information that was known to be false. Maybe he and other police officials enjoyed making the chief appear foolish. If that was their objective, it was certainly accomplished. To this day, I don't understand why the chief did not fire the people who deliberately lied to him and showed no respect for his authority.

Why did they want to lie about Leslie's weight and height? It appeared to us that they were trying to establish a picture in the public's mind of this huge monster, who posed a threat to the safety of police and others, and it took four police officers to control him. I wish that at least one of the officers had possessed the critical thinking skills to determine that there were alternatives to resolving the situation. In lying about Leslie's size, maybe they were trying to copycat an altercation between Nathaniel Jones and the police department in Cincinnati. Jones, who was reported to be more than three hundred pounds and more than six feet tall, died on November 30, 2003, from asphyxia during an altercation with several police officers. His case was nationally publicized and widely known.[12] It seemed too much of a coincidence that the Chattanooga Police Department would use the weight and height identified with Jones to falsely describe Leslie. The coroner in Cincinnati reported Jones to be three hundred and fifty pounds. He also ruled the death a homicide.[13]

I asked the chief for clarification regarding the use of mace. When Chief Dotson spoke to me on the Saturday before the meeting, he told me that no mace was used. However, in a journalist's interview with Dotson and printed prior to our arrival in Chattanooga, he stated that pepper spray was used by two officers.[14] Maybe Dotson was "splitting hairs" in terms of the use of mace versus pepper spray. After we arrived in Chattanooga, we were told that pepper spray was used. In fact, in the Monday meeting, we were told that two officers sprayed Leslie with no effect, so each sprayed Leslie again. We asked, "Could this take a person's breath away?" Chief Dotson and others on the platform affirmed that it could. We understood that pepper spray was essentially the same as mace. The name "pepper spray" designates a substance that can cause death and be used as a torture device.[15]

Family members continued to question the officials. We asked, "Why did they have him facedown after spraying him four times with

pepper spray?" The response was that the officers were trying to restrain him and that one officer checked Leslie's breathing and another
officer came and turned his head to the side. When we later talked to
an eyewitness, he stated, "Your son would be alive today if they had
just turned his head to the side." We had been told that officers had
gotten a defibrillator out to use prior to the arrival of the emergency
vehicle. Dwight asked, "Why were you going to use a defibrillator on
our son if he was only unconscious? Wouldn't it be dangerous to use
a defibrillator on a person's heart that is beating normally?" The response to that question was that the defibrillator was not used because
of the timing of the arrival of the emergency vehicle.

The department had issued a statement that there was no trauma
to Leslie's body. We asked for clarification, considering that we had
been at the funeral home earlier that day and discovered that there was
trauma to the body. Dwight asked them to explain their definition of
trauma, since we had also been told that Leslie's arm was broken. Actually, the word "arm" was used synonymous with shoulder here, based on
the location of the injury described by the funeral home staff member.
Angel quickly responded, "There was no broken arm bone; it was dislocated." Dwight responded, "This is a conflict with what we were told,
but even if his arm was dislocated instead of broken, that is still trauma."
The anger continued escalating in that room with every unsatisfactory
answer. An official who had attended the autopsy mentioned that Leslie had an enlarged heart. Dwight's brother Michael stated, "It seems
strange to me that people are walking around with an enlarged heart,
but they only die from the enlarged heart after physical contact with
police officers." Family members asked, "Who were the people present
at the autopsy?" The names mentioned included pathologist Dr. Frank
King, his assistant Allison Leach, and police officials Mike Tilley, Tim
Carroll, Dave Emerson, and Steve Angel.

Chief Dotson stated that he would take responsibility for making certain that a full investigation was completed regarding the circumstances
of Leslie's death. I confronted him with the question, "You have already
announced your retirement, so how can you make this promise?" The
chief appeared shocked that I was aware of his plans to soon retire. Although we no longer resided in Chattanooga, I still remained connected
to a lot of people and also read *Chattanoogan.com* on a daily basis. Chief

Dotson had announced his retirement plans weeks prior to Leslie's death. It was public knowledge, even to someone living in Missouri.

The chief responded, "Yes, I am getting ready to retire, but the department would be committed to this investigation, including the person replacing me." Although he may have thought I was operating from a position of ignorance, I knew that the minute he was no longer the chief, he had no jurisdiction over the behavior of departmental personnel. The truth is that his staff had already demonstrated that they had no respect for him, based on their lack of remorse or accountability for lying to him. The chief was clearly a "lame duck" and was treated as such. After the plaques were presented, the photographs taken, and the cookies and punch consumed, that would be the end of his six-year reign. Also, I wasn't convinced of his interest in doing the right thing in securing the truth and advocating for justice. He was already guilty of lying to the press and lying to me.

As Chief Dotson and I engaged in continued dialogue, I was watching closely the body language, and especially the facial expressions, of other persons on the platform. I learned tips for evaluating body language when I was working on my master's degree in counseling. One person in particular appeared to have a smirk and half-smile on his face. It was as though he was enjoying that Dotson was being interrogated by angry family members. That person was Steve Parks, who was an internal applicant to replace Dotson as chief. Possibly he felt that he was next in line to be named for the position.

On January 14, 2004, just twelve days after Leslie was killed, Mayor Bob Corker announced his choice of Larry Wallace as the city's next police chief. Wallace, who had not even applied for the position, was in fact the consultant paid $8,500 to assist the mayor to find a replacement for Dotson. As you might imagine, although he did return the consultant's fee, the appointment did not pass the "smell test" for Chattanooga residents, the police union, or the city council. Possibly because of the uproar and lack of transparency surrounding the appointment, on January 21 Mayor Corker announced that Mr. Wallace had withdrawn his name from consideration.[16]

Steve Parks got his wish. On February 4, 2004, one month and two days after Leslie's death, the city council confirmed him as Chattanooga's next police chief. Maybe the smirk on his face was because he believed that he was going to be the new chief and that Dotson's words would have no influence in his administration, or in his oversight of the investigation into Leslie's death. Not everyone was convinced that Parks was the best person for the job. One mother spoke out against the council's decision. Her son, Tory Hardy, was shot and killed in 2003. She expressed that Parks, as the deputy chief providing oversight of that investigation, had mishandled the case.[17] I was also unhappy with Parks's selection. Although I had not met him prior to Leslie's killing, I had some knowledge of his background. When he was a rookie cop, he killed a person armed with a shotgun, a married white businessman and father of two daughters and a son.[18] I had personal knowledge of that situation. When that incident occurred, one of the victim's daughters was a student in my class, and I taught the other one a few years later. Based on the circumstances surrounding their father's death, I believe Steve Parks was remorseful. In that tragic situation, it appeared that he had no choice, in order to preserve his life and the lives of others. Because of how he felt about his killing a citizen, my concern was that his empathy would be directed more toward police officers, not with us, and certainly not with Leslie.

I cannot recall all of the questions family members asked that evening, especially those that were not captured in the written notes. What I do recall is that police departmental administrators were blasted with questions from family members. I also recall that the officials had few, if any, responses that were satisfactory to us. Near the end of the meeting, the chief asked, "Who would be the contact family member for us to report progress on the investigation?" Frankly, I was surprised by that question. Obviously, he made the inaccurate assumption that because Dwight and I lived out of town, the department would contact a Chattanooga relative to receive updates. I suppose they believed that we would just go away and passively await the police department to contact us at their convenience. Possibly that was their practice in the past with other families, other cases, other wrongful deaths.

Dwight and I made it very clear that we, as Leslie's parents, would be the contact source. At the conclusion of the meeting, I sensed that the chief and his staff got the message that their rehearsed and canned responses and process of handling similar situations in the past would probably not work with this family. Because of the history of in-custody deaths in Chattanooga, I imagined that they had a system for how to deal with families in these matters. However, we were not intimidated by them in any way, and we were determined to get to the truth of how Leslie died.

At least two police officials should have had an idea that Leslie's family was going to present a challenge. The day prior to Dwight and me arriving in Chattanooga, Detectives Angel and Tilley had already talked to Leslie's cousins, Spen and Ronnie. The two detectives assigned to the case requested that the brothers meet with them. According to Ronnie, the conversation was mostly one-sided. Police officials did most of the talking, and Ronnie and Spen just listened. Leslie was like a little brother to them, so they were still in shock. Questions asked by officials focused on what they knew about Leslie's life and his activities on January 2. During that meeting, police officials offered no explanations about how Leslie had died. Spen did tell them about seeing Leslie on the Friday afternoon of his death. He and Leslie talked briefly, mostly about Leslie's excitement regarding his job interview at the Coca Cola office the following Monday. Spen told the detectives that Leslie was not intoxicated, nor was he running around downtown Chattanooga screaming all day, as reported in a prior fake news item.[19] Spen drove a Coca Cola delivery truck and encountered Leslie on his route. According to Ronnie, at the conclusion of the meeting a detective asked if they had any questions. Ronnie responded, "No, but when Dr. Prater gets here, she will have plenty of questions." He said that detective looked shocked and immediately asked, "Who is Dr. Prater?" Ronnie responded, "Dr. Prater is Leslie's mother, and she will definitely have questions."

The insensitive actions and attitudes of police officials toward families serve as building blocks that erect a tower of anger. There were many other circumstances, from law enforcement officials as well as others, that added more blocks. Days before Leslie's funeral, I was approached by a member of the local National Association for the Advancement of Colored People (NAACP) on the parking lot of our church who said, "We get along well with the police. We have been conducting workshops focused on how people should respond when stopped by the police." My anger was fueled, because I thought, "Here we go again, always blaming the victim." I wondered who was teaching the police about how to behave when they stop citizens.

The words from the NAACP member were not comforting to me. Often, especially if police use firearms, victims don't have an opportunity to use any of the techniques suggested in a workshop. For example, if you are stopped by the police, you have the legal right not to speak and can say, "I would like to remain silent."[20] Sometimes police officers discharge their firearms first and ask questions later, as in the case of unarmed Jonathan Ferrell, mentioned previously. If you recall, Mr. Ferrell was immediately tased and fatally wounded from several gunshots. According to reports, there was no verbal exchange between Mr. Ferrell and the police officers.[21] Maybe he had attended NAACP's workshop, but didn't get the chance to use any of those recommendations. Sometimes it doesn't matter what you do or don't do. If you encounter a rogue, aggressive, or hateful police officer, your well-being is in danger. The majority of police officers most likely would have helped Mr. Ferrell or Leslie, but those were not the officers answering the call.

Other than a responsible public servant employed in the role of a police officer, what could have saved the life of fifteen-year-old Jordan Edwards? On April 29, 2017, in Balch Springs, Texas, Jordan died after a police officer fired a rifle into a car, shooting Jordan in the back of the head. Jordan, a straight-A student, talented athlete, and African American, was riding in a car driven by his brother. The assailant white police officer was not threatened or in fear for his life, although he tried to cover up his actions with lies. There were no weapons or drugs in the car—just young African American males leaving a party. On May 2, 2017, the police officer was fired. Subsequently, he was arrested for murder.[22] I am grateful there was a body cam recording to document that homicide. I cringe when thinking about how many wrongful deaths were not recorded and the words of the guilty were accepted as facts, their actions justified with the infamous phrase "I felt threatened."

In the absence of effective public relations guidance, and in the presence of insensitivity, Chief Dotson telephoned our pastor to offer assistance to the family. The pastor forwarded the message to me that the police department had offered to escort the funeral procession from the church to the cemetery. I was furious. My initial thought was "They kill Leslie and now they want to escort him to his grave." If they wanted to help the family, they could have arrested those officers who killed him. Of course, the family refused the offer.

During the week, after Leslie was killed, police department officials were consistent in demonstrating insensitivity to what we were experiencing. Nothing prepares you for planning a funeral and burial of your child, which is listed as the fifth life stressor on the Social Readjustment Rating Scale.[23] Within a period of seven days, I had talked to Leslie, who was well and happy; was notified of his untimely and violent death; had traveled from Cape Girardeau, Missouri, to Chattanooga; selected a funeral director and identified Leslie's body; met with police departmental administrators; initiated the process of planning a funeral and completing all of the related activities; talked with an attorney; completed arrangements for a second autopsy; talked to numerous friends and relatives; conducted interviews with media representatives; and selected a burial site. It was exceptionally difficult to devote so much energy to all of these matters, especially since we were still in shock, eating very little, and hardly sleeping. Yet the police department continued to anger us by asking us to come out to the Police Services Center again to meet with detectives. They knew who killed Leslie. Why did they need more meetings with us? The four officers were preparing to go back to their original assignments, even before Leslie was buried.

Anger even surfaced while the pastor was delivering Leslie's eulogy. He talked about his fondness for Leslie and his infectious smile and winning personality. He shared his memory of the last time he saw Leslie. One could sense that he was sincerely distressed by Leslie's death. He appeared more saddened when speaking about the many other young African American men whose lives were lost to violence. He said, "As a society, we are losing because of the untimely death of, yet another, young black male." I could identify with the pastor's words, while also selfishly thinking of how Leslie was blessed with artistic talent to create paintings and drawings, but there would be no more future works from him. Leslie's future on Earth was gone forever. Our family would not have any more conversations with him. We wouldn't receive any more greeting cards or embraces from him. Stefan no longer had a "big brother" with whom he could interact. I was especially heartbroken when Stefan viewed the body for the last time. He loved his brother so much. I felt so helpless, because I couldn't shield him from the pain that he was obviously suffering.

I could write another book on just the many instances of anger that have been surfacing and resurfacing from the time of the notification of Leslie's death until this very day. I sincerely hope that the anger will subside one day, because anger consumes a lot of energy and obstructs peace of mind. Sometimes it occurs in the strangest places, at the most awkward of times. Anger has surfaced while attending weddings, because Leslie had not experienced marriage. When I am around the grandchildren of others, I think about how there is no potential to grandparent Leslie's children. Somehow, I experience anger during the changing of seasons. My thoughts are "This is another spring that Leslie won't experience." I especially fight feelings of anger during holidays, on Leslie's Christmas Eve birthday, and when I visit his grave. When the jazz artists Leslie loved release songs, I get angry because I want him to hear these new works.

From talking to other mothers of sons killed by the police, I know that many are struggling with the same kind of anger. Marcia Riley continued to express anger about the death of her unarmed son. She was determined to get more mothers involved in this fight for justice. Marcia's dream of justice ended with her death in 2016. I know that the mothers of Derek Hale and Brandon Miller were angry about police killing their sons. And the anger is heightened by the lack of accountability for these homicides.

After fighting charges in the shooting death of unarmed Walter Scott, former police officer Michael Slager finally entered a guilty plea in federal court in Charleston, South Carolina. Two years earlier, Slager had shot Mr. Scott several times in the back while the victim was running away from him. Slager had stated that he feared for his life, but on May 2, 2017, Slager finally admitted that was not true. Mr. Scott's family responded to the announcement, "We can now begin to heal, because the truth was told."[24]

Families want justice, but they are usually overpowered by a system that is reluctant to bring criminal charges against police officers in these homicides. Usually, the only recourse for the family is to engage an attorney to file a wrongful death lawsuit in civil court. Even then, there is no guarantee that there will be a ruling in favor of the family. Whatever the outcome, the family is still the big loser, because nothing can replace the life that was taken.

Immediate family. Front row, left to right: Dwight A. and Loretta Prater. Back row, left to right: Leslie and Stefan Prater.
Courtesy of Author

Left to right: Louise Arnold, aunt of Leslie Prater, and Leslie.
Courtesy of Author

Happier times at Stefan's wedding in 2000. Left to right: Stun Easley, Rick Bakewell, Stefan, and Leslie.
Courtesy of Author

Happier times: Leslie's graduation
Courtesy of Author

The last picture of Leslie with Stefan, a week before Leslie's death. Taken in December 2003, Atlanta, Georgia.
Courtesy of Author

A view of a Prater protest march in downtown Chattanooga, Tennessee, in 2004.
Courtesy of Author

LESLIE VAUGHN PRATER
DEC. 24, ✝ JAN. 2,
1966 2004
NEVER BE ANOTHER YOU

Leslie's gravesite
Courtesy of Author

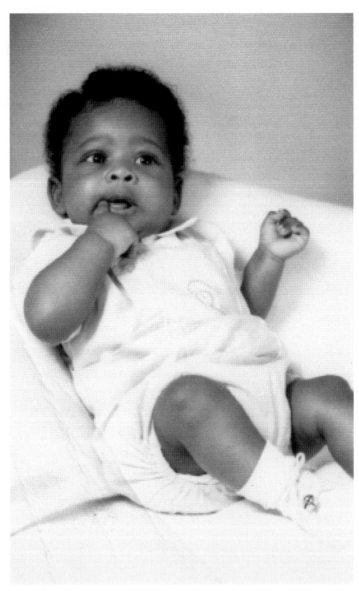

Leslie's baby picture
Courtesy of Author

Left to right: Lezley McSpadden, mother of Michael Brown, and Loretta Prater.
Courtesy of Author

Left to right: Loretta and Connie Hale. Connie is the mother of Derek Hale.
Courtesy of Author

6

TO SETTLE OR NOT TO SETTLE IN WRONGFUL DEATH CASES INVOLVING POLICE OFFICERS

If anyone had told me that I would be in the middle of a legal battle with a police department and the city of my birth, I would have immediately said, "No way." After all, I am a law-abiding citizen, with friends and relatives who are police officers. At the time of Leslie's death, I was an academic dean, leading a college that included a Department of Criminal Justice and Sociology and the Regional Police Academy. I was instrumental in the employment of faculty who researched criminal justice issues and taught hundreds of students about those matters. I was a champion for criminal justice instruction and recruiting future professionals to enter careers in law enforcement. I approved requests for faculty to continue their professional development by attending national and international criminal justice conferences. Also, while living in Chattanooga for fifty years, I was significantly engaged in numerous civic relationships and boards. Some of those activities were connected directly to the police department.

For most of my life, I believed in the expression "We are the police and we are here to help you." That was my introduction and early interaction with police. When Leslie was killed, I was thrust into circumstances that forced me to reevaluate my idealistic beliefs. Consequently, I shifted from trust to mistrust and from respect to disrespect and disappointment in the Chattanooga Police Department and some other members of the judicial system. With some initial difficulty, I came to realize that there is a dark side of policing.

My introduction to police officers began as a six-year-old in the first grade. The stories in our early readers were mostly about white families and others in their community. A police officer was among those always pictured as a neighborhood staple, sort of akin to the roles portrayed on *Sesame Street*. The residents were characters that were predictable and easy for children to remember. In those early readers, the police officer was always a white male, never a male of any other identity or a policewoman. He was always friendly, helpful, well liked, and respected. Often the policeman was pictured assisting children to cross the street en route to and from school. Through those readings, I developed a very positive attitude about police officers. At that time, I had never met a police officer.

In 1948, seven black police officers were hired to walk beats in black neighborhoods in Chattanooga, but I don't recall ever seeing them. It was not until 1960 that black officers could patrol all neighborhoods and even arrest white citizens. Chattanooga is credited with integrating its police department decades earlier than most departments in the South.[1] That is amazing, because 1960 doesn't seem to be very long ago.

I don't recall having any direct interactions with police officers prior to adulthood. I did see police officers on local television. I would sometimes see officers cruising through communities in their cars or on foot patrol in commercial areas. Also, the fathers of some of my classmates from school were police officers, but I didn't know them personally. In adulthood, I became acquainted with police officers mostly through church, civic, or professional situations. There were police officers as members of our church. Some of my high school classmates joined the Chattanooga Police Department. I had relatives and neighbors who became law enforcement officials. I greatly respected police officers and the sacrifices they made as public servants. I want to be very clear that, before Leslie's death, direct interactions between police officers and me had been positive.

The majority of my positive associations with officers occurred during my professional role as an educator. As a teacher in junior and senior high schools, police officers were often invited into my classroom, depending on the subject discussed. As a teacher of family and consumer sciences, there were opportunities to discuss security and safety topics directly impacting families. "Just Say No" drug education programs were popular during that time. One comical situation occurred when an officer presented a talk to my students about the dangers of drugs. He brought an educational kit with him that contained a number of drug samples. When he burned the marijuana sample to illustrate the smell, one of the assistant principals frantically raced down the hall in search of the student culprit whom he believed was smoking marijuana in the building. My classroom was directly across the hall from the boys' bathroom.

After fourteen years of classroom teaching in secondary schools, I accepted a position as the first administrator of Chattanooga Public Schools' Drug Free Schools federal program. In that role, I experienced numerous other opportunities for positive interaction with police officers. I served with them on various committees, including the Operation Prom/Graduation Committee. We were charged with providing education and safe strategies targeted to the issue of teenagers' illegal use of alcohol and other drugs, and the occurrence of date rape among that population. For example, the California Coalition against Sexual Assault found that approximately 50 percent of reported date rapes occurred among teenagers, and the high levels of alcohol consumed on prom night increased these odds.[2] The combination of graduation celebrations and alcohol consumption also leads to the likelihood of increased motor vehicle accidents. I spent many hours with dedicated and respected police officers working on those issues.

While employed in that administrative position, the most significant interaction with police officers resulted from my role as Chattanooga's cofounder of the Drug Abuse Resistance Education program, more commonly known as DARE. I worked closely with Ralph Cothran, Chattanooga's first African American police chief. He served admirably until his death from cancer in 1995. Chief Cothran often referred to me as Chattanooga's "Mother of DARE." I was instrumental in selecting the urban schools that would implement the program. I interviewed prospective DARE officers, forwarded my recommendation to the chief, and interacted closely with those police officers after the program's implementation. I worked with DARE until I left the school system to accept a position at the University of Tennessee at Chattanooga. DARE was ended in 2005, after Chief Parks read an article questioning the effectiveness of the program.[3]

Police departments have existed for decades; yet people still commit crime. Should we get rid of police departments and conclude that those social service agencies are not working? No, we do just the opposite. We employ more police officers and continue to increase budgets for law enforcement efforts, including correctional facilities; yet crime continues. Ironically, 75 percent of public funds for incarceration are from budgets originally intended to fund health care, housing, public assistance, and education.[4] Where are our priorities? We continue to report that prevention is the best course of action to address social problems, yet we continue the same failed strategies. I have heard that insanity is the expectation of a different outcome while continuing the same behavior. In addition to drug abuse education and strategies to avoid negative peer pressure, one of the most positive outcomes from DARE is the positive relationship developed between elementary school students and police officers. Today, the media outlets are flooded with inquiries about how police can regain trust and respect in urban communities. From direct observations between police officers and youth in DARE programs, I witnessed the development of friendship, trust, and respect that students held for DARE officers. DARE is a worthwhile component of community policing. I continue to stress that attitudes are formed early.

When I moved from Chattanooga to become an administrator at Eastern Illinois University, I connected with the Charleston, Illinois, police department. In response to their chief's request, I became a volunteer consultant. In that role, I conducted a series of workshops for parents who were court-ordered to participate in parenting workshops. I continued my relationship with that department until we moved from Illinois to Missouri. I was recruited as the Dean of the College of Health and Human Services (CHHS) at Southeast Missouri State University. As previously discussed, that administrative position was significantly intertwined with criminal justice initiatives. Also, during my time as dean, the Cape Girardeau police chief served a term as the president of the college's advisory council. My many situations of direct contact with police and other law enforcement officers were positive experiences.

Prior to Leslie's death, I could have easily led a fan club for police departments. My experiences with police officers supported the belief that, collectively, officers upheld the law and were law-abiding citizens themselves. For the most part, I had stereotyped current police departments as positive, different from the days of Jim Crow in the South, when a racial caste system of government-sanctioned racial oppression made it common for police to be involved in assaulting or killing black people.[5] They covered up their crimes and the actions of others involved in similar crimes. Now, we are being told that there is a new Jim Crow, characterized by more black people being killed by police officers than during the times of the first Jim Crow.[6] How could I have been so blind?

In more modern times, I was totally aware that there were a few "bad apples," but I felt that those officers would be disciplined or fired, depending on the violation. In fact, I had known of situations in which officers accused of theft or insubordination were subjected to disciplinary action, sometimes leading to termination. I was mostly unaware that officers could kill unarmed citizens who were of no obvious threat to their safety without any consequences. Also in 2004, technology was unavailable to readily record those incidents in real time, and social media was in its infancy. Because of my ignorance of the far-reaching "Blue Wall of Silence" and my blind trust of officers I knew personally, I was shocked by the immediate response of the Chattanooga Police Department. It was as though I was hit by a bolt of lightning that thrust me into another world, the world of reality.

On January 1, 2004, I was a friend of the police, and after January 2, 2004, I was treated as an enemy. How could this have happened overnight and through no fault of my own? Within days, my trust and respect for officers and administrators of my hometown police department dissolved and vanished. The real police department, free from all of my perceptions and those of others, was revealed to me. Those imperfections had been there all the time, but I didn't see them; my view was clouded by seeing only what I wanted to see. From that day forward, our family was in a battle like no other we had ever experienced, or anticipated.

When engaging in a battle, one does not go forward without preparation. We had no experience, training, or armor for what we were about to face. Dwight had been in the air force during the time of the Vietnam War, but even his military experience could not help us. Dwight, Stefan, and I had love and support from family and friends, educational credentials, good jobs, a spiritual foundation, a respect for the law, and no record of illegal infractions. Those were the only resources we initially had to take to the battlefield. We were the underdog David and the police officers and the system of law enforcement were collectively Goliath.[7] They had the police union, a system of protective devices couched within the judicial system, a staff of taxpayer-funded attorneys, a lot of experience avoiding accountability in wrongful death accusations, the support of public opinion of those who believe that the police could do no wrong, and the established connection to media outlets. To us, it seemed as though they had all of the advantages. What they did not have was our passion for seeking truth and justice at all costs. They didn't have our spiritual foundation and belief that God would help us. They didn't have the love for Leslie or the memories we shared with him. Also, we had the unwavering belief that Leslie was a homicide victim.

Given our limited resources in comparison to those of the police department, where was our help? Where did we need to start? What should be our next move? These were some of the questions that were tormenting us during our sleepless nights. It was clear that the police department would be of no help to us. Their energies were consumed with spreading lies, engaging in cover-up activities, and profiling Leslie as a monster. I always thought that in a homicide case, especially as determined by the autopsy reports, the office of the district attorney would be of help to the victims, rather than the perpetrators. Support was denied our family. We discovered that if the accused are police officers, there is a completely different set of rules and procedures. We were very disappointed that the district attorney, a former police officer and son of a former local judge, would not even take the case before the grand jury. In fact, he never made any direct contact with the family. In my opinion, he joined others in the role of our enemy and the friend of the police. Our experience with the Chattanooga Police Department was that existing laws applied to others, not to their police officers. There was only one time that any degree of sensitivity was extended to us from the district attorney's office. Years after Leslie's death, an attorney from that office attended one of our memorial services. My impression was that she was representing herself, as a compassionate citizen, rather than representing the district attorney. After the service, she introduced herself to me and personally expressed her sympathy. In fact, I'm not even sure her boss knew that she attended Leslie's memorial service. I was glad when that district attorney later retired.

Initially, our help came from friends and relatives. One of our friends and church members was a longtime community advocate. Johnny suggested to us that we needed to seek advice from an attorney. He knew of one who had a reputation for representing persons with complaints against police officers. Because of the social justice focus of his cases, this attorney was disliked by officers and the local police union. With our approval, he facilitated a meeting between us and attorney John Wolfe. As you might imagine, most attorneys "run away" from these cases. They want to maintain a positive relationship with the police department, rather than participate in situations that could potentially create a wedge between them and police officers. They anticipate their need of officers' cooperation in winning their future cases. In other words, they don't want to "rock the boat," and they will avoid controversial lawsuits against police officers. Because Mr. Wolfe had previously angered Chattanooga police officers, he did not appear intimidated by the police union. The perception communicated by the attitude of the police union is that police officers are right and everyone else is wrong, regardless of the facts. Even now, with all of the video evidence of excessive force, the union is fierce in support of police officers in cases of police killings of unarmed citizens. For example, in the well-known case of the death of Eric Garner in New York, there were no criminal charges filed.[8]

Our first meeting with Mr. Wolfe was very helpful. There was no mention of any lawsuit. It was more of a consultation, as we were seeking some direction and an idea of what we might expect, based on Mr. Wolfe's experience. The first advice was to arrange a second autopsy independent of Chattanooga or Hamilton County. That seemed reasonable to us, since police officials were at Leslie's autopsy in Chattanooga and still there were lies about the condition of his body, his weight and height. Mr. Wolfe made the arrangements to transport Leslie's body to Nashville for the second autopsy. As lay citizens, and as parents dazed by the shock of Leslie's death, we would not have been able to accomplish that task. From that meeting, we got an idea of the monumental ordeal that we would be facing, especially in a city with such a long history of police brutality allegations without any accountability. It's still hard for me to believe that after fifty years living in Chattanooga I had been unaware of the long history. It would be an understatement to say that we were overwhelmed at the end of that meeting. After the meeting, there was a sense of trust emerging that this man could be of help to us as we pursued justice for Leslie's death.

We left the meeting with an assumption that we would need some form of continuous legal advice throughout this process. We felt the precariousness of solely depending on the judicial process in seeking justice. The justice system is an abstract concept. At the micro level and at every step of the process, the living, breathing organisms responsible for justice are the individuals in charge of each unit couched within the system. These individuals hold attitudes that might be inconsistent with punishing police officers for killing an unarmed young black man, regardless of the circumstances. We needed someone within the legal community to be on our side, even if it meant employing the person for that role.

The next glimmer of assistance came from a relative on the day of Leslie's funeral. I received a call of sympathy and support from Janice, a cousin living in New Haven, Connecticut. During our discussion, she insisted that I needed to get in contact with attorney Emma Jones, of New Haven. Prior to calling Emma, I researched news articles that reported her situation. Malik, Emma's twenty-one-year-old unarmed son, had been shot and killed approximately seven years prior to Leslie's homicide.[9] When I later contacted Emma, she was very understanding and compassionate. Her response to me was not as an attorney but as one grieving mother to another. More of my interaction with Emma is shared in chapter 8.

As a university professor, my next action was to research publications dealing with matters of police brutality. I found very little that addressed helping families impacted directly by police misconduct. Most articles are more descriptive in reporting quantitative data. I found only one gem that was focused on guiding families in these matters. That helpful information was presented by the Stolen Lives Project, a joint effort of the Anthony Baez Foundation, the National Lawyers Guild, and the October

22 Coalition.[10] The Anthony Baez Foundation was established in memory of the unarmed twenty-nine-year-old victim of police brutality killed on December 22, 1994, in New York.[11] The National Lawyers Guild was founded in 1937 and is the oldest and most extensive network of public interest and human rights activists working within the legal system.[12] Beginning in 1996, October 22 is the national day of protest chosen by the group identified as the October 22 Coalition, with the goal of stopping police brutality, repression, and the criminalization of a generation.[13]

Certainly, the idea of Stolen Lives caught my attention. Through their book project, Stolen Lives has documented thousands of cases of unlawful deaths from police brutality. The significance of their effort is that, rather than just reporting numbers, there is a face to these tragedies. They tell the stories about the circumstances surrounding these deaths and recognize that victims are a part of family units. In their book publication, there is direct information to assist families. They developed the "Family First Aid Kit" to help families who have lost a loved one to police violence.[14] We followed their guidelines, as best we could, and found them to be very beneficial.

According to the coalition, the untimely death of a loved one begins the tragedy for the family. With police killings, the grief is compounded in the following ways:

- *Your world is filled with confusion, as those sworn to protect you destroy your loved one.*
- *You are made to feel isolated, as the police force mobilizes to protect its own at the cost of the truth.*
- *To diminish their guilt, they publicly demonize the victim.*
- *Your natural support system may be unsympathetic when you turn to them for emotional or spiritual solace, as they have been influenced by the police slant that always receives most of the media attention.*
- *Even the strongest family's integrity is challenged by this onslaught, and, at best, you and your family must assume a defensive posture instead of seeking the necessary closure in your grief.*
- *The natural search for justice shall set many tasks and obstacles before you.*

To further cope with this trauma, the October 22 Coalition suggested that families do the following:

- *Develop a support system and pursue legal strategies.*
- *Document all related interactions and collect all pertinent records.*
- *Do your own investigation and present your case to the media.*

We quickly discovered that the police department mobilized to protect their own. They were steadfast in their uncooperative actions throughout the legal process. Departmental officials used every available vehicle to keep information from the family and to cover up their actions. For example, on June 15, 2004, at 3:15 p.m., Dwight and I went to the Police Services Center to ask for a use-of-force report. The person at the window informed us that they did not release these reports. I knew that statement to be untrue. I then asked for an incident report. I was told that someone would have to approve their releasing the report. A few minutes later, we were told that someone would come out and talk to us. We waited patiently, but no one ever came out. At 3:40, we were called back up to the window and handed a four-page report that was very incomplete and provided little to no information of value. That a professional, taxpayer-funded department would distribute such *trash* to represent a Chattanooga Police Department incident report is an embarrassment. In fact, more information had been reported in the newspaper and on television than was listed on that report. However, the report did list Leslie's height as five feet, eleven inches and his weight as 235 pounds (not more than six feet and more than 300 pounds). The date and time listed on the report was January 2, 2004, at 19:25 (7:25 p.m.). The next date near the bottom of the report was very interesting. According to the report given to us, the incident narrative was entered on April 1, 2004, at 8:11:56 a.m., one day shy of being three months later than the original January date. I guess that was appropriate, since it was April Fool's Day, but we were not fools. The narrative had many inaccuracies and missing details and was written in a manner that favored the police. Here is the wording of that report narrative, exactly as written:

On Jan 2, 2004 at 1925 hours, Officer Tilley responded to 810 Central Ave and witnesses called in reporting a naked male running around acting abnormal. Officers responded to the scene and, after locating him at 810 Central Ave. approached him. The man resisted the stop and a struggle ensued. During the struggle the man lost consciousness and was transported to Erlanger where he was later pronounced dead. Major crimes and crime scene unit investigators responded and notifications were made to administration.

Beneath the report narrative, the case status was listed as "inactive." As far as they were concerned, they were through with the case, but we were just beginning. Prior to leaving the Police Services Center, I asked for information regarding the process for viewing the public records and personnel files of the officers involved in Leslie's death. This was a part of conducting our own investigation, as directed by the "Family First Aid Kit." I was told that I needed to call the office of the police chief. I called his office and told his secretary why I needed to talk with the chief. I was told that he was out of the office and that I needed to speak with another person. I called that person and got a voice message. I left a message with my name and phone number, but I never received a call. On that person's voice recording, it stated that if the matter was dealing with internal affairs, I would have to go to the internal affairs building on Martin Luther King Boulevard. It was clear to me that I would be wasting my time to continue playing on their merry-go-round. They may have enjoyed the ride, but our family did not. This is another example of how badly the public is treated. On that day, I gave up trying to get them to provide requested information directly to me and decided to rely on an attorney to retrieve future documents, even if a court order was required. I believe that departmental staff had been told to not cooperate with the Prater family. It appeared as though there was a "shutdown" when it came to any requests from us.

We became convinced that the police department was aggressively forming a coalition against us. It became evident that we would need to officially engage an attorney. We started with Mr. Wolfe, who soon employed attorney Amelia Roberts to add to the case. Somehow, I still felt that we needed more of a team to help us fight this uphill battle. You may have often heard the expression "You can't fight City Hall." Yes, you can fight City Hall, if you can find someone to represent you and if you have the physical stamina to endure the process. However, it is very difficult and unlikely that you will win, in the legal sense, if you are

fighting the police department. Even if the legal dynamics are resolved
to the family's satisfaction, there is no winning. The hole in your heart
can never be filled after the senseless homicide of a child.

Throughout the years, there have been wrongful death complaints
filed against the Chattanooga Police Department and accusations of
police brutality. Consistently, the department and city have won. That is
why I felt such a dire need for an unusually strong legal defense. To my
knowledge, no Chattanooga police officer has been sentenced or made
to serve one day of imprisonment resulting from killing an unarmed
citizen. As cited in chapter 2, the police officer indicted for the shooting death of unarmed John Eric Henderson was not convicted.[15] Rarely
are officers fired in Chattanooga due to allegations of police brutality or
wrongful deaths. Because of that knowledge, I believed that our family needed a team of attorneys, in addition to the two who practiced in
Chattanooga.

As with their previous wrongful death claims, the Chattanooga
Police Department was handling our case as "business as usual." After all, they had established a pattern of dealing with these matters
that ended with their officers being blameless. As part of their usual
process, Chief Steve Parks set up a meeting on June 29, 2004, with
Dwight and me to disclose the outcome of the internal investigation.
Others present and sitting with the chief and us at a long conference
table included our two local attorneys, the city attorneys, a couple of
the chief's support staff, and the medical examiner. Leslie was also in
the room: We carried a 12 × 14 poster of Leslie's picture, attached
to a wooden frame and handle. This picture was placed in an empty
chair, near us at the table. We felt the need to personalize Leslie in
those discussions, because they were about him. He was a real person and not just a faceless statistic or a name on a police report. The
administrative assistant of Chief Parks was there to take minutes. I
began to take my own notes, but the chief told me that would not be
necessary because he would have a copy of the minutes forwarded to
me. I made the mistake of trusting him. He never sent those notes to
me. Therefore, I don't recall exactly who else was there, except for an
armed, unidentified person the chief invited to sit in the back of the
room. I knew that he was armed because I noticed his large gun on the

side of his belt. In an effort to intimidate us, I believed, he wanted to make certain that we saw that gun, because his suit coat was opened and pushed back to clearly reveal the weapon. I suppose he was there to shoot us if we made any abrupt moves.

I felt much anxiety in awaiting the big announcement from Chief Parks about the results of the Internal Affairs investigation. In a million years, I could not have imagined the extent of his creativity in crafting such an outlandish outcome. According to Chief Parks and based on the department's internal investigation, Leslie's death was an accident. I asked, "What kind of an accident? Was it an automobile accident, a drowning, did Leslie's death result from a fire, just what was the nature of the accident?" Parks's immediate response was "They said that they didn't intend for him to die." When he made that statement, I quickly responded again in anger: "Anyone whose body was treated like Leslie's was treated would surely die." Furthermore, I challenged anyone in the room to volunteer to have their body treated in like manner as Leslie's and see if they could survive. Of course, there were no volunteers. It is an understatement to say that we were dissatisfied with the outcome of their bogus investigation. They had investigated themselves, with the predetermined result that they were blameless. In fact, we were more outraged, because the chief ignored the reports from two medical examiners. Why employ medical examiners if their investigation and reports mean nothing? The medical professionals had determined that Leslie's death was a homicide. How is it possible that those officers could kill Leslie and just say, "Oops," and the department would defend those fatal actions?

Furthermore, those officers did not even receive a reprimand identified as negative discipline, a process sanctioned in the department's policy manual, issued on April 28, 2005, and signed by Chief Steve Parks. It stated:

> *Negative discipline, on the other hand, is strictly punitive in nature and always takes the form of punishment or chastisement. Ideally, negative discipline should only be used in cases where positive discipline would obviously be inappropriate or when serious, willful violations of policy or procedure occur. Even when negative discipline is used, the department should always consider the co-application of some aspect of positive discipline, i.e. training, etc., to encourage and reinforce correct behavior.*

Although use of excessive force is listed in the manual as serious, nothing happened. If an officer is guilty of insubordination, there would more likely be action, even if it is only a letter of reprimand placed in his or her file. I still cannot understand why there was no negative discipline administered to those officers. If homicide by positional asphyxia is not serious, what would Parks consider a serious violation? The manual describes forms of negative discipline to include a written reprimand, suspension, demotion, probation, or termination. Those officers received none of that. They were given seven days of administrative leave, comparable to a week's paid vacation, as a reward for killing an unarmed black man.

Wrongful death accusations against the Chattanooga Police Department, without accountability, were not unusual. I should have expected that they would not champion justice for Leslie's homicide, but I was hopeful for justice. Because the officers resumed their work assignments after their one week's paid vacation, that nonverbal message was that Leslie's death didn't matter. The officers would not be disciplined. It is decisions like this that have contributed to the Black Lives Matter movement.[16] Yes, people around the country are angry about these wrongful deaths. Surely the chief must have known that we would challenge his ruling, but he also knew that citizens' complaints against the Chattanooga Police Department usually went nowhere.

Immediately after that meeting, the chief held a prearranged press conference in a different room. We were told that we were not welcome. We complied, because we did not want to create a scene and feared for our safety and freedom. We were surrounded by a sea of police officers, were on their turf, and understood their capacity for dishonesty. As we were walking toward the building's exit, a departmental employee passed by me and whispered, "Don't leave." We followed that person's instructions, which is why we had the opportunity to have an unscheduled press conference following the one scheduled by Chief Parks. At the conclusion of the chief's conference, television reporters asked us if we would talk with them about the meeting's deliberations. We would have already left the premises if it had not been for the advice of that helpful employee. Our attorney, Mr. Wolfe, joined me and Dwight outside on the lawn near the front entrance of the Police Services Center. Newspaper reporters were also there. I noticed that during our press conference, the chief had sent his public relations officer and another plainclothes officer out to spy on us. They were standing behind bushes, but we noticed them. There was no need for them to hide, because we spoke openly about our reaction, knowing that the reporters would share our comments with the public. We were recorded holding Leslie's picture and spoke frankly that Leslie's death was a homicide, not an accident. Despite our trust in attorneys Wolfe and Roberts, it appeared as though the local police department had little respect for local attorneys. I sensed a need for attorneys with no connection to Chattanooga, or even the state. Through a series of fortunate "miracles," the New York law firm of Johnnie Cochran, Peter Neufeld, and Barry Scheck joined attorneys John Wolfe and Amelia Roberts as our unified team on August 4, 2004. The New York firm is now Neufeld, Scheck, and Brustin. Partner Nick Brustin, assisted by attorney Debi Cornwall, was the New York attorney with whom we mostly communicated. Former partner Johnnie Cochran died on March 29, 2005.[17]

Fortunately, we had infinite trust in the collective expertise of our team. We were not disappointed. The local attorneys were very familiar with Chattanooga, its city attorneys, police department, and history. Interestingly, Amelia Roberts was the daughter of Gene Roberts, a past fire and police commissioner and a former mayor of Chattanooga. She was also a student I taught when she was in high school. She and John Wolfe were experienced with representing clients in social justice matters. The New York firm included attorneys with years of experience and success with social justice litigation, including clients involved in high-profile cases known nationwide. The collective experience and documentation of successful litigation positioned the New York firm's attorneys as legal experts in handling wrongful death and police misconduct cases.

Our attorneys were experienced in these matters, but we were not. I accumulated boxes of documents related to police brutality. In preparation for this manuscript, I went to attorney Wolfe's office a few years ago to review his Prater lawsuit files. I was shocked by the volume of information he had compiled. As I reviewed his documents, I was thrust into "information overload." I can only imagine the amount of information collected by the New York attorneys. All things considered, our case created a lot of research material.

The wrongful death lawsuit filing was officially documented on January 11, 2006, two years and seven days after Leslie's homicide. Federal case 1:04-cv-00385 was filed in the United States District Court, Eastern District of Tennessee at Chattanooga. Dwight, Stefan, and I were identified as the plaintiffs. Listed among defendants were Jonathan Mance, Keith Hudgins, Daniel Anderson, and Gregory Chambers, the four officers whose irresponsible actions caused Leslie's death. A number of other officers and supervisors with particular relationships to the case were also named as defendants. Additionally, Chief Steve Parks and former chief of police Jimmie Dotson, in their individual and official capacity, and the City of Chattanooga, a Tennessee Municipal Corporation, were listed as defendants. Former mayor Bob Corker and another person representing the Chattanooga City Council were called to the scene of Leslie's death but were not named in the lawsuit. Prior to filing the lawsuit, a scheduling order conference was held on January 10, 2006. Representing us at that conference were local attorney Amelia C. Roberts and Deborah L. Cornwall and Nick J. Brustin by telephone from New York. Present and representing the defendants were Phillip A. Noblett, Michael A. McMahan, and Crystal R. Freiberg.

The language in the lawsuit was very precise legalese, and I won't burden this account with the details of the document. It is easy to locate it through social media for those who are interested. However, the following thirteen items were listed as Claims for Relief, plus the final entry of Prayer for Relief:

- First Claim for Relief: Individuals Defendants
- Second Claim for Relief: Substantive Due Process
- Third Claim for Relief: Conspiracy to Violate
- Fourth Claim for Relief: Supervisory Liability
- Fifth Claim for Relief: First, Fourth, and Fourteenth Amendments and Privacy Violations
- Sixth Claim for Relief: Monell Claim (Monell is shorthand for a legal principle under the federal civil rights laws, particularly what is called Section 1983, which is the law that allows one to bring suit for a civil rights violation)[18]
- Seventh Claim for Relief: Failure to Provide Medical Treatment
- Eighth Claim for Relief: Failure to Intercede

- Ninth Claim for Relief: Wrongful Death
- Tenth Claim for Relief: Loss of Consortium
- Eleventh Claim for Relief: Negligence
- Twelfth Claim for Relief: Negligent Training and Supervision
- Thirteenth Claim for Relief: Assault and Battery

Under the heading of Prayer for Relief, the Plaintiffs pray that the court:

- Award Plaintiffs compensatory damages against Defendants in an amount to be determined at trial, including but not limited to pain and suffering of the deceased;
- Award Plaintiffs punitive damages for their civil rights claim against individual Defendants an amount to be determined at trial;
- Award Plaintiffs the reasonable funeral and burial expenses incurred as a result of this wrong death;
- Award Plaintiffs damages for their loss of consortium, pain and suffering;
- Award reasonable attorney fees;
- Declare Defendants actions unconstitutional and enjoin Defendants from the unconstitutional violations complained of herein;
- Grant the Plaintiffs a trial by jury; and
- Grant such other relief as may be just and equitable.

As in all lawsuits of this nature, there is a possibility of the case being resolved by settlement, but that potential outcome is initially unknown. At the beginning of the lawsuit, we felt that we would follow the scheduling order and proceed to court. The pretrial conference was set for April 2, 2007, followed by the jury trial beginning on April 16, 2007. With the trial date being more than three years after Leslie's homicide, it was anticipated that the trial date could be only one of the likely changes. The most interesting change to me was that we ended up dealing with three different judges.

Whenever there was a change in judges, the newly assigned person requested time to become familiar with the case, which resulted in slowing the process. One judge stayed on the case for six months and then decided to recuse himself. It angered us, because his actions caused months of wasted time. During all that time, there was no activity on the case. I didn't understand why it took him so long to feel that he had a conflict of interest. He belonged to the same church we attended when we lived in Chattanooga, but our only other similarity was that we were all African Americans. In two prior cases, potentially high profile and involving African American males with status in the community, he recused himself. Was this a trend?

We considered that judge to be a part of the suspicious slowing-down process. He was probably less familiar with us than the other judges were with some of the defendants, considering the suspected inbreeding environment often common within the judicial system. White judges handle cases of white people all the time. So, why couldn't an African American judge handle our case? We weren't seeking favors. It didn't matter to me the skin color of the presiding judge. Clearly, we received no advantages based on skin color, but we didn't want to be disadvantaged either. When Leslie was killed, the chief of police was African American, one of the officers named in the lawsuit was African American, and the first judge assigned to the case was African American. I think that there are times when blacks, in those law enforcement positions, are harder on other blacks. They go overboard in proving to whites that they are not giving African Americans "a break." We were not seeking special considerations, only fairness and justice.

I always felt that the city did not want a jury trial. As confirmation of those feelings, the city attorneys contacted our legal team to request a mediation. Attorney Nick Brustin informed me of their request. My initial response was "No." There had been no indication that they wanted to extend fairness and justice toward us. I just wanted to go to court. Mr. Brustin advised that it would be useful to meet with them to see what they had to say, but we did not have to agree to anything. Because we trusted our attorneys, we agreed to the mediation.

On May 16, 2006, mediation occurred in Knoxville, Tennessee, at the Howard Baker Federal Building. Dwight, Stefan, and I attended with three of our attorneys. Nick Brustin and Barry Scheck had flown in from New York, and John Wolfe drove over from Chattanooga. The Chattanooga city attorney and his two associates attended. The Chattanooga chief of police did not attend, sending an assistant chief instead. That assistant was an African American man who happened to have been friends with one of Dwight's sisters when they were teenagers.

Of course, that fact was not revealed at the meeting. The facilitator of the mediation was a retired federal judge who convened mediations as a consultant.

Dwight and I had never been involved in a mediation of this nature, and this was the first meeting that Stefan had attended related to Leslie's death. The mediator began by explaining the process. Dwight, Stefan, and I were primarily in the role of students. Everyone else in the room had prior experience with these types of mediations. I felt that the information was presented clearly and in a manner that did not make us feel intimidated. In fact, I was very impressed with the professional posture of the facilitator. We had no choice in his selection, but I was pleased.

The joint proceeding was held in a very nice conference room, with audiovisual equipment available. The city's representatives and our team sat at opposite sides of the conference table, with the mediator at the head. Barry Scheck sat to the immediate left of the mediator. Prior to the official beginning of the meeting, I remember that the facilitator seemed thrilled to be in the presence of Mr. Scheck. You would have thought that a rock star was in the room. In the legal profession, I suppose Barry did hold that seat of prominence. He told Barry that he had long admired his work and had read his books.

The mediator officially opened the session with introductions. I was surprised that one of the city's attorneys was dressed in a wrinkled suit. My impression was he wasn't serious about the meeting. The mediator explained that we would begin with a joint session in which both sides would hear the same discussion, mostly about the process and expectations for the meeting. After our initial time together, the two sides would be separated into different rooms. We would remain in the conference room, and the city's representatives would go to another room. The mediator would go back and forth between the two groups to inform each group of the other's deliberations. The mediator would also maintain order and guide the discussion toward an anticipated conclusion of what would be offered by the defendants and what would be accepted by the plaintiffs. At the end of the process, there would be another joint time with both sides to present their decision and, if needed, further work toward a combined agreement. The process was fascinating.

Before we separated into two groups, I asked if everyone had seen the video in which Dwight, Spen, and I shared memories of Leslie. The response was "No." I expressed that, in order for everyone in the room to have the same sense of the impact the family felt from Leslie's death, the video should be shown. Stefan had not seen the video. All of the city's representatives had viewed it, except the police department's representative. The mediator agreed to show the video, which was difficult for Stefan to watch. He cried during the entire showing, because he loved his brother so much.

At the end of the video presentation, the city attorney, the one wearing the wrinkled suit, made an ignorant statement directed to Stefan. I cannot imagine what prompted him to say to Stefan, "Those police officers are very nice guys. If you got to know them, you would want to be their friends." Immediately, I said, "Stefan would not want to be friends with those officers, because he does not have friends who are murderers." During that dialogue, I noticed the facial expressions of the other attorneys with him. Their nonverbal cues seemed to be screaming at him, "Please shut up." Instead of trying to bring us toward a place of conciliation, his words definitely widened the gap between us and them. After his words, my feeling was that we were not going to agree to anything they proposed that day. I wanted to see them in court. Interestingly, Barry Scheck stated with passion, "This case will probably end up being settled, because I would really like to try this case in court."

I can't tell you what was said when the mediator met with the city's representatives. I only know his expressions to us confirmed our feelings that we had a good case. He based his comments on his legal knowledge and experience. We believed that we had not only a good case but also attorneys who were more experienced and better prepared than theirs. Because they were the ones who asked for mediation, they were in the position of trying to get us to agree to their offers. We were in the position of saying, "No." After the "back-and-forth" period, the two sides came together again. I was disgusted that there was never any feeling that they were willing to offer some degree of accountability for the officers' actions. They only wanted to offer money. Obviously, they came prepared with a figure. They offered more than one amount as a settlement. Each time, we would say, "No," including the top figure that they had been authorized to offer. They didn't understand that our wrongful death lawsuit was not about money; it was about some sem[?] justice, change, and accountability.

The mediation ended in a stalemate, but it wasn't a waste of t[?] We all learned a lot that day. We learned more of how they do business[?] just hurry and give family members a check so that they will disappear. They learned that we were not in a hurry and did not need their money in exchange for accepting Leslie's homicide. The mediator's attitude toward us is also etched in my memory. He seemed very compassionate and empathetic. In fact, I thanked him for his words of comfort, and his response to me was "I have sons."

After the mediation, we met with our attorneys to process and further discuss our case. Fortunately, our attorneys were experienced with similar cases. Our challenge was to be patient. Because our attorneys had gotten to know us and understood our motives for legal action, they were not surprised that we rejected the monetary offer. After all, we came to mediation for information, not to get a check. We knew that we were fortunate that our attorneys were patient and also not money hungry, as documented by the fact that they took the case pro bono.

As the case proceeded toward a jury trial, numerous people contacted us with information they hoped was helpful. Some communication was about them or their loved ones being unfairly incarcerated, because of lies told by Chattanooga police officers. Other discussions were about aggressive and unnecessary tactics by police officers that resulted in physical injuries sustained by them, or injury or death of their family members. I mostly heard from mothers of sons. In one case, a sister called from the East Coast to talk about the police brutality death of her unarmed brother in Hamilton County, near the city limits of Chattanooga. In another case, my interaction was with a daughter of a victim; another letter was from a wife. It was interesting to me that they felt they could get some form of justice through us if we were able to receive justice for Leslie's death. I now understand those feelings. When we hear of a rare instance in which a police officer is indicted and convicted of the murder of an unarmed citizen, we are pleased that the family received some degree of justice. In some strange way, their grief is our grief. I often wondered if the families who reached out to us felt disappointment because we eventually settled. Ultimately, our plight mirrored theirs in that we received no justice either.

ss extended is a strategy to have more time
...bat the accusations. It also serves to exhaust
...e deceased. Our experience was very differ-
...l by the family members of Freddie Gray in
...cott in North Charleston, South Carolina.[20]
...quick actions signaled an admission of guilt
.... for police misconduct, even before the investigations
were conclusive or any lawsuits filed. In the Gray and Scott cases, the
city initiated legal action against the officers. In our case, everything
seemed to proceed at a slow pace except for their sending the officers
back in the field and trying to seek a quick settlement. There was never
any indication that the officers would be held accountable. Judicial officials were slow to release documents; slow to set up dates for requested
depositions; and, when we were moving forward to go to court, slow to
reschedule a trial date.

To further complicate matters, we also dealt directly with three different police chiefs: Jimmie Dotson, who was replaced by Steve Parks
on February 1, 2004; Parks, who retired at age fifty on December 31,
2006; and Freeman Cooper, who was confirmed by the Chattanooga
City Council on December 19, 2006, to replace Parks. I never understood why Dotson didn't do the right thing. He had nothing to lose,
since he was already preparing to leave Chattanooga when Leslie was
killed. Also, Dotson was known as the Bible-carrying chief and ought
to have been more attuned to Christian values. From our interactions
with Parks, we felt that his actions were targeted toward preserving the
officers' jobs and reputations. Cooper was fair with us and showed a
sense of empathy, but irrevocable damage had already occurred before
his appointment. Cooper provided oversight of some of the ongoing
demands of the lawsuit until his retirement in March 2010. At my request, he agreed that I could provide sensitivity training to police cadets
indefinitely. When Cooper became the police chief, I sent him a copy
of Norm Stamper's book *Breaking Rank*. I can only hope that it helped
him to avoid the mistakes of his predecessors. After Cooper's retirement, none of the subsequent chiefs in Chattanooga would allow me to
speak with academy cadets. The department has tapes of my sessions,
but I am not certain if they are using them.

While still preparing to go to court, we experienced other challenges. We received a letter from the United States Department of Justice. In summary, the letter stated that they had reviewed the case and determined that the Chattanooga Police Department and the city of Chattanooga were not responsible for Leslie's death. I was shocked to read that letter, just as shocked as I was to find it in the mailbox. Neither our family nor any of our attorneys were ever notified that the Department of Justice was conducting an investigation. The investigation could not have been thorough. In a legitimate investigation, all sides of the issue are scrutinized. The federal government's so-called investigation was very similar to the one reported by the Tennessee Bureau of Investigation; they received information from the Chattanooga Police Department and merely sanctioned the self-serving outcome of that internal investigation.

The Chattanooga Human Rights Commission also concluded that police officers were blameless in Leslie's death. Their information and interviews were all connected to the Chattanooga Police Department, including the commission's leadership. The chairperson of that citizens' advisory group was on the police chief's executive team. His serving in that role was a clear conflict of interest. Again, the cards were stacked against us. In their official capacity, the local human rights group only reviewed materials provided by the police department. One of the members expressed sympathy to me, as one mother to another. She also said, "I believe there was a problem with the officers' training." Procedures like these confirm why citizens feel helpless in trying to get justice. I must raise the question: "Is there a conspiracy against victims and their families?"

There were other disturbing activities initiated by the city's attorneys. In their attitude of cold calculation, or perhaps in an effort to further discredit Leslie as a human being, the city hired a faculty member from the Department of Economics at the University of Tennessee at Chattanooga (UTC) to determine the monetary value of Leslie's life. Of course, I was angry and disgusted that the professor would accept such a soulless consultant's job, all in the name of money. I have no idea what variables were used. I suppose he developed some magical valuation formula, as if Leslie were merely a commodity or tradable asset rather than a human being. The outcome was that he determined Leslie's life to be worth between $70,000 and $80,000. I often wondered whether his life would have been worth more if he had not been an African American, had been married with children, or had kept a big bank account. I was especially saddened because I knew this professor and had previously had positive interactions with him as a former faculty colleague at UTC. I sent him an e-mail and told him how I felt. I asked him, "What price would you put on your child's life?" If nothing else, I hope he felt some shame when he cashed his check.

For most of 2006, our attorneys continued to prepare to go to trial and, as it appeared to us, the city attorneys were preparing to avoid going to trial. We were able to complete some depositions and secure some documents requested while being challenged by the city's slow response time. In June 2006, before all of the anticipated depositions were completed, the city's special counsel, Philip A. Noblett, sent a letter with an offer to settle the lawsuit. The document stated that the City of Chattanooga offered the plaintiffs a judgment of $1,500,000 in full and final settlement of all claims of all plaintiffs against all defendants. It was interesting that the judge who earlier had recused himself was still listed on the document. There was one paragraph in that letter that demonstrated a bullying tactic:

> As I explained in my earlier letter, an Offer not accepted shall be deemed withdrawn and evidence thereof is not admissible except in a proceeding to determine costs. If the judgement finally obtained by the Offeree is not more favorable than the offer, the Offeree must pay the costs incurred after the making of the Offer. This could be a significant monetary risk for your clients based upon any contingent fee agreement you have with them in this case and for your firm based upon Marek v. Chesny and the applicable Sixth Circuit authorities.

For clarification, I researched *Marek v. Chesny*. This is a case that was argued before the United States Supreme Court and decided on June 27, 1985. The original lawsuit involved a wrongful death claim resulting from police officers answering a domestic disturbance; the respondent's adult son was shot and killed by officers. A timely offer of settlement of $100,000, including costs and attorney's fees, was rejected. The case went to trial and the award totaled $60,000 but did not include attorney's fees and other costs. The court's decision referred to Federal Rule of Civil Procedure 68. In plain language, if a pretrial settlement is not accepted and the judgment resulting from a trial is less than the offer of settlement, the plaintiffs are responsible for attorney's fees. Obviously, the purpose of Rule 68 is to encourage settlement and avoid litigation.[21]

Even with Noblett's threat, we did not accept that offer. We discussed the situation with our attorneys and decided to counter with demands referred to collectively as injunctive relief. This is a legal remedy that may be sought in a civil lawsuit in addition to (or in place of) monetary damages. Rather than offering money as payment for a wrong in a civil action, injunctive relief is a court order for the defendant to stop a specified act or behavior.[22] Prior to our lawsuit, I was unfamiliar with the term, but I knew that we wanted changes within the police department's policies and procedures. After praying and engaging in further discussions with our attorneys, we decided to settle, but only if our demands for injunctive relief were honored. I also recalled a conversation with my friend Emma, who went to court with her case. She told me to avoid the court route if possible. She explained the years of ongoing stress, reliving Malik's killing over and over in courtroom settings. She also cautioned me that even if we received a favorable court ruling in the initial trial, the city would most likely appeal. That process could go on for years, which is what she experienced. The years of a possible open legal wound is something I wanted to avoid. Of course, I later discovered that nothing could bring complete closure.

What we really wanted was for those four officers to be indicted and convicted of second-degree murder and serve time in prison. We realized that was not going to happen, especially not in Chattanooga. The next best thing was to seek changes to help someone else's child to remain alive. There were four demands. We felt that an external investigation of the Chattanooga Police Department was warranted; this was our first demand. The outcome of the Internal Affairs investigations favored police officers in accusations of officer-involved assaults on citizens and wrongful deaths. Outcomes that went against officers usually occurred in non-life-threatening situations. For example, a Chattanooga officer shoplifted a $10.88 watch from Walmart; the outcome of the Internal Affairs investigation was that the officer resigned to avoid termination.[23] But if an officer steals someone's life, instead of an inexpensive watch, nothing is likely to happen. We demanded that they reinstate the academy training to avoid the death sentence of positional asphyxia, our second demand. An important component of effective police training is sensitivity education in the prevention of these wrongful deaths. Our third demand was for sensitivity training workshops, taught by me, to be presented to cadets at the Chattanooga Police Academy. I felt that the best place for sensitivity intervention was prior to persons becoming police officers, and not after they were possibly tainted by seasoned officers. Most people were amazed that I volunteered to do this training. Our fourth demand was that the four police officers must meet with Leslie's immediate family.

Our attorneys received a letter from Mr. Noblett dated July 14, 2006, regarding our case, in relation to our nonmonetary demands. Our four demands were addressed. It was reported that the city was in agreement with an audit of its Internal Affairs division to be conducted by an independent expert and that the city would assume the costs of such an audit. The cost of the audit was $30,000. According to the letter, the Chattanooga Police Department had already implemented training to avoid positional asphyxia. The city council was not averse to my providing an approved presentation, whether in person or on videotape to future police officers. The impact of in-custody death would be the subject, and I would not receive compensation for the presentations. I never expected or requested compensation. The fourth demand was the one of highest importance to us. The demand was for the four officers who had hands-on contact with Leslie on January 2, 2004, to meet with Dwight, and Stefan, and me. We were amazed and angered that the response letter included the following statement:

> The City Council is willing to encourage but does not feel it can compel these officers to attend any meeting, if they do not desire to attend for their own personal reasons. Any such meeting should be accomplished in a manner where neither party to the meeting feels threatened to attend. I do believe such a meeting could provide important closure for the officers and your clients if it is closely monitored and the parties remain civil to one another. Any such meeting could be conducted with the assistance of the mediator, if advisable, after a Release of All Claims and a Final Order dismissing this case has been entered with the court.

That statement was especially infuriating to us because it seems that considerations are always targeted to the desires and comfort of the police officers, without primary concern for the victim or the victim's family. We were not seeking a social visit; our beloved Leslie's life was ended by their actions. Because they received no discipline, the very least they could do was to face us. In the last paragraph, it was mentioned that $1.5 million was the monetary offer for settlement.

As a follow-up to that letter, our attorneys told us that two of the officers had agreed to meet with us, and two said they would not. Our response was that if all four of those officers would not meet with us, then we would not settle. That was a deal breaker. We would just go to court if that was our only recourse to see all four of those people. I wanted to end my nightmares about those faceless officers responsible for Leslie's death. After a few days passed, Mr. Noblett informed our attorneys that the two officers initially unwilling to meet with us had changed their minds, but there were conditions: they did not want the meeting in Chattanooga; they did not want media present; and we could not publicly share the details of the discussions that occurred during the meeting. We agreed to those conditions, because my main purpose was for the four of them to face us. We had only been in the room with the officer who had given a deposition.

At the October 17, 2006, meeting of the Chattanooga City Council, our lawsuit was an agenda item. Dwight, friends, relatives, and I attended that meeting. City attorney Randy Nelson reported on the lawsuit identified as "Prater and the City of Chattanooga." He stated that at the time that Leslie Prater passed away, the police department had ceased its training with positional asphyxia, which is what caused his demise. "It is our understanding that we will be liable in this case." Also in the meeting, it was stated that the top priorities for Parks, the new chief, would be staffing, training facilities, and career development. There was a motion and a second to authorize the city attorney to move forward with the proposed settlement agreement. I will tell you that $200,000 is the maximum amount that the city is authorized to pay in these types of lawsuits, unless there is proof that there was a problem with the training. When insufficient training is proven, there is no limit to the award.

On December 6, 2006, the family held a televised press conference. I read from a three-page, single-spaced document that I wrote. The following are some excerpts from that statement:

On January 2, 2004, our lives changed forever. That was the date that our son, Leslie Vaughn Prater, was a victim of a homicide. Leslie was the victim of police brutality, an ongoing travesty in America that has reached epidemic proportions.

Let me pause and thank all of those who have stood by us, supported and prayed for us, during almost three years of pain and suffering related to Leslie's death and the subsequent activities following the senseless and cruel actions that stole his life. I won't call individual names, because you know your identity. I would like to express appreciation to the law firms of Cochran, Neufeld, and Scheck of New York City and their partner, Nick Brustin and the Chattanooga Law Firm of John Wolfe and Amelia Roberts. I would also like to thank the representatives of the media who are here today.

The settlement included a fiscal settlement of 1.5 million dollars and four injunctive relief agreements that are summarized as follows:

1. *The City of Chattanooga agrees to contract with an independent expert, agreeable to the parties, to conduct an audit of the Chattanooga Police Department's Internal Affairs Division.*
2. *The City of Chattanooga agrees to consult with an independent expert, agreeable to the parties, regarding existing and recommended policies and procedures for current training on positional asphyxia and related topics by police training agencies.*
3. *The City of Chattanooga agrees to allow me, Dr. Loretta Prater, the mother of Leslie Prater and a university professor and Dean, to teach a workshop at the police academy for the next three classes of new police officer recruits. The class will focus on the preventable death of Leslie and the real-life and permanent consequences of police actions on the street. For this service, I agree to receive no fiscal compensation.*
4. *The defendants Jonathan Mance, Keith Hudgins, Gregory Chambers, and Daniel Anderson must meet, face-to-face, with the Prater family.*

On Thursday, December 7, 2006, the day following the press conference, Dwight and I went to Knoxville. The purpose of the trip was to meet, face-to-face, with the four police officers. As previously agreed, there were no media present. A mediator facilitated the meeting within a tight secure environment. In honor of another condition, I have never shared the details of the meeting's dialogue, which is why that information is not included in this book. Stefan chose to not attend that meeting. He said to me, "There is no way that I could be in the same room with the guys who killed my brother."

Because people knew that we had an excellent case and some nationally renowned attorneys, many continued to ask, "Why did you settle?" I feel that the people of Chattanooga deserve an answer. For our family, money was not the issue. There was no dollar amount listed on the original wrongful death lawsuit. We love Leslie very much and no amount of money can fill our emptiness. We could have been awarded millions of dollars if his case had appeared before a jury, which is what I believe city officials feared. After nearly three years of non-action by the police department in this matter, it was evident to us that we had to force changes. The only vehicle we had, in a sincere desire to prevent this from happening to another family, was to make demands in a settlement arrangement.

Some people confuse receiving money with receiving justice. The two are not comparable. When people congratulate us on receiving money in exchange for Leslie's life, it saddens me. I know they mean well, but they actually have no understanding of the impact of their words. Yes, the money serves as a tangible implication of the officers' guilt and a way for the city to express some accountability for the actions of its employees. I have been told that the $1.5 million is the largest amount that Chattanooga has ever awarded in a wrongful death lawsuit, but Dwight and I could never put a price on Leslie's life.

There can be some good to come from our lawsuit, but only if the city acts in good faith. We are hopeful that the city will follow through on the actions they are obligated to complete, according to the settlement agreement. We will be watching, and I am asking two groups, especially, to join us in making sure that these agreements are honored. The first group includes taxpayers and the second group is composed of hard-working, honest police officers who are tired of professional policing being disrespected because of the criminal actions of a few. If this happens and there is a zero-tolerance policy for police brutality, senseless killings of residents by police officers will stop. No one should be denied the right to life, liberty, and the pursuit of happiness.

For our family, the settlement of the lawsuit is a beginning. We will continue to oppose these wrongful deaths. I pray that police brutality will end and that abusive police officers will be purged from employment roles everywhere. This epidemic of senseless killings must stop. None are safe until all are safe. We are all at risk as long as there is no accountability. What happened to our family can happen to your family. I would like to close this chapter with a quote from Robert Kennedy: "Let us dedicate ourselves to the challenge presented by the Greeks so many years ago—to tame the savageness of man and make gentle the life of this world."

7

SILENT NO MORE

Strategies of Advocacy to Elevate Public Awareness

This chapter provides a glimpse of what a family might have to endure in bringing attention to a wrongful death at the hands of police officers. I summarized some of the engagement that took place between the public and family members. There were far too many television, newspaper, radio, and online reports of our case to touch on them all. In fact, I feel certain that there are some reports of which we are still unaware. Although we thought our media experiences were extensive, they were minor in comparison to some other families.

The family of Michael Brown from Ferguson, Missouri, is the first that comes to mind. I feel saddened every time I hear his name, because I am reminded of how his life was stolen. But imagine how his family must feel, considering the infinite public reminders of Michael's death. After reading the book *Tell the Truth and Shame the Devil*, coauthored by his mother, Lezley McSpadden, her feelings are no longer left to the imagination.[1]

Because of the volume of materials I had accumulated, it was challenging to decide how to organize the information for this chapter. I began to establish categories, such as newspaper articles; television presentations; protest activities; city council meetings; special invited presentations; and research conference presentations. As I started writing, that format quickly became cumbersome. Instead, I will share selected events mostly within a chronological structure. The information is not all-inclusive but provides an overview of the activities involved in bringing attention to the injustice of Leslie's death, especially those events that can be initiated by families. Some activities have been referred to in other chapters but not discussed. You will notice that some situations are briefly mentioned and others are discussed in more depth. A majority of activities occurred in the earlier years after Leslie's death.

ACTIVITIES JANUARY 2, 2004–DECEMBER 31, 2004

When media representatives were notified of Leslie's death, they wasted no time in reporting information that they received from the police. As previously noted, the first report appeared prior to any notification of Leslie's death to family members. After that initial televised report on January 2, 2004, there were other televised stories, newspaper accounts, and articles posted on the internet. The top story reported on January 5, 2004, by WTVC, Chattanooga's local ABC affiliate, was "Chattanooga Opens Personnel Files for Officers in Leslie Prater's Death." On March 26, 2004, their report was "Man Dies in Police Custody: Several Injuries on Body." Another of their top story reports on June 16, 2004, was "Parents of Leslie Prater Seeking Answers." Accessed from the internet on January 13, 2004, was a breaking news item from *Chattanoogan.com*: "Prater Family Claims Chattanooga Police Have Pattern of Aggressive Force." On February 16, 2004, the *Chattanoogan.com* article was "Leslie Vaughn Prater Family Says His Death Unnecessary."

There were numerous local newspaper accounts of Leslie's death and our subsequent struggle for justice. Because I did not live in Chattanooga, I depended on others to furnish me with copies of those articles. Their loyalty to our cause was tremendous. Friends and relatives were constantly sending me copies of the articles, sometimes resulting in duplicates of the same information. On Friday, January 9, 2004, the *Chattanooga Times Free Press* article was titled "Court Won't Block Release of Officers' Photos." However, the police department never released pictures of all four officers. On February 17, 2004, a relative faxed me the *Chattanooga Times Free Press* article, "Family Pays for Private Autopsy in Son's Death in Police Custody." An interesting quote in that article was from Chief Parks, who stated, "The four officers were suspended without pay for one week, and are back on the job." Previously, we were told that the officers were on a one-week administrative leave with pay and returned to their prior assignments, which I believe to be accurate. After the February 18 article, the *Southeast Missourian* in Cape Girardeau printed on its front page, "Cape Couple Seeks Second Autopsy in Son's Death."[2]

During those earlier months of intense grief, I also exhausted my brain trying to think of every way possible that I could engage the public in our story, including sending information to the producers of the *Oprah Winfrey Show* and ABC's *20/20*, their weekly news magazine show. Those actions were to no avail, but I quickly established contact with Chattanooga media outlets. I participated in a local radio talk show there and established communication with local television and newspaper reporters. Early in the process, reporters were anxious to talk to me, and I was willing to talk to them, although I am usually a private person. I didn't want the circumstances around Leslie's death to be a secret, so my priority was to let the public know that Leslie's death was a homicide. For as long as it lasted, I took advantage of that attention from the media, more commonly referred to as one's "fifteen minutes of fame."

During that first year, I spent a lot of time talking to people, especially those living in Chattanooga. The communication contacts were very much two-way. People were contacting me to discuss their problems with the Chattanooga Police Department or incidents of police brutality that they had witnessed. I was following up on leads from people who had filed lawsuits against the department or those who were rumored to have witnessed Leslie's homicide. Social justice advocates from Chattanooga contacted me to share their long-standing concerns about police brutality in the community. I will admit that even I was amazed by the number of people who wanted to talk with me.

At our first appearance at the Chattanooga City Council, we prepared copies of a flyer and passed them out at the meeting. The flyer, with a picture of Leslie, was titled "The Lord Giveth: The Police Taketh Away, The Death of Leslie Vaughn Prater."

The following is a list of the issues contained in the flyer:

- The police neglected to do their job, which is to serve and protect citizens. Because Leslie was a citizen in need of help, his situation was a perfect opportunity for the four police officers to demonstrate how they serve and protect citizens.
- The police stated that, upon their arrival, they were unsure whether they were dealing with a medical or mental problem, but they neglected to follow departmental policy in dealing with such situations.
- Four police officers used excessive, unreasonable, and unnecessary force.
- The four police officers violated the constitutional Fourth Amendment rights of Leslie Vaughn Prater.
- The four police officers were perpetrators of a homicide.
- The body of Leslie Vaughn Prater was severely beaten, as evidenced by two independent autopsy reports showing twenty-one rib fractures, a broken arm, a dislocated shoulder, blunt trauma to the scrotum, and numerous other bruises and lacerations.
- Two officers on two separate occasions used pepper spray, which compromised Leslie's ability to breathe.
- Homicide by positional asphyxia was the cause of death. After Leslie was severely beaten, deliberate actions of the four police officers further prohibited him from breathing. These actions included keeping him facedown in the dirt after his hands were cuffed behind his back, and while the knees of officers were pressing him in the back until he stopped breathing.
- Leslie was unarmed, as police could clearly determine, because he was nude and posed no threat to the well-being or safety of the police officers or any citizens.

We demanded to see the incident report and the public files of the officers, and have an independent and objective investigation completed. We demanded justice for Leslie and an end to the double standard of justice when police officers are the perpetrators. We also demanded that the police officers be released from duty, pending the outcome of the investigation. Furthermore, we demanded that Mayor Bob Corker dismantle Chattanooga's "Blue Wall of Silence."

You might wonder if any of our demands were met. The family received a very vague incident report, and, much later, our attorneys received some of the public files. Only after the lawsuit settlement was there an independent investigation of the department. Otherwise, none of our other requests were honored. The officers returned to their positions one week after killing Leslie. They were not released from duty pending the outcome of the investigation. Justice was never received and, in my opinion, the double standard is still current. In most cases of unlawful deaths and injuries perpetrated by police officers, the "Blue Wall of Silence" is as strong as ever, although we live in a country of acclaimed freedom.

I taped an interview for the local Cape Girardeau CBS affiliate station, KFVS12. The purpose of the interview was for me to give my version of the dynamics surrounding Leslie's death. For security reasons, the interview was taped without my face being shown, with the camera facing the reporter. Only the back of my head was shown. When one speaks out against police officers, you can become a target for violent behavior from police sympathizers.

Dwight and I attended the Southside Reunion in Chattanooga. Many African Americans currently or in the past resided on the Southside. During overt segregation, blacks were strictly prohibited from living in certain sections of the city, even if you could afford to live in those neighborhoods. Consequently, the Southside was home to African American doctors, teachers, business persons, and laborers. Economic status didn't matter; the common thread was the color of your skin. There was a positive outcome of that diverse economic demographic. African American children living in urban settings had the opportunity to interact directly with positive role models, from all economic levels. All of the hardworking residents were their family members and neighbors, regardless of the numbers on the paycheck.

We anticipated that many persons attending the Southside Reunion would be people we knew from our former neighborhood or who were former classmates. We attended the reunion and placed signs around the grounds about the killing of Leslie. We also passed out information describing similar incidents in Chattanooga, in which other unarmed citizens, mostly African American men, were killed by police officers. I had hoped that we could have a rally during that time. I spoke with one of the organizers, an elected state representative, about that possibility. She denied support for that request, stating, "The Southside Reunion is a time for socializing and eating barbeque." I was disappointed in her response. Years later, she approached me about sending her some information about police brutality and possibly coming to Nashville to testify. I sent her the information and agreed to testify before a committee in Nashville. She never contacted me again.

Since June 1982, Chattanooga has held the Riverbend Festival, an annual two-week event on the Tennessee River. On the Monday after the opening weekend, the Bessie Smith Strut occurs. For this event, a section of Martin Luther King Boulevard is blocked off for participants. Noted blues singer Bessie Smith was born in Chattanooga on April 15, 1894. Bessie Smith Hall, located on Martin Luther King Boulevard, is named in her memory. The Strut is similar to a street festival with live music, fellowship, and food, especially barbeque. The Strut, which reminds me of the year-round social events on Beal Street in Memphis and Bourbon Street in New Orleans, has been a popular feature of the Riverbend Festival. The people are usually just walking up and down the street, eating and stopping to listen to various musicians and chatting with acquaintances. Street vendors are located all along the route with a variety of food and beverages for sale.

I anticipated that there would be hundreds of people at the 2004 Strut. I was correct. I saw that as an opportunity to continue to inform people about police brutality in Chattanooga. Family members joined me in carrying signs about Leslie's killing. We walked up and down the street with everyone else, but the difference was that we were carrying our signs. Several people stopped me, especially out-of-town tourists, to ask questions about the situation. My sign read, "The Lord Giveth, the Police Taketh Away," and it had a picture of Leslie as a baby on it. Media were present. One photographer took a picture of me holding the sign and posted it on *Chattanoogan.com*.

I saw numerous people I knew along my way. They stopped me to talk. They expressed sympathy and talked about how awful it was that nothing was done to the officers who killed Leslie. Some people who were strangers to me stopped me to say that they knew Leslie and were friends. There were others who stated that they would help us if needed. Persons approaching me were of both races. In one instance, I made eye contact with one of the white Chattanooga police officers. In his eyes, I saw compassion. However, he was surrounded by several other officers and did not dare to let them know that he even knew me.

With our eye contact, I sensed that he recalled me as one of his teachers. We both recognized that the current environment did not allow us to communicate.

As mentioned earlier, the Bessie Smith Strut attracted many people, local residents as well as persons residing outside of Chattanooga. When I assumed a stationary position with my sign, I was able to observe and identify more of the attendees. While reviewing the crowd, I noticed that Mayor Bob Corker had passed by on the other side of the street. Responding to my instincts, I immediately hurried in his direction and approached him. I introduced myself and told him that Dwight and I would like to meet with him to discuss Leslie's death. He agreed to meet with us and gave me the information to contact his assistant. I must admit that I was surprised that he did not appear to be reluctant at all. I often wondered if he ever regretted that action, because I'm sure the city attorneys would have advised against it, considering that Corker was called to the scene the night that Leslie was killed. I saw the taped television newscast that showed Mayor Corker at the scene, talking with police personnel.

On June 18, Dwight and I met with Bob Corker and his city manager in his conference room. The city manager was there as an observer, and I don't recall his joining the conversation, other than to introduce himself. It was a very cordial meeting. I took numerous pictures of Leslie in various family settings over his life span. I wanted Mayor Corker to get the sense that Leslie was very much a part of a family unit and very much loved. He was our son, not just "something" that the police could squash just like someone stepping on an ant. I asked him if he had children, and he responded that he was a father of two children. We talked with Bob Corker as parent to parent. He made no commitments but appeared sensitive to our feelings. While I am disappointed that Corker never spoke publicly about Leslie's homicide, I appreciated that he hosted that meeting. He listened to our concerns and treated us in a nonjudgmental manner. He seemed sincerely compassionate, maybe considering how he would feel if one of his children was treated as Leslie had been treated. In December 2009, one of his daughters was carjacked in Washington, D.C. As a parent, I wondered if he reflected on our situation, and how quickly life-changing circumstances, over which one has no control, can occur. Fortunately and thankfully, his daughter was unharmed.[3] From our meeting with Bob Corker, I sensed that he loved his children as much as we love ours.

We attended the Chattanooga City Council meeting on June 29, 2004. We had several friends and relatives with us. Dwight and I spoke, as did others in support of us, although other speakers were unsolicited. One person, who had prior employment experience as a professional at a mental health facility, stated that there are techniques for physically interacting with unarmed persons without killing them, even persons who are naked. Tom, the individual who spoke, had known me for years when we both were employed at the University of Tennessee at Chattanooga. I was so pleased to see him again, although I had no idea that he would be at the meeting to speak on our behalf.

A number of council members made public statements to suggest that they planned to pursue our concerns. I will tell you that two of those council members were observed at the scene the night Leslie died. One was the council member representing the district in which the death occurred. The other, a funeral director, was conducting business at the location directly across the street from where Leslie was killed, and he did go over to the scene. They made "politically correct" statements at the meeting, but their words were just empty promises. I left the meeting with the feeling that the matter of Leslie's homicide was just beginning.

The *Chattanooga Courier*, a local newspaper in Chattanooga, identified as "A Progressive Voice in the African American Community," printed the family's story on July 12, 2004. Through this opportunity, we were able to tell our side and the impact Leslie's homicide had on the family. The title of the article was "Prater's Family Wants to Change Negative Images Painted by the Media, Police Department." Stefan's poem, "Never Be Another You," was included in a separate section called "The Poet's Corner." The editor gave us front-page coverage, with a picture of Leslie and Stefan posing together when they were young children. The article was extensive and concluded on page 5, consuming approximately one-third of that page. The last statement from the article was provided by Stefan. He said, "If I can prevent another family from going through it, then my brother hasn't died in vain."

On September 21, I spoke at the University of Tennessee at Chattanooga (UTC) in a social science class. The presentation focused on sharing research on police brutality, coupled with my personal experience.

There was a diverse group of approximately twenty-five students of varying ages and races. As an experienced and award-winning teacher, I was confident in presenting to the class but less comfortable when I opened the session for questions. I was sure that I would be challenged in my assertion that police officers were responsible for Leslie's death. As expected, I was confronted. An older white female student wanted to know how I could feel certain that the lives of the police officers were not in danger. I calmly responded with the facts that Leslie was nude, clearly unarmed, and pinned facedown on the ground with his hands cuffed behind his back. There was no way that he could have harmed those four officers, especially with their combined weight pressing on him. The exchange between us was cordial and ended with that response.

Later that evening, Dwight and I, family members, and supporters attended the Chattanooga City Council meeting to conduct a silent protest. The chairperson of the council was someone I knew personally. When I lived in Chattanooga, I served on the board of directors for Big Brothers/Big Sisters, and Jack was its executive director. I felt comfortable approaching him because of our interpersonal connection and my knowledge of his legacy as a person of integrity. I also had a personal relationship with the administrative assistant for the council. Carol was the youngest sister of Cheryl, one of my childhood friends and high school classmates. At the end of the meeting, it probably seemed odd to observers that those two persons greeted me with an embrace.

I was the spokesperson for the family. If you recall, this was not my first council meeting. My objectives for attending that meeting were for the city council members to be more aware of police brutality in Chattanooga, introduce a resolution denouncing police brutality, and request that they convene a public hearing on the matter. Our family members and friends were there for moral support and to carry posters. The posters had different messages. Dwight used his expertise in technology and his creativity to design the posters. Some had a picture of Leslie only, others depicted Leslie with family members, and some included statements under the picture. As always, it was wonderful having the consistent support of family members and friends. We were truly blessed to have them by our side throughout this struggle for justice. In some ways, it must have been more difficult for them, because they lived in

Chattanooga. We would travel there, attend events, and leave town, while they remained in Chattanooga. I heard rumors that some people described us as "troublemakers." They charged that we came to town to stir up trouble. If seeking justice for an unlawful homicide is "stirring up trouble," then I will accept their label as a "troublemaker."

After reading about the significance of October 22, I began planning to participate in the annual national movement to speak out against police brutality. I started back in March, when I ordered posters that had "Police Brutality did not die on September 11th" printed on them from the October 22 Coalition in New York. All during the spring and summer, I was working on organizing the event. On August 30, I invited attorney Emma Jones, from Connecticut, to be the keynote speaker. If you recall, Emma is the person who suggested that I appear at city council meetings.

On October 22, we facilitated a program in observance of the annual National Day of Protest to Stop Police Brutality. We called it a Rally for Justice. It was held at Second Missionary Baptist Church, the congregation in which Dwight and I were active when we lived in Chattanooga. Financially, the rally was supported by private donations, including the family, the Unity Group, and the Clergy Koinonia. The Unity Group is composed of leaders from a cross-section of Chattanooga. Members are mostly African Americans, similar to the racial composition of the Clergy Koinonia, an organization of ministers in Chattanooga.

The annual October 22 observance was started years ago by the organizers of the Stolen Lives Project, which contends that one of the greatest tragedies of police brutality is the suffering of family members who must struggle, sometimes with virtually no help, to seek justice for the brutalization or loss of a loved one. As described previously, the Stolen Lives Project is a joint venture of the Anthony Baez Foundation, the National Lawyers Guild, and the October 22 Coalition to stop police brutality, repression, and the criminalization of a generation. The mission of the Stolen Lives Project is to assemble a national list of people killed by law enforcement agents from 1990 to the present. More than two thousand cases were documented in the second edition of *Stolen Lives*, a book published in 1999. The project aims to restore some dignity to the lives stolen and not allow those lives to be forgotten.[4]

It was significant to have Emma as our speaker. In addition to her being a community activist and humanitarian, she is the mother of a son killed by a police officer. Malik, Emma's unarmed African American son, was shot and killed by a white police officer in East Haven, Connecticut, on April 14, 1997. Malik was shot multiple times while sitting in his car. The officer was never held accountable for his actions. Subsequently, he was promoted and eventually retired in 2012 as the department's spokesperson.[5]

On October 13, we mailed out a flyer and a letter discussing the rally. This communication was sent not only to our friends and relatives but also to supporters of other victims of police brutality in Chattanooga. To reach our supporters directly, we sent letters to persons who had signed the memory book at the visitation prior to Leslie's funeral. The local CBS television station assisted us in spreading the word. I was an invited guest on local talk show *Point of View*. Although I discussed the program for the rally, my focus was to increase awareness that police brutality is a nationwide problem. Also, the rally was announced in the *Chattanooga Courier*. In the newspaper article, it was stated that everyone was invited to attend and join other concerned citizens to learn strategies to deal with police brutality. The article summarized items communicated in the flyer:

> If you believe in justice for all; believe in upholding The Constitution of the United States; believe that there should not be a double standard for justice; believe that no one should be above the law; believe that terrorism perpetrated by police officers in communities should end; believe that police officers should serve and protect all citizens, not just some; believe that the Blue Wall should be dismantled; and believe that enough is enough and that there has been too much suffering already; then come to the Rally. Join other concerned citizens for justice, and the family and friends of victims of police brutality, as well as victims who have survived these brutal attacks. Your support is needed and welcomed to voice your belief in human rights for all citizens.

In addition to individuals, community groups were represented to support the cause. These included our church, the Unity Group, Clergy Koinonia, United for Democracy and Justice, Concerned Citizens for Justice, the Nation of Islam, and the local Rainbow Push Coalition.

The local chapter of the National Association for the Advancement of Colored People (NAACP) had not reached out to us, but I asked their president to give the welcome on the program and he agreed. His brief appearance on the program was the local NAACP's only presence in our fight for justice.

Based on our goals, the rally was a success; it was well attended and attracted media presence. There were probably some curiosity seekers in attendance, but that was all right. Hopefully, they were able to learn something from the speakers. I invited representatives from a cross-section of the community, and they attended. I also invited the police chief, but he chose not to attend. I had hoped that law enforcement officials in Chattanooga would attend as a way of publicly standing for justice, which was the focus of our activities. I guess that was asking too much. It seemed as though they were always on the defensive to protect the interest of police officers, or cover up their misdeeds, regardless of the circumstances. I always felt that the absence of the police chief was a missed opportunity to make a statement that he supported justice for everyone. If there were any representatives of the police department or the mayor's office there, they did not make their presence known.

ACTIVITIES JANUARY 2005–DECEMBER 2005

Our making noise continued into 2005. I didn't want Leslie's homicide to become a cold case. As Martin Luther King Jr. stated, "Justice delayed is justice denied." We needed to continue activities to seek justice and to let law enforcement officials know that we had not forgotten Leslie. I felt like the police chief wished that we would just ride off into the sunset to Missouri, never to be heard from again. I even sent an e-mail message to filmmaker and author Michael Moore to ask him to write about this epidemic of police brutality sweeping the country. Fortunately, many Chattanooga residents didn't forget Leslie. They continued to contact me with their stories of injustice or expressions of concern about Leslie's unlawful death. I heard some horror stories from others who were abused by Chattanooga's "finest" but managed to survive their injuries. All of the accounts didn't involve excessive force. Some instances were of police officers lying and using their power to arrest people without cause, resulting in incarceration or loss of income from having to pay court fees and attorneys.

On February 28, I was contacted by a consultant who was under contract with the National Association of the Mentally Ill (NAMI), on behalf of the Tennessee Highway Patrol. She was working on a training video for troopers but felt that police departments could benefit from the same training. The focus was to present strategies to avoid aggressive behavior and employ safe practices after encountering motorists with suspicious behavioral issues. She wanted to interview us as part of the video. We agreed and traveled to Chattanooga for the interview and filming. After completion of her video, the segments including Leslie's case were not accepted by the Tennessee Highway Patrol. She was told to delete that footage.

On April 26, I sent an e-mail to an assistant producer with *Dateline/* NBC News. She responded by thanking me for the information. She also stated, "I am going to review all of this carefully and then I will get back to you on what, if anything, I can do." That was the end of her correspondence with me.

Stedman Graham spoke on the campus of Southeast Missouri State University on April 27. I was among those invited to attend a private dinner with him. I knew that I could not have a one-on-one meeting with him, so on the back of my business card, I wrote a brief summary of why I would like contact with Oprah. I asked him to give the card to her. I never received a response. I imagine that he was accustomed to getting many such requests, but I had to try anyway.

In the June 2, 2005, edition of the *Chattanooga News Free Press*, a quote from Chattanooga City Councilwoman Rutherford was printed. Her statement, which she voiced during the public council meeting, was "Do I want police officers to treat each citizen equally? Yes I do. But do I want to hammer this subject in the ground? No I don't."

I imagined if she had an unarmed son killed by the police, she might have felt differently. Also, one might ask, "Should there be a time limit when seeking justice?" In addition to our family, other residents had publicly pleaded with council members to address their concerns about police brutality. Rutherford, a white female, represented District 6, an area highly populated with African Americans. Based on Rutherford's statement, I suppose she didn't want to hear any more about police misconduct from her constituents. In my opinion, she was abusing her positional authority, which has been identified as the socially constructed understanding of one's world and oneself.[6] What could possibly have been her motives for making such a statement, unless she perceived herself as living in a different world from her constituents?

After reading the newspaper article mailed to me from my friend Ingrid, I was furious. Dwight and I traveled to Chattanooga to attend the council meeting on June 14. I felt that a public reaction was warranted, because she had made such an outrageous statement in public. I read a prepared a statement. Among my comments, I noted that statements of that nature served as a green light for police perpetrators of brutality. Attitudes expressed verbally, comparable to her statement, secure a system of injustice. I also noted that I recognize that there are good officers who serve and protect. Because of the lack of accountability in Chattanooga for deaths from police brutality, I asked council members, "Who serves and protects citizens, all citizens, from the police?" and "Who protects constitutional rights and ensures due process for all citizens?"

My prepared statement also included the following:

> I have friends and relatives who reside in District 6. They have assured me that they will not vote for Marti Rutherford in the future. They believe in justice for all. They believe in accountability of persons who commit crimes, even if they are wearing a uniform and badge. I pray that all eligible voters in District 6 will vote. For all voters in the district who want equal and fair treatment for themselves, their families, and neighbors, even if the subject has to be hammered in the ground, I plead with you to not vote for Marti Rutherford. Do I believe that police should be respected? Yes I do. Do I believe that this respect comes merely from putting on a uniform, accessorized with a badge, gun, baton, pepper spray, and a Taser? No I don't.

ACTIVITIES JANUARY 2006–DECEMBER 2006

Connections to the public continued during 2006, including more media contacts. During that year, we assumed more roles with audiences outside of Chattanooga. We still had been unable to attract national attention to Leslie's homicide, but we could expand our activities to other markets. In addition to visibility in Chattanooga, we sought other opportunities to expose persons in other cities and states to the problems with police brutality.

On January 2, the Chattanooga-Hamilton County Branch of the National Association for the Advancement of Colored People (NAACP) held its annual Jubilee Day program. Printed in the program was the statement, "It is significant that Black Americans come together to celebrate their freedom from slavery and to reshape the strategies for facing equality for justice for the future." That may sound good, but on January 2, 2006, the second anniversary of Leslie's death, our attendance was not an experience that supported those words. In the printed program, it further stated:

> For nearly a century now, socially conscious individuals from all walks of life, from all parts of the political spectrum, of all races and religions, have done something wonderful. They have dared to speak out for that which is right and against that which is wrong. They've all believed that civil rights are for everyone, that democracy is for everyone, and not just for some. They are unafraid to speak the truth. The primary focus of the NAACP continues to be the protection and enhancement of the civil rights of African Americans and other minorities.

We discovered that the local NAACP president did not practice actions corresponding to the words in the program. This was a different president from the one present at our 2004 rally. The president we encountered that day displayed actions toward us that were disgraceful and totally opposite the expectations one might have of a declared champion for civil rights.

Prior to the beginning of the program, Dwight and I were outside the church, passing out flyers with accurate information about Leslie's homicide. To enter the church from the sidewalk, one had to walk up several steep steps to reach a landing, where we stood. We offered the flyers to persons who wanted them. We did not try to intimidate anyone or force attendees to receive a flyer. Because of our decades of residency in Chattanooga, we knew many of the people in attendance and chatted briefly with them. Everyone seemed supportive, interested, and pleased to receive a copy of the flyer. Our plan was to join the audience when the program began. We had no plans to pass out any information inside the church or be disruptive in any way.

Approximately fifteen minutes before the program started, the NAACP president came out of the church, approached Dwight, and immediately began a dialogue. I was standing in an area near him but could not hear the discussion. I then walked over to where they were standing. According to Dwight, she asked us to leave. To make sure he heard her correctly, he asked her, "What did you say?" She said, "I am asking you to leave and maybe go to the parking lot." Dwight said, "Are you asking me to leave the church property?" She then said, "You are trying to put words in my mouth." Dwight responded, "No, I am interpreting the words that just came out of your mouth. Don't you believe that our struggle is connected with your program?" There was no response. I asked her, "Are you saying you don't want us to attend the program?" Again, there was no response. The confrontation was quickly escalating into an argument. It was not our intention to create a scene, especially with the media being present. So, we decided to go to the bottom of the steps and stand on the public sidewalk to continue passing out the flyers.

As we were on the sidewalk, Booker, a close friend, came up to us and expressed his excitement at seeing us at the event. He asked, "Are you all going to be on the program?" My response was "No, the NAACP president doesn't even want us at the program and we were asked to leave." Booker shared in our amazement of how we were treated. Another person I will mention is the late Judge Bob Moon, a respected judicial figure in the community. He approached us and expressed his sympathy for Leslie's death and support for our cause. Without divulging any confidential information, he did say to us that something was going to happen soon that he felt would please us. Later that year, it was publicly announced that Chief Steve Parks was going to retire. I'm not certain, but I always felt it was that information to which Judge Moon referred, because Steve Parks's announcement certainly pleased us.

We have an extensive network of relationships in Chattanooga. That NAACP president was not a native Chattanoogan and was unaware of our circle of influence. When we told members of the audience how we were treated, many expressed their disgust at the actions of that NAACP president. Some of those people were longtime NAACP members and officers of the organization. In fact, I personally knew six members of the branch's executive committee. Until we shared our experience, they were not aware of the incident. As originally planned, we did attend the event, which was open to the public. A friend of ours, who also happened to be an officer with the local NAACP, came and sat with us as she entered the church. We told her what had just transpired. She expressed shock and outrage and vowed to find out why we had experienced such treatment. Immediately prior to the conclusion of the program, we went back to our sidewalk location and continued to pass out flyers. As other persons were leaving the program, some volunteered to help us and asked for multiple flyers. They positioned themselves at various other locations along the sidewalk to distribute our information.

While we were still distributing flyers, our friend and NAACP officer approached us with the outcome of the conversation she had just completed with the president. In response to her direct question of why the Praters were asked to leave, the president said, "Because they are suing the police department and the city." That response was even more shocking than her misguided actions. If she had been supporting the collective mission of the NAACP to struggle for justice and confront injustice, the local NAACP branch would have joined us in the lawsuit. Instead, they avoided interacting with us.

Dwight wrote a commentary prompted by our reaction to that experience and submitted it to a local media outlet, but it was never printed. Here are questions he included in that opinion piece:

1. Has the local chapter changed its name from the National Association for the Advancement of Colored People to the National Association for the Abandonment of Colored People?
2. Have you changed your agenda to do only those things that are expedient and politically correct?
3. Have you ever considered the question, "Why is the membership decreasing?" Could it be that your vision has become that of short-sightedness?
4. Have you considered the fact that your current agenda does not tackle the core issues that are common in today's life?
5. When do you deal with the core issues of injustice and brutality against the people?

At that time, the presiding NAACP president had no concept of the real message of Jubilee Day. Simply because slavery was officially outlawed decades before January 2, 2006, didn't mean that African Americans were free from being enslaved. I liken her actions to those of slave masters, who were gatekeepers of oppression and opposed freedom. To be free requires more than a piece of paper stating that one is free. Yes, on January 1, 1863, President Abraham Lincoln signed an executive order, the Emancipation Proclamation, the document that freed the slaves. And even in 2017, many African Americans are pondering the question, "Are we free yet?"

In response to an invitation, I spoke at the Thirty-Third Annual National Black Family Conference in Louisville, Kentucky, on March 10, 2006. The title of my research paper was "Terror in the Neighborhood: Police Brutality as a Barrier to the Health and Longevity of Black Males." When I discussed my situation, others in the audience volunteered to share their accounts of police brutality experiences. I sensed that people were surprised that I and others in the room had such horrible experiences. Their reactions further document that anyone can be victimized by aggressive police officers.

On May 18, 2006, Dwight and I, along with the generosity of other family members and friends, established the endowed Leslie Vaughn Prater Memorial Scholarship in Criminal Justice at the University of Tennessee at Chattanooga. We wanted to establish the scholarship as a lasting tribute to Leslie's life, demonstrate our commitment to justice, and help students in their pursuit of education. As a part of completing the formal application, students would be required to write and submit an original essay, "I Believe in Justice for All." Because the scholarship is endowed and contributions are continually applied to the book value amount, it is anticipated that the scholarship and Leslie's name will outlive us.

During the public announcement of the award, I said, "It is the family's sincere hope that the recipients of this scholarship will embrace justice and embark on a successful professional career to ensure that justice is enjoyed by all." Throughout the years, scholarship recipients have sent us thank-you messages, which mean a lot to us. The following is one of those correspondences. I chose to protect the student's identity.

Dear Mr. and Mrs. Prater, first and foremost, I would like to show my appreciation for being awarded the Leslie Vaughn Prater Scholarship by writing this letter. I am sincerely thankful to be honored and blessed by the both of you. This scholarship means a lot to me and will contribute to my college education. I am approaching my senior year and am one step closer to graduating. Going to college has always been a dream of mine, and with the assistance of wonderful people like you, I have been able to afford college costs. Again, I'd like to say thank you for being so kind to students like myself. Thank you for making this award possible. Sincerely,

―.

In response to another invitation, on October 16, 2006, I spoke at the National Social Science Association's annual research conference in San Francisco, California. As the organization's name implies, there were presenters and attendees from all over the United States. The research I presented was based on a secondary analysis of data focused on social systems impacted by police brutality.

On November 21, I completed a telephone conversation with a contact person from the Commission on Accreditation for Law Enforcement Agencies (CALEA), Inc., regarding the accreditation of the Chattanooga Police Department. I knew that there were problems with the training of police officers in Chattanooga. I felt that the department should not be reaccredited without some conditions for them to improve. Based on my administrative role over the Department of Criminal Justice and Sociology and our regional police academy, I had some familiarity with CALEA. I wanted to seek more information regarding the process used by CALEA.

In addition to the lack of training regarding avoidance of positional asphyxia, there were other concerns. Equipment was substandard. On more than one occasion, we requested information and were denied and told that it was unavailable because of computer equipment malfunctions. There were public relations concerns, such as police releasing information to the media prior to contacting the immediate family. Certainly, there were problems with departmental procedures and policies with regard to approaching an unarmed person with questionable behavior. There were other concerns as well, such as their procedure for filling out incident reports when more than one officer is involved. Maybe you can understand why I felt a need to discuss these matters with a CALEA representative. To my knowledge, the Chattanooga Police Department has maintained its CALEA accreditation status.

On December 8, I was contacted by an ABC news correspondent from New York. She was assigned to the law and justice unit and expressed an interest in interviewing me on the topic of police brutality, but she would have to get clearance from her supervisor. Unfortunately, she did not get the approval. Later in 2007, she contacted me four more times, but she could never get the approval to move forward with an interview. I always felt that she sincerely was interested in my perspective.

Jason, a young white college student from Georgia, whom I had never met, telephoned me on December 11. He stated that he had experienced an episode of police brutality perpetrated by Chattanooga police officers and was calling me to give me encouragement because he understood Leslie's situation. He had been unarmed and had been beaten and tased. Another young man had been with him at the time, but his injuries were not as severe as Jason's. A camera on the parking lot site of the incident had captured footage of several officers beating and kicking the two young men after they were down and handcuffed; they never resisted arrest. He said, "I can relate to what happened to Leslie, because Leslie was alone and without camera footage." After a newspaper report of the incident, the unwarranted charges of resisting arrest and disorderly conduct were dropped. Jason's situation ended with a civil lawsuit settlement. In addition, two officers were terminated, two others were suspended for twenty-eight days without pay, and another suspended for ten days without pay. Chief Steve Parks ruled on the decision. Jason told me that he never wanted to return to Chattanooga. Rogue police officers are equal-opportunity abusers. One has to wonder if the officers would have been disciplined had there been no videotaped evidence. Would that event have been simply "all in a day's work," or would Parks have ruled the injuries as accidental?

ACTIVITIES JANUARY 2007–FEBRUARY 2017

After the lawsuit was settled, I continued activities focused on promoting public awareness of police brutality. Activities initiated by others became more infrequent with the passing of time. I continued to have interactions with news people, law enforcement administrators, and residents about the topic of police misconduct. Also, I continued to research the literature on police brutality and share that knowledge with others. During 2007–2016, more of my time was also concentrated on completing the manuscript for this book, which was an emotional struggle.

On September 28, 2007, I was a guest speaker in a criminal justice class at Southeast Missouri State University. My presentation was a combination of research and personal experience. As usual, the audience seemed shocked that I was a mother of an unarmed son killed by police officers. People tend to profile family members involved in these situations. I was introduced as the dean of the College of Health and Human Services, their dean. Part of my purpose was to document that anyone could be the object of police brutality. At random, I pointed to various students and said, "It can happen to you, and you, and you." I felt it important to stress that no one is immune. Certainly, I sensed that their original perception of mothers identified with those circumstances was shattered.

October 4, 2007, was the first date I spoke to candidates enrolled in the Regional Law Enforcement Academy in Cape Girardeau. Their training curriculum, which was carefully designed to abide by CALEA guidelines, routinely allowed for guest speakers. I had discussed with the academy director that I was willing to speak on the matter of police brutality. He was familiar with my situation and was the first person to tell me that Leslie's death was probably the result of positional asphyxia. His conclusion was actually my introduction to the term, even prior to the completion of Leslie's autopsy report, which documented positional asphyxia as the cause of the homicide.

Dwight and I prepared the presentation, which included a Power-Point and the video presentation about Leslie that had been filmed to potentially present in court. Although I was the speaker, Dwight accompanied me to provide technical and moral support. For me, the presentation was practice for the talk that I would later give to the police academy in Chattanooga. During the presentation, I was observing the body language of the audience, and sensed an interest in the information. I stressed that when their lives or the lives of others are not in danger, their actions should be focused on preserving life. I also asked them to think about the fact that residents, with whom they will come in contact, have people who love them too.

On October 22, 2007, I presented a workshop at the Chattanooga Police Academy, the first of three opportunities granted to me as part of the lawsuit settlement. An interesting coincidence is that October 22 is the annual National Day of Protest to Stop Police Brutality. That workshop is discussed more in chapter 9.

As part of the observance of Black History Month at Eastern Illinois University (EIU), I was invited to speak on February 26, 2008. My presentation was titled "Guilty until Proven Innocent: Experiences of African American Males and Police Brutality." Attendees included students; faculty; the interim Charleston, Illinois, police chief; and the chief of the university police department. In announcing the campus lecture, the *Eastern Daily News* printed an article on February 26 titled "Death by Brutality Inspires Mother." As a follow-up, in the next day's edition of the *Daily Eastern News*, a summary of my lecture, audience feedback from interviews, and my picture were featured on the first page.[7]

The news article also included statements from those in attendance. One African American male student stated that he grew up in a neighborhood where residents frequently experienced police brutality. He said, "Neighbors have lived with it for so long that they do not think of the violence as police brutality anymore." During the presentation, I stressed that silence can be deadly. When the reporter interviewed the interim chief of police, he said, "Training should never be underestimated." After the lecture, the chief approached me to share his reaction. His remarks were encouraging and supportive of my intentions to increase awareness. He was not defensive. He noted that he agreed that a crucial intervention strategy to decrease police brutality is to focus on recruiting the right people for those positions. He shared with me his personal challenges in completing the recruitment process. He and I agreed that everyone who applies is not necessarily the best fit for the role of police officer. As a bonus, a DVD was created of my presentation and placed in EIU's library as a resource for future research on the subject of police brutality.

On March 15, 2008, I returned to make another presentation to a different group of cadets at the Southeast Regional Law Enforcement Academy in Cape Girardeau. I asked another mother to join me in the presentation. Connie had also experienced the homicide of an unarmed son resulting from police brutality, and she saw the value in addressing the issue, as well as the opportunity to express her family's pain. Connie's son Derek, a former Marine sergeant who had survived a tour in Iraq, met death on American soil. Connie and I had been brought together by a similar tragedy. It was the glue that sealed our common bond. I am African American and Connie is white, but our pain has no racial boundaries.

The August 23, 2008, edition of the *Chattanooga Times Free Press* printed an article titled "Man in Police Custody Died of 'Excited Delirium.'" I have found no organization that recognizes "excited delirium" as a cause of death except police departments. It appears that "excited delirium" is a successful defense in the acquittal of homicides when police officers are the defendants. I was interviewed for the article and clearly stated my disagreement with their report. I could not understand how such a "condition" could have caused bleeding and all of the numerous injuries to Leslie's body. The police department never provided any explanation. Of course, police officials can say anything they desire, even if it is totally irrational, and the comments are accepted as fact. After all, "they" are the police.

In November, researching materials dealing with police brutality, I discovered a DVD that I thought was excellent: *Every Mother's Son*, a film by Tami Gold and Kelly Anderson, distributed by New Day Films. The video features the mothers of three victims killed by police officers. I wanted more insight into what other mothers experienced. The following is an excerpt from a statement written on the back cover of the DVD case:

> *Iris Baez never meant to become an activist. Kadiatou Diallo never meant to live in the United States, fighting for justice for her son. And Doris Busch Boskey never thought she'd become a spokesperson against police brutality. This film profiles three New York mothers who unexpectedly find themselves united to seek justice and transform their grief into an opportunity for profound social change.*

The *Tennessee Tribune*, a weekly newspaper in Nashville, Tennessee, included an insert in its December 4–10, 2008, edition. The report was designed by Jennifer L. Milele as a special community exclusive: "United for Change: The Movement Continues." The headline was "Wanted!! Mothers Whose Sons Were Killed by Law Enforcement."

This publication was arranged by Dr. Marcia Riley. Three mothers wrote articles about the deaths of their unarmed sons in that edition. Marcia wrote "Another Senseless Murder in a Texas Jail." "Arizona Teenager Shamelessly Shot in the Back" was written by Sandra Robertson, and I wrote "Unarmed and Murdered by Police Officers in Tennessee." Connie's son was featured in the article "Death Squad in Delaware: The Case of the Murdered Marine." That piece was written by William Norman Grigg.

The book *Africana Cultures and Policy Studies: Scholarship and the Transformation of Public Policy*, edited by Dr. Zachery Williams, was published by Palgrave Macmillan in 2009. I accepted the invitation of Dr. Williams to write a chapter for the book. My contribution was "Institutionalized Terror: A Social Systems Analysis of Police Brutality."

I accepted an invitation from the Unity Group in Chattanooga to give a presentation on January 17, 2009, focused on police brutality. The title of the lecture was "Black Males and Police Brutality: A Research Summary." The presentation was part of a group of programs planned during the annual Martin Luther King Jr. celebration.

On June 28, 2009, I sent a letter of appreciation to the mayor of Birmingham regarding how he responded to a police brutality incident. According to a news report, five police officers brutally kicked and beat an unconscious suspect after a high-speed chase through Birmingham, Alabama. The incident was caught on camera and discovered a year later. The five officers were fired.[8] Unfortunately, the officers mounted a successful appeal and the Jefferson County Personnel Board reinstated the officers.

Dwight and I attended the Twenty-Third Annual National Conference of Parents of Murdered Children (POMC), which convened on August 21–23, 2009, in Cincinnati, Ohio. The organization, identified as a self-help group dedicated to helping the families and friends of those who lost loved ones to violence, has more than three hundred chapters and one hundred thousand members.[9] The conference theme for 2009 was "Broken Hearts Healing with Help, Hope and Hugs." In comparison to research conferences, the workshops at this event were mostly personal and akin to testimonials, as well as self-help sessions and some research presentations. Here are a few examples of sessions: "Victim to Survivor Panel"; "How Much Did My Loved One Suffer?"; "The

Investigation—What Really Happens"; "Collaborative Efforts—Victim Advocates and Law Enforcement"; "Sibling Grief"; "Mother's Grief"; "Intimate Partner Homicide"; "How Dreams Heal"; "Murder/Suicide"; "Created Out of Justice"; "Alive Alone—No Surviving Children"; "Victim's Rights: Where, What, and Why"; and "Does Grief Come in 'One Size Fits All'?"

Although I am glad that we attended the conference, I don't know if I will attend another one. I left distressed because I didn't identify with the majority of parents who were helped by the police to punish the murderers of their children. I sat through sessions in which there were expressions of praise for police officers and the district attorney. I attended a session that informed participants of the victim rights' resources provided by the federal government. I specifically asked if there was any help for victims of police brutality. The response was "no." It was explained to me that the federal resources were administered by police departments.

There were four mothers in attendance whose sons died from encounters with the police. We came together, with the leadership of Marcia, and formed the informal MOMS support group. That group also included Connie, who traveled with us, and Deborah from Virginia. I felt like no one else at the conference understood the challenges we faced in seeking help from the justice system. We did find common experiences with other conference participants, such as the grief process and the struggle to accept the "new normal." On the last page of the conference booklet, we were left with the statement, "May we find comfort in gentle memories and while we grieve their loss always, may we too not forget that they lived."

The *Chattanooga Times Free Press* printed an article about the public forum for residents and law enforcement officials to speak to a team charged with gathering data for CALEA. I felt that the title of the article, "Public Backs Police at Forum," was misleading. I attended the forum on December 15, 2009, and asked the investigators to more closely examine the training standards and use-of-force policies used by the department. I stressed that there was concern with the training of officers on procedures for handling encounters with unarmed persons who are demonstrating confusion. My remarks were taken out of context. The reporter stated that Leslie had mental health problems. I believe in total health and well-being and feel that mental health is just as important as other conditions of physical health. Yes, Leslie was intoxicated when killed by the police, but he was not mentally ill. I believe that mental illness is a health condition that we, as members of society, should address in a thoughtful manner, especially considering that approximately one in five Americans suffers from a diagnosable mental disorder in a given year.[10] After reading the article, I immediately contacted the reporter and asked her to provide the family with the information of what doctor had diagnosed Leslie as mentally ill and when she received that information. She never provided any documents to support her conclusion.

I wasn't the only person who testified at the forum. Another parent confronted CALEA's team. The father of a man fatally shot multiple times by Chattanooga police the previous July asked investigators to consider whether police follow proper procedures and are properly trained. He further stated that some residents felt oppressed and that the police were out to kill or control them. I felt that the few residents who praised the police were carefully selected to appear before the team. For example, one man was a part of a community patrol program in concert with the police department. Other testimonials of praise were from the sheriff of Hamilton County and other public officials. When the reaccreditation process was completed, apparently the team dismissed the statements made by me and the other parent. The department was reaccredited and praised as Chattanooga's finest. That outcome was a signal of empowerment to continue business as usual. The team chairperson had stated, "The accreditation process makes you do what you're supposed to be doing."

The Unity Group sponsored its annual Martin Luther King Jr. community-wide birthday celebration on January 17, 2012. The Rev. Dr. Paul McDaniel was selected as the speaker. If you recall, he was our pastor and the spiritual leader who accompanied our family to the first meeting with the Chattanooga Police Department. I did not attend the event, but I was sent a video copy of the proceedings. As a former county commissioner, he was very familiar with situations of concern in Chattanooga, especially as related to racial divisions. He spoke about an array of situations in which improvement was needed. He talked about Leslie, whom he knew personally. He stated that the city would not have paid more than $1 million to a black family if there had not been a sense of guilt. Considering the mixed audience, including law enforcement officials, I thought it took a lot of courage for him to make that statement. During his speech, he did announce that he had nothing to lose by saying what he felt was needed. Political correctness did not guide his remarks. I was very touched that, eight years after Leslie's homicide, he was still speaking about police brutality.

Concerned Citizens for Justice (CCJ), a social justice advocacy initiative in Chattanooga, invited me to attend a meeting on June 25, 2013. The private discussion was hosted by the police chief, Bobby Dodd, and was by invitation only. The meeting's purpose was to listen to the concerns of CCJ, based on numerous complaints of police brutality from persons living in neighborhoods heavily populated with African Americans.

Ash-Lee Henderson, the leader of CCJ, contacted me and asked if I would attend the meeting with her and Jannelle, another devoted CCJ member. The chief had given her permission to bring a few people with her. He insisted on keeping the number small but did not specify the identity of those persons. I consented and traveled to Chattanooga to attend the meeting. The chief had not anticipated my attendance. When he walked into the room and recognized me as one of the people sitting around the conference table, he appeared shocked. He and I were not on good terms, because he would not allow me to continue the sensitivity training at the police academy.

The chief had carefully orchestrated the meeting, or so he thought. His assistant chiefs were present, as well as representatives from the mayor's office. He came prepared with his data, such as the number of arrests in certain urban neighborhoods and the nature of the criminal offenses. He had anticipated the concerns that CCJ would bring forward, because those had been publicly voiced over a period of time. The citizen complaints were mostly clustered around racial profiling, physical assaults, and unlawful arrests by police officers. It was clear that there was little or no trust or respect of police officers who patrolled the neighborhoods discussed. Contrary to the expectations of the chief, CCJ representatives also came prepared with information to counter the police chief's data.

CCJ members and I had discussed our planned approach. Ash-Lee would take the lead as CCJ's primary spokesperson. She had a lot of knowledge about misconduct of police in Chattanooga and had been involved in social advocacy for many years. Jannelle and I would contribute as needed and as deemed appropriate at the time. Actually, my role was closer to that of a volunteer CCJ consultant, since I did not live in Chattanooga and charged no fee for my service. I think the very fact that I was a surprise guest seemed to upset the chief, because he had no idea what I might say. I know that he didn't like the fact that I was present because he made a comment that Ash-Lee had brought haters of police to the meeting. Calmly, I reacted by stating that if he was referring to me, I did not hate the police, but I was opposed to injustice. Jannelle also reacted to the chief's statement and blatantly responded that she did dislike the police. She shared some of the reasons why she felt that way, including some personal knowledge of police misconduct. Jannelle, a professional with a bachelor's degree in criminal justice, also countered when the chief talked badly about people committing crimes in mostly African American neighborhoods. She shared that she lived in a predominately white neighborhood. There were white people committing crimes in that neighborhood, but rarely were there police patrols or people arrested. In the predominately black neighborhoods discussed, residents had complained to CCJ that police occupied those areas and frequently profiled and harassed residents. I guess that was Chattanooga's version of community policing.

When the question of the low number of minorities on the police force was asked, again, Chief Dodd referred to his data. He talked about the number of African Americans who had been considered but disqualified when the background check revealed a felony. As usual, it seemed to me that he was always prepared with negative comments about African Americans. I felt that he was implying that African Americans were mostly criminals and unqualified to serve among Chattanooga's finest. I was sitting there thinking, "What about the police officers already on the force who commit felonies but are not convicted because they are already police officers? What about African Americans wrongly convicted of felonies?" My feeling is that there are many African Americans with no felonies who would never consider law enforcement as a career. Why is that?

At the end of the meeting, I didn't sense that there were any bridges built. The wall between the police department and CCJ constituents remained. I suppose the chief could report to the mayor that he did have the meeting. The mayor could make a politically correct statement that the police department is reaching out to the community. It is clear that the "city fathers" don't want any race riots scaring off the downtown tourists, which I believe was the hidden agenda. The meeting was cordial, but I didn't feel that any opinions were changed or any progress was made. We listened and commented and they listened and commented. And that was all.

I accepted an invitation to present in a class at Fontbonne University in St. Louis on February 18, 2015. The class focused on racial issues and social inequities, past and present. Dr. Corinne Wohlford, a brave professor, developed the course in response to the situation in Ferguson after the death of Michael Brown. I identify her as brave because I had read hateful comments printed in an editorial page of the *St. Louis Post Dispatch* in response to her announcing the intention to develop such a course. The audience included students of varying ages and different racial backgrounds, as well as other guests from the university and lay community. I invited attendees associated with the Missouri Foundation for Health (MFH), an initiative focused on improving the health of Missourians through partnership, experience, knowledge, and funding. Currently, I serve as the chairperson of MFH's Community Advisory Council.

Dr. Wohlford allowed me to use the entire two and one half hours of class time. I provided a research overview of police brutality during the first hour, followed by a fifteen-minute break. The remainder of the class time was for an informal discussion to present a case study, our family's experience with police brutality and Leslie's death. I showed a brief video about Leslie and then I joined class members, who were already seated around a long rectangular table. I sat and talked with them, not as a researcher, but as a mother. At the end of the class, several students approached me and offered condolences and voiced appreciation for my visit; a few asked permission to hug me; and some approached me in tears.

As a capstone project, students presented a journal to the faculty member. This activity was part of the requirements for the class. The faculty member wrote an e-mail to me regarding the last entry of one student. She wrote, "I am usually not brought to tears, but tears flowed as I read the entry. If I would ever question whether or not I need to continue to do these presentations, all I need is to recall the words of that young man. It meant so much to me that 'he got it.'"

The faculty member shared the student's entry and she agreed that I could include some of his reflections in this book. This young white man, probably in his early twenties, was from a rural community in Missouri. Prior to enrolling in college, he had little to no direct exposure to black people. There were no black people in his K–12 classes and no black people living in his community. In his writings, he shared that he grew up thinking that there were no more problems with race, other than sentiments of the KKK and white supremacists. He admitted that one of his uncles was extremely racist and other family members were blatantly racist. They stereotyped black people as criminals and without good family values. According to this student, "When I was able to drive to St. Louis, I was told to never go past Delmar or into any part of North County." Family and friends told him that there was a difference between someone who is black and someone who is the n-word. He even began to use the n-word. As he continued his writings, he did take responsibility for his accepting those racial stereotypes as factual. He noted that the class had an impact on his thinking and he thanked the professor for that. He stated, "I can already see big differences in the way I think about race."

Additional excerpts from his journal are as follows:

When I first heard about Ferguson, it was from a friend who said something along the lines of "Did you hear about all the crazy stuff going on up in Ferguson?" I was shown a few videos of the folks who were looting and burning the QuikTrip. So I figured here we go, a bunch of black people who were angry and taking it out on hard working folks and their businesses. To me this reinforced stereotypes of black people as criminals and, from that point, I thought any protest was basically a riot. Then I walked into your class and it was the very first time that I was of the minority in a classroom. Even after reading "The New Jim Crow," I found myself right back where I started in November the night of the Wilson decision. I even made some racial remarks about welfare checks and telling black people to go get a job, but something ended up being different about this class.

I think the first huge thing for me was when Mrs. Prater came in. Actually hearing a woman teaching a lesson about how her child was killed; I just could not believe it. I could not even imagine my own mother, who is very strong, being able to go through that and talk about it the way Mrs. Prater did. I think I listened more and really began to question and look at some of the systems that were in place. It always seemed like whatever *particular thing we talked about in class, like how racially segregated St. Louis is or being able to see how colorblind policies effected the amount of black people that were in jail, would pop up in my life outside of this class. I also really began to see all of the stereotypes of black folks being talked about where I live. It began to be a really eye opening experience for me. I realized that these people did not know what they were talking about, but I couldn't blame them because they did not have the knowledge that I was obtaining through this course.*

On June 12, 2015, I responded to an opinion article posted in *Chatta-noogan.com*. The article gave examples of police officers who were compassionate and performed deeds determined to be heroic. I know there are officers who fit that profile. I know some of them, so I am aware that they do exist. My concern was that the author did not mention that there were police officers whose behavior was more criminal than heroic.

In my response, I discussed examples of cases where police officers were not compassionate. In fact, their actions killed unarmed residents and violated their constitutional rights. I mentioned that sensitivity workshops are needed, similar to the ones I was no longer allowed to teach in Chattanooga. I also challenged citizens to question the amount of their taxpayer dollars applied to defend police officers and settle lawsuits. That money, whatever the amount, could have been used in addressing social service needs.

In the closing paragraph, I asserted that the author of the original opinion piece was writing from his knowledge and experience, and I was writing from mine. I added that I was familiar with criminal justice/policing research, which documents numerous accounts of police misconduct. Many people are dead today because the "good cops" did not respond to the call. I ended by stating:

I think the world will be a better place if we are ever a post racial society. Unfortunately, we are not there yet. The variable of hatred is alive and well. As the words of a familiar song recount, "What the World Needs Now Is Love, Sweet Love."

I wrote a "mother-to-mother" letter to Lezley McSpadden on June 8, 2016. There is a level of understanding that precludes our having to explain our pain. I feel that Lezley, other mothers in similar situations, and I could provide strength to each other and work toward awakening more people to the reality of a failed justice system. I live two hours south of St. Louis, but Lezley and I did not meet until July 2, 2016, in New Orleans. Dwight and I attended the Essence Festival and attended Lezley's book signing for *Tell the Truth and Shame the Devil: The Life, Legacy, and Love of My Son Michael Brown.* Although I had already purchased and read her book, Dwight and I bought another copy and attended the signing. Instructions were to write your name on a piece of paper provided and hand it to her when you approached the table. When I handed her the paper with my name, she immediately recognized it. She got out of her seat and ran around the table and we embraced. Our instant communication was without words. We didn't need words, because our common pain spoke loudly. I felt as though I knew her in so many other ways, because of reading her memoir. Lezley is much younger than my children, and it seemed as though I was hugging that sweet little girl, with the red suitcase, described in her book. We took a picture together and she invited me to attend her next "Rainbow of Mothers" event in St. Louis.

On August 7, 2016, I attended the "Rainbow of Mothers Gala" facilitated by Lezley. The mothers present had a common bond, that of grieving the loss of a child, although there were varying causes of death. I identified more closely with the mothers who had lost children from violence, especially in cases where police officers were the perpetrators and there was no accountability for those homicides. In addition to mothers, other family members, and friends, there were community advocates in attendance. I invited my cousin Dot to attend with me. Her son and my dear cousin Anthony Winton had died within a year of this event. Although his death was nonviolent, Dot's grief was still very real and fresh. Some names of deceased children, their mothers, and most participants were unknown to me. Others were recognizable, because of media attention to their cases. In addition to Lezley, the mothers of Eric Garner, Tamir Rice, Sandra Bland, Sean Bell, and Oscar Grant attended. Also, Rev. Al Sharpton and Congresswoman Maxine Waters were there and each gave a compassionate address. In general, I felt a spiritual connection to all of the grieving mothers. It was as though we were in a room filled with people who understood our sorrow, and provided unconditional support.

I spoke on November 29, 2016, to members of Alpha Phi Sigma, the Criminal Justice Honor Society chapter at Southeast Missouri State

University. I was invited by Dr. Raleigh Blasdell, an associate professor in the Department of Criminal Justice and Sociology. My presentation focused on the circumstances and aftermath of Leslie's death and our family's interaction with the Chattanooga Police Department during the process of the wrongful death lawsuit. I was pleased to have the opportunity to speak with potential professionals, who will have influence within the law enforcement community.

I was featured on the front page of the *Southeast Missourian* newspaper on November 30, 2016. The article "Pain in Our Eyes" was the result of an earlier interview of me and others regarding Leslie's death, the related investigation, and the subsequent lawsuit. The subheading was "Cape Girardeau Woman Says She Hopes Her Son's Death Will Lead to Better Policing." There was also a video developed, which was featured on *semissourian.com*.[11]

I accepted an invitation from Dr. Corinne Wohlford to return to Fontbonne University on February 14, 2017, to present another lecture. I titled the presentation, "My Experience with the Two Faces of Policing: Before and After January 2, 2004." I feel it is my responsibility to continue telling the "behind-the-scenes" story of a family that experienced the homicide of an unarmed loved one resulting from police brutality.

Mother Teresa said, "I alone cannot change the world, but I can cast a stone across the waters to create many ripples." I have cast many stones and will continue to do so. I have cast enough stones to build a fortress, but am only sharing a sampling with you. Actually, I consider my various interventions as seeds. I keep planting seeds in the hope that some will germinate and grow. I will continue to reach out to others for help. I am facing the biggest challenge of my life, that of seeking social justice for victims of police misconduct. Even more of a challenge is to increase sensitivity to the fact that a problem exists that will impact public policy. Like so many other family members of these tragedies, this fight found me. I didn't go seeking trouble, but I must not and cannot remain silent. Families and supporters of other victims have also created ripples. We must unite and continue to resist injustice using peaceful strategies, without violence. I am inspired by the words of Mohandas Gandhi: "A small body of determined spirits fired by an unquenchable faith in their mission can alter the course of history."

8

MOMS
(MOTHERS OF MURDERED SONS)

Unarmed and Killed by Law Enforcement

In the prologue, I mentioned the special relationship between mothers and sons. In this chapter, I want to highlight that bond, although a couple of mother-daughter dyads are included. The mothers discussed in this chapter share a bond not only with their children but also with each other through the tragedy of their child's death. Unfortunately, our tragedies are not so uncommon anymore. Technology has uncovered the ugliness of police misbehavior. Most of the mothers featured in this chapter were not interviewed on the national news, but they do share similarities with mothers whose names may be familiar to you. Most of their unarmed sons were killed by police officers, whether or not there was any admission of guilt, a conviction, or imprisonment. Although no two circumstances were exactly the same, the outcomes were the same. Their child is dead, and without just cause.

Emma Jones was the first mother I spoke to who truly understood the depth of a mother's trauma and grief after her child is killed by law enforcement. The sudden death of a child from any circumstance is a shock. I would never dismiss that fact, but the unanticipated repercussions of how families are treated by police departments only add to the devastation. In memory of her son, Emma started the MALIK Organization to support others who had children killed by police officers. I told

Emma the details of what had happened to Leslie. In the following, I paraphrase the first of many conversations I had with her, based on the notes I took. This is what Emma said to me:

> *I did not have the opportunity to grieve. At the hospital, I was trauma-tized and screaming out for someone to help me. I couldn't begin to con-ceptualize what had happened. I didn't talk to the press or any media until July. Beginning in July, I contacted individuals within the state to come and help me to make a plan of action. Representatives from various racial and ethnic organizations came. As an attorney, I knew how the criminal justice system worked, and how politics worked. I talked to prosecutors. It was hard to find attorneys who knew the situation. Usually, attorneys only look at civil lawsuits. I wanted an attorney to fight for civil rights. I held a press conference to call for an independent investigation. Subse-quently, I asked for the justice department to investigate. The department responded that they didn't have enough evidence to show that a crime was committed. They suggested that I write letters to the Department of Justice to express my concerns as a mother.*
>
> *You need to be very strategic about how you handle their questions. Frame the issue and keep with the issue. Stick to the facts that four po-lice officers used excessive force that was unreasonable and unnecessary. Leslie's constitutional rights were violated, they caused his death, and you want answers and justice. It is important to not argue with them, but write a fact sheet and begin distributing it right away. Your son was brutalized and he was positioned so that he could not breathe. Pound on the issue of what they did to him. While he was unarmed, handcuffed, and lying facedown on the ground, police officers had knees in his back. Someone should be held accountable. You need to go after these officers profes-sionally and personally. You need to get justice for your son and end the double standard of justice for police officers. There should be a thorough investigation, and they should be relieved from duty pending the outcome of the investigation. There should be objectivity in the investigation and a request to stop using excessive force. Request that criminal charges be brought against all of the officers that were involved in this egregious behavior.*

From 1997 to 2017, there have been many twists and turns to Em-ma's fight for justice. She first initiated a federal wrongful death lawsuit against East Haven, Connecticut, its police department, and the officer who killed Malik. All officers in that department were white. The accused officer was cleared of any wrongdoing. He never demonstrated any remorse. In 2003, the civil court jury ruled in Emma's favor. The ruling included a Monell claim, which is difficult to win. The Monell claim suggests that there was a violation of civil rights.[1] The jury awarded her $1.7 million for attorney fees and $2.5 million for punitive damages. East New Haven appealed, and in 2007 the verdict was reversed. In 2010, a federal jury awarded $900,000 in compensatory damages, but East Haven appealed that decision and won in 2012. A panel of three judges ruled that the town was not liable for the shooting. Emma then filed to have the US Supreme Court hear her case. On October 7, 2013, the US Supreme Court declined to consider Emma's appeal of a lower court ruling. Sadly, twenty years, two jury trials, and several appeals after April 14, 1997, Emma and her family have not received justice for the shooting of Malik, an all-too-typical outcome in police-involved deaths. There is no end to Emma's pain.

On January 31, 2006, I contacted Cynthia through one of my attorneys in Chattanooga. John Wolfe also represented her family in the wrongful death lawsuit of her son, Brandon Miller. He was killed on June 27, 2003, in Cleveland, Tennessee. Brandon was a handsome twenty-nine-year-old African American. He was law abiding and an employed college-educated professional. Unfortunately, Brandon was alone when he encountered a person who should never have been a police officer. Any well-trained officer would not use deadly force against an unarmed person merely for a speeding violation—if the claim of speeding was even accurate. Brandon had no criminal record or outstanding warrants, so there was no documentation to portray him as a villain. The officer claimed that Brandon was speeding when he was stopped and subsequently tried to flee and run over him. Witnesses living nearby contradicted the officer's version in sworn depositions.[2] The grand jury cleared the officer of any wrongdoing. The testimonies of key eyewitnesses were not heard. The grand jury only considered the police department's version of what happened. In reference to the grand jury, Cynthia was quoted as saying, "They don't want the witnesses talking for some reason. They just don't want the truth."[3] The officer was not held accountable for the murder of Brandon. No justice was served.

There were several mothers with whom I connected but never met. I never met Sarah, who didn't live in Chattanooga, but I did contact her in November 2004 to offer my condolences and to discuss her experience with the Chattanooga Police Department. We communicated by telephone and exchanged e-mail messages. The circumstances that caused the death of her daughter were very different from most of the mothers I contacted. Her case, which occurred approximately two years before Leslie's death, involved a traffic accident that was caused by a patrol officer. In that tragedy, Vanessa, an eighteen-year-old white university student, was killed. The officer was driving at a high speed through a red traffic light without using the emergency siren. The driver of the vehicle in which Vanessa was a passenger thus had no awareness of an emergency vehicle approaching. When she attempted to drive through the green light, the police cruiser hit her vehicle on the front passenger side. Vanessa died instantly.

Although Sarah and I were strangers, we talked at length about our children. When she sent her only child to college, she never expected to receive the "chilling" phone call that Vanessa was dead. Vanessa's death occurred on December 13, 2002, just a few days prior to ending the first semester of her freshman year. As grieving mothers, Sarah and I had a lot in common, although our experiences with the police department were different. The officer responsible for Vanessa's death was remorseful, expressed his sorrow, and, subsequently, resigned his position. According to Sarah, he was the only person in the department to show any remorse. The police investigation found that the officer was driving too fast for conditions and sped through a traffic light without "utilizing due caution." There was a lawsuit settlement. Police Chief Steve Parks told the family that the department would adopt new, year-round training methods in an effort to keep officers focused on proper emergency vehicle operation. In our case, we were only met with defiance and disdain. After Parks told us that Leslie's death was an accident, his expressions to us ended. Sarah and I agreed that legislation should be changed to bring attention to police abuse, neglect, and outcomes in which police are put above the law. In an e-mail message from Sarah to me, she said, "I grieve with you for your loss. The pain will always be with you and your life is changed forever, as you know. Being a Christian, I hope to be reunited with my daughter someday. If you have the same beliefs, you will also see your son."

Connie was the mother who traveled with me and Dwight to the Parents of Murdered Children's Conference. We both live in Missouri. In the local November 28, 2006, edition of the *Southeast Missourian*, there was an article about twenty-five-year-old Derek Hale, who had been shot and killed in Wilmington, Delaware, on November 6, 2006.[4] Derek, a veteran and former US Marine Corps sergeant, had survived in Iraq. He had fought for the safety of Americans, only to return home to die on American soil at the hands of a police officer charged to serve and protect. Derek lived in Manassas, Virginia. He had gone to Wilmington to participate in a "Toys for Tots Run," sponsored by his motorcycle club. Derek was unarmed and sitting on the steps of a friend's house when he was approached by several police officers. Police claimed they suspected the club of criminal activity. Like Trayvon Martin, Derek was wearing a hooded sweatshirt. Could this have been his crime? Derek had no criminal record, and there was no evidence that he was involved in any crimes. On that fateful Saturday afternoon, Derek posed no threat to anyone and did nothing to invite aggressive behavior from the police. Dr. David Crowe was interviewed for the article. This is what he said about Derek:

> *Derek is a true hero in my life for what he did for my son Taylor. In elementary school when Taylor was in the throes of autism, Derek was right there helping him and involving him in the mainstream; coming over on weekends or any free time Derek had. He was an extraordinary young man. What an unspeakable irony and tragedy, when you survive two tours in Iraq and then are killed by law enforcement in your own country.*

The circumstances leading to Derek's death were that Derek was tased three times in rapid succession by two officers. Additionally, one officer shot him in the chest at close range. This occurred all within three minutes, without any attempt of appropriate dialogue to diffuse a potentially deadly situation. Actually, there was no "situation," prior to the arrival of the police officers. After he was tased, the officer told him to put up his hands. He was trying to comply but could not get his hands up because of his body's reaction to being tased. A contractor working next door was an eyewitness. He said, "He didn't deserve to be shot. He wasn't any kind of threat. They had him surrounded. They could have grabbed him."[5] People claim that citizens are safe if only they comply with the demands of the police. But complying or trying to comply, as in Derek's case, is not a shield against the intentions of an abusive police officer. In 2010, the city of Wilmington, Delaware, settled the federal lawsuit for $875,000, paid to Derek's widow, Elaine, in exchange for the release of all legal claims. The city and police officials defended the officers' actions. The officer who shot Derek was cleared of any wrongdoing and was later promoted.[6] There was no justice in Derek's death.

On Thanksgiving eve in 2007, the ringing of the telephone interrupted my cooking responsibilities for the next day. "Is this Dr. Loretta Prater?" I wondered what stranger would be calling me to chat on the night before Thanksgiving. Even telemarketers don't do that. The caller introduced herself as Dr. Marcia Riley from Atlanta. She explained that she wanted to talk to me about Leslie's death because her unarmed son had also died from an altercation with law enforcement officers.

Marcus Nygel Elliott, her twenty-two-year-old son, was killed in Plano, Texas, on June 30, 2007, within forty-eight hours of being detained in a Collin County jail. When she first talked to her son, after his arrest, he said to his mother, "They are going to beat me, Mom; I'm scared." His fear was understandable, considering that he only weighed 130 pounds and, as he told his mother, there were about twelve jailors. After that initial conversation, she called numerous times to speak with him, but each time she was told that he was "housed" and did not want to speak with her. Finally, he called her and was much calmer; he talked about his plans for the future. That was the last time she heard his voice. The next phone call she received was from a social worker at McKinney Medical Center. She said to Marcia, "Marcus hung himself in jail." After her initial hysteria at hearing that news, the first person she called was her brother, a police officer for more than twenty-five years.[7] According to Marcia, "Marcus was talented and had much potential. He only wanted a new start, add a new story to his life."

Someone who is looking forward to a future doesn't commit suicide. Marcia received conflicting reports of how Marcus died. Dr. William Rohr, the Collin County medical examiner, listed the manner of death as "homicide" and the cause as "sudden death after struggle and restraint" on the death certificate.[8] In the July 2 issue of the *McKinney Courier-Gazette*, the medical examiner stated that suicide was not the cause of death. Another news item reported information provided by a sheriff's spokesperson. It stated, "Marcus Nygel Elliott, 22, of Atlanta stopped breathing while being held down by officers. Officers noticed Mr. Elliott lying on his bunk with a thread around his neck that had been removed from his jail uniform. As officers tried to remove the string, Mr. Elliott began kicking and swinging at them. After Mr. Elliot's arms and legs were shackled to a restraining table, a nurse discovered he was not breathing."[9] Marcia sought legal counsel, but no one would take the case.

The evening of my first conversation with Marcia marked the beginning of a friendship, spanning years, although we were initially drawn to each other through tragedy. We also had a common interest in writing. Marcia was a journalist, owner of her own business, and the author of the book *Hot-lanta*. Our desire was to bring attention to police brutality and ways that families can unite to support one another. One of those strategies was to start the support group MOMS (Mothers of Murdered Sons: Unarmed and Killed by Law Enforcement). As previously mentioned, we joined with two other mothers at the 2009 Parents of Murdered Children's conference to initiate MOMS. We were two white mothers and two black mothers grieving the deaths of our sons. Unfortunately, the MOMS group did not expand as we had hoped. We discovered that there are so many groups with a similar purpose. The challenge is to unite under one umbrella, comparable to Mothers Against Drunk Driving (MADD). We understand that may never occur, because MADD has the support of law enforcement and the larger community.

On February 14, 2008, twenty-three-year-old Zachary Snyder, an unarmed white male, was shot and killed by a Fugitive Unit Investigator, with the Missouri Department of Corrections. Snyder was shot while avoiding his parole officer. Zachary's nonviolent offense was a parole violation and failure to appear. According to a newspaper report, the officer pulled out his service revolver as he approached the victim. Snyder was initially compliant but then turned and ran. The officer shot Zachary in the back. As usual, the officer's defense was that he feared for his safety. Clearly, Snyder was not attempting to threaten the officer's life, considering that he was running away from the officer.[10]

When this story was first reported, I searched for information to locate Snyder's mother. Edith lived approximately fifty miles from me.

It did not matter that she wasn't African American. She was another grieving mother in need of compassion. In a "cold call," I introduced myself, expressed empathy, and alerted her to some of the challenges she would face. In all likelihood, her help would come from outside the justice system. As the victim, her son would most likely be profiled as a villain and blamed for his death. The killer would probably not be held accountable or serve one day of jail time for his actions.

Edith expressed worry about her preschool grandchildren, who would not have the benefit of her son in their lives. She said that her son was a nonviolent, loving person. I could not help but think about the irony that her son was killed on Valentine's Day. She thanked me for my call of support. We have never spoken again. The eventual outcome of the case was that the officer was charged with involuntary manslaughter but was later acquitted. However, Zachary's father had expressed to news reporters that his son was assassinated. As the result of the family's civil wrongful death lawsuit, a jury awarded Snyder's children $1 million.[11]

I talked with Angella Henry once, but I never met her. I saw a news report about the shooting of unarmed Danroy "D. J." Henry Jr., her twenty-year-old son in New York. In their case, her husband Danroy Henry Sr., an executive with a Fortune 500 company, was the family's primary spokesperson. As a mother, I wanted to reach out directly to Angella. I made a "cold call" to their home and asked to speak to her. Angella was cautious and seemed rather anxious at receiving a call from a stranger, which I understood. There are so many haters out there who want to bring harm to anyone who speaks out against unlawful actions of police officers. After I provided more information about myself and the reason for my call, she was more relaxed and inviting of my expressions of empathy and understanding. As I had hoped, we talked as one grieving mother to another, which described our new and unwelcomed role in life. We will always carry the burden of our children being murdered and the judicial system's cold response of no justice. As I experienced with other mothers, it seemed to me as though we were friends, instantly bonded by our common pain and compassion for one another. I later read a statement Angella had given to a reporter. She said, "The pain of losing our son so suddenly is insatiable and not only has his absence changed us forever, but his suffering will always haunt us as well."[12]

D. J. was shot on October 18, 2010. He was a junior and football player at Pace University. From my review of information about the Henry family, and D. J. in particular, he was a young man from a beautiful family. He was pursuing a college degree, with potentially a bright future ahead of him. He embodied high moral standards, was never in any trouble, had a winning personality, and was highly regarded by friends, teacher/coaches, and loved ones. The Henry family, living the American dream in middle-class suburbia, was very different from the negative picture of the African American family characterized by former New York senator Daniel Patrick Moynihan.[13] I mention this because many people are comfortable with thinking that there is no way that they, or any of their family members, could be the victim of police brutality. I continue to stress that anyone can become a victim, even unarmed law-abiding persons. All that is needed is for circumstances to place you in contact with an abusive or trigger-happy officer. This can happen even if you do nothing wrong and obey the officer's commands. Once bullets are released, they don't discriminate. No demographic criteria will serve as protective armor.

On the evening D. J. died, police responded to a call of a disturbance at a restaurant. D. J. and two other football players were in a car, parked outside. D. J. was the driver. According to one of the others in the car, an officer approached the car and knocked on the window. They thought the officer wanted them to move the car, because they were in a fire lane. As D. J. slowly began to drive away from the disturbance, of which he was not a part, an officer jumped from behind another car onto the hood of D. J.'s vehicle. That officer immediately started shooting D. J. multiple times at close range through the windshield. Another officer shot into the car, injuring one of the other passengers. This was the report from eyewitnesses. The police version was that when they knocked on the window, D. J. tried to speed away, striking one officer and pinning another against the hood.[14] As usual, the justice system accepted the officer's version and D. J.'s killer was cleared of any wrongdoing. He provided the defense that always seems to work: he felt threatened.[15]

A video of the event showed that the police threw D. J. to the ground, handcuffed him, and stood around without offering any paramedic aid, which they were trained to give.[16] This was another example of white police officers demonstrating no regard for the life of an innocent and unarmed African American male. In recognition of D. J.'s life, the family established the D. J. Dream Fund, which has benefited hundreds of children. This nonprofit 501(c)(3) organization provides funds to support youth from families with low incomes to participate in various sports, music, dance activities, and summer camps. D. J. was known to be involved in healthy lifestyles, so this initiative mirrors his life. There was no justice for the homicide of D. J., but the Village of Pleasantville, New York, agreed to a settlement of $6 million awarded to the family for his wrongful death.[17] Money is not justice, although it is a signal that there was wrongdoing.

A former faculty colleague contacted me to tell me about her grandson. He had been shot and killed by a police officer in California. James, her twenty-five-year-old grandson, had a prior diagnosis of mental illness and was on medication. Crisis intervention teams had been called to the house on nine occasions and were able to diffuse the situation without violence. On the day of his death, James had another episode, believed to be caused by his not taking his medicine. His mother called the police for assistance. James ran outside his home with two knives from the kitchen. An eyewitness stated that he never saw James rush toward the police and questioned the police officers' ability to handle that situation. The police asked James to drop the knives, but he did not immediately comply. Two shots were fired at James by one officer. James's mother, my friend's daughter, was in a bedroom and his father was not at home. When she heard the shots, she assumed that he had been shot in the leg, to stop any threat. She was not allowed to accompany James in the ambulance. At the hospital, she was told that James had died in surgery.

The experience of James's parents is common to other parents of victims of police violence. Information was withheld from them, and many inquiries remained unanswered. I was asked to send a letter to the mother because she was too distraught to talk about her son's death. On April 5, 2014, I sent her a letter of support and understanding. Their case was eventually resolved with a lawsuit settlement.

There are so many mothers of this "sisterhood" whom I have never met, and I probably will never have a face-to-face discussion with them. I never met Deborah Jenkins, the mother of unarmed Larry Jenkins, killed in Milwaukee on September 19, 2002.[18] I never met the mother of Jonathan Ferrell, who was killed trying to seek help from a police officer after surviving an automobile accident.[19] The officer did not help Jonathan but instead shot and killed him. He was found innocent of any wrongdoing. That case was settled in 2015 for $2.25 million. Ferrell's mother received no justice.

Thirty-one-year-old Donte Hamilton, an unarmed black male suffering from schizophrenia, was killed in Milwaukee on April 30, 2014. I haven't met Maria Hamilton, Donte's mother, who started the group Mothers for Justice. The white officer was fired but not charged with a crime. Donte became paranoid after missing his medication because of insurance problems. He was resting in the park, causing no harm to anyone, but was shot fourteen times.[20] The officer's appeal to get his job back was unsuccessful.

Marcella Holloman was the mother of thirty-one-year-old unarmed Maurice Donald Johnson, killed by police in Northeast Baltimore on May 19, 2012. Maurice, her firstborn child, was diagnosed with bipolar disorder in 2009. Marcella called the police for assistance because of Maurice's disruptive behavior.[21] She wanted an ambulance to take her son to the hospital for treatment. According to Marcella, her son was shot twice in the chest and once in the back within minutes of police entering her home. Marcella has also said that there have been many inaccuracies reported of the incident.[22] I do believe that there is inadequate training of police officers in confronting persons diagnosed with mental illness. Surely they are not told to just show up and kill them.

It seems as though the number of "sisterhood" members is inexhaustible. Valerie Bell's life changed when Sean Elijah Bell died. Her twenty-three-year-old unarmed son was killed on his wedding day in New York on November 25, 2006. Police officers fired a barrage of fifty shots into the car in which Sean was riding. Although the officers were charged with criminal offenses, they were acquitted of any wrongdoing. Valerie Bell is the founder of Mothers of Never Again (MONA).[23] New York City paid the Bell family a settlement of $3.25 million. In Sean's memory, the New York City Council designated a portion of Liverpool Street in Queens as "Sean Bell Way."

There are countless other mothers suffering from the results of police brutality. Who is Jeralynn Blueford? She is the mother from Oakland, California, whose unarmed eighteen-year-old son, Alan Blueford, was shot and killed on May 6, 2012, just weeks before his high school graduation. She founded the Alan Blueford Center for Justice.[24] Dallas resident Collette Flanagan is another grieving mother. Her twenty-five-year-old son, Clinton Allen, though unarmed, was shot seven times and killed on March 10, 2013. Colette spoke during a Mothers Against Police Brutality candlelight vigil in front of the US Department of Justice in Washington, D.C., on December 10, 2014. Collette has also given a powerful interview near her son's gravesite.[25] I also completed an interview at Leslie's grave, and I was so proud of Collette, because I know the magnitude of strength required for gravesite interviews. Why do we expose ourselves to that suffering? We do it for our sons and daughters, and for the children of others, dead and alive. For those still alive, we want them to continue living and pursue their constitutional rights.

Thirty-four-year-old Rumain Brisbon, an African American father of four daughters, was shot and killed by a white police officer in Phoenix, Arizona, on December 2, 2014. As usual, the police's version of the killing contradicts reports from eyewitnesses. Also typical, the officer said he shot Brisbon because he felt threatened, although Rumain was unarmed. The police officer was not charged with the fatal shooting. Nora Brisbon is Rumain's mother. Our direct paths have never crossed. I viewed a news report in which she pleaded for the killings to stop. She stated her belief that lack of training and fear, more than race, are factors leading to these killings.[26]

I identify with Gwen Carr, whom I met in 2016 in St. Louis. In so many cases, guns were used to end the life of unarmed persons. In the case of both Leslie and Gwen's son, Eric Garner, they were not shot but died from positional asphyxia. In both cases, no criminal charges were filed against the officers responsible for their deaths. Gwen has stressed that mothers need to fight through the grief. She noted that the deaths of our sons is yesterday's news, but to us those deaths remain a headline in our lives. Gwen quit her job to become a full-time advocate and is one of the leaders of Mothers of the Movement, a social justice initiative comprised of mothers of sons and daughters whose deaths resulted from violence. The majority of the mothers represent sons who died from interactions with law enforcement officers, but not all. Sandra Bland is a daughter of one of the Mothers of the Movement. Also represented are sons and daughters whose death resulted from lay citizens, as with the death of Jordan Davis and Hadija Pendleton. Hadija, a fifteen-year-old who performed at President Obama's inauguration, was shot in a Chicago park. She was a beautiful, innocent child, but that didn't seem to matter to gang members.[27] Mothers of the Movement is believed to be the inspiration for Black Lives Matter, which was created in 2012 after Trayvon Martin's murderer was acquitted.

Since Leslie's death, I have had several mothers and others contact me to share accounts of police brutality resulting in homicides or assaults of their loved ones. Many of these persons live in Chattanooga, and some of the situations occurred years prior to Leslie's homicide. It seemed to me that they just wanted someone to listen, to express compassion and understanding without judging or blaming them or the victims. In some instances, many were without partners to share their sorrow. Many expressed having experienced harsh words from strangers, acquaintances, or social media. Some persons approached me when I was in Chattanooga presenting lectures or participating in marches.

We are mothers who love our children. I use the present tense, because that love will never fade, nor will the memory of how they died. The scary thing is that if I continued gathering information from mothers with experiences of police brutality, I could fill volumes of books. The fact that there are so many of us is distressing. Please, stop the violence, on all sides. We don't want to see any more mothers bury their sons or daughters, including mothers of police officers.

I want to thank Hillary Clinton for listening to grieving mothers and giving Mothers of the Movement a national platform to share their stories. Featuring those nine mothers at the 2016 Democratic Convention in Philadelphia allowed millions of Americans to confront these issues of violence. Three mothers spoke on behalf of all. Those appearing on the stage were Sybrina Fulton, mother of Trayvon Martin; Gwen Carr, mother of Eric Garner; Geneva Reed-Veal, mother of Sandra Bland;

Maria Hamilton, mother of Dontre Hamilton; Lucia McBath, mother of Jordan Davis; Lezley McSpadden, mother of Michael Brown; Annette Nance-Holt, mother of Blair Holt; Cleopatra Pendleton-Cowley, mother of Hadija Pendleton; and Wanda Johnson, mother of Oscar Grant.[28] Their experiences represent the experiences of many. That national exposure was an opportunity to acknowledge that our sons and daughters matter too. For parents reading this book who love their children, all I am saying to you is that we love our children too, just as much as you love yours.

9

POLICE ACADEMY WORKSHOPS

A Proactive Strategy to Address Police Misconduct

I felt strongly that the Chattanooga Police Academy needed sensitivity training. Regardless of what its training manual may have said, it was evident that sufficient training was lacking in that area. The history of interactions between unarmed citizens and Chattanooga police officers in which the citizens died or were seriously injured indicated that recruits, as well as seasoned officers, were not getting the message. Sensitivity training, in comparison to some of the other topics taught at a police academy, should not be just another assignment conducted by a veteran police officer. There is a need for the "face and voice" of victims of police misconduct to be represented as part of the curriculum. As Leslie's mother and an advocate for social justice, I felt a calling to accept that role. I was more than a mother of a victim; I was an experienced educator, and one with knowledge of criminal justice issues and police academy curricula.

I was allowed to teach in three classes at the Chattanooga Police Academy. An alternative would have been for me to make a video and have that available for others to present. I felt that the more powerful approach would be for me to present the workshops in person. I didn't want someone to merely drop a video into a recorder and "check the box" that sensitivity training had been completed. Only someone who had experienced a wrongful death of a loved one at the hands of police officers could assume the role of the "face of a survivor."

Speaking to groups of people was familiar to me and not intimidating. I had conducted many professional workshops and class presentations. I had spoken at local, state, and national conferences for a combined period of decades. However, although I had spoken to cadets at the academy in Cape Girardeau, speaking to a group of police officer recruits in Chattanooga was emotionally challenging. I anticipated an unwelcoming and cold reception in Chattanooga because a legal settlement was obligating the department to allow my presentations.

The structure of the academy presentations in Chattanooga was similar to the one I used in Cape Girardeau. Dwight was at each, providing technical assistance and moral support. After the introductions and prior to the audiovisual presentation, I conducted a brief research activity. I asked each recruit to write an anonymous response on an index card provided. The question was "Why did you want to become a police officer?" I collected the cards. Near the end of the session, I read some of the responses, commented, and facilitated a discussion.

The presentation lasted approximately ninety minutes. We showed a brief video in which Dwight and I were interviewed and shared memories of Leslie and how we felt about losing him. The PowerPoint was mostly focused on what happens with families after the burial and closure of any related legal matters. I boldly stressed that Dwight and I were parents who represented families they had read about in newspaper accounts of police brutality. I included the poem "Never Be Another You," written by our son Stefan. In introducing the last slide, I said, "The family is left with this." That slide is a picture of Leslie's gravesite. A question-and-answer period immediately followed the PowerPoint presentation. In the first presentation in Cape Girardeau, few questions were asked. Of the inquiries voiced, most were about the outcome for the police officers and the lawsuit settlement agreement. One recruit approached me after the session. He wished us well and congratulated me on the presentation.

The first academy presentation in Chattanooga was scheduled on March 26, 2007, from 9:00 to 10:00 a.m. at the Police Training Center. Chief Cooper, who had approved the content of the presentation, had informed me that I would be allowed additional time to respond to any questions from recruits. When Dwight and I entered the building, we were greeted warmly. I'll admit I was surprised but cautious. I knew that we were expected and easily recognizable from the many local television appearances.

The training officer who greeted us ushered us into his office to explain the logistics we needed to know. He gave us information about the room arrangements and the computer and video equipment. Another officer would video the presentation for possible future use. Although we had our own laptop computer as a backup, he explained to Dwight the particulars of using the department's equipment. My interaction with this particular officer was cordial but rather guarded, as I noted that his last name was the same as a departmental executive administrator who had publicly expressed support of the police officers who caused Leslie's death. He also looked like a younger version of that administrator, and I thought they could be related. Nepotism is common among personnel in police departments, especially father/son pairings employed in the same department.[1]

At the department's request, I had already sent a written description of the workshop's objectives and content, which closely followed the workshop presented in Cape Girardeau. The main difference between the two presentations is that I provided no handouts in the prior workshop. For the Chattanooga recruits, I brought a handout that described the Leslie Vaughn Prater Memorial scholarship, available at the University of Tennessee in Chattanooga. The handout also included a picture of Leslie and Stefan's poem, "Never Be Another You." Because the scholarship is in the Department of Criminal Justice, I thought that there might be persons in the session with an interest in applying or who might share the information with others.

While the recruits were on break, we entered the classroom with the training support staff and proceeded to set up, test the equipment, and adjust the lighting. I placed a blank index card at each recruit's seat for them to write a response to the research question.

As the recruits entered the room from their break, other training officers also came into the session and sat at the back of the room. There were approximately twenty-five recruits present. They were mostly white males, with a few women and African Americans. The supervising training officer introduced Dwight and me and told them why we were there, and he provided some information about my past as a resident of Chattanooga. To my surprise, he also gave some examples of my years of positive relationships with the Chattanooga Police Department. When I spoke about why we were there, I didn't mention anything about the lawsuit but talked about how this initiative was about saving lives, theirs and citizens. Before beginning the official presentation, I asked them to respond to my research question on the index card.

I began by expressing my understanding that many honorable people with integrity choose to become police officers. I applauded them for their consideration of this career, given the potential personal risks involved and the relatively modest pay. We then showed the video of Dwight and me talking about Leslie. This was followed by the Power-Point presentation. Next was the question-and-answer period. I will admit that I dreaded this last part because I had experienced so much negativity from the Chattanooga Police Department. I felt that I was perceived as the enemy, the evil mother of Leslie Vaughn Prater. Regardless of those feelings of anxiety, I still invited their questions.

I asked, "Are there any questions?" I looked from one side of the room to the other. My glances were met with silence. I was about to move on to my closing activities when a young white man stood up slowly at the back of the room. He was very tall and physically imposing. My heart sank because I immediately thought, "Well, here it is. He is going to blast me." I was shocked by his words. He thanked me for the presentation and stated, "I knew your son Leslie, and he was just as you described him." I was practically mesmerized. He continued by sharing that Leslie was a wonderful person. He said that Leslie was very kind, was well liked, and had a lot of friends. He didn't know of anyone who had any negative interactions with Leslie. According to this recruit, he had gone to school with Leslie and was shocked and could not believe that this had happened to him. He gave such a positive tribute to Leslie's memory that I could not help but wonder, "How could God have known that I needed that?" My other thought was "Does this young man know how brave he is, to stand up before this audience and say such positive things about Leslie?"

I then identified some of the other materials I had brought and discussed the significance of each. These included the books *Driving While Black* by Kenneth Meeks;[2] *Both Sides of the Fence* by Bob Martin;[3] and a copy of Norm Stamper's book *Breaking Rank*.[4] Before retirement, Mr. Stamper had served as the police chief of San Diego, California, and Seattle, Washington. In his book, he was very open about his knowledge of accounts of police brutality. His writings confirmed my belief that unwarranted acts of police misconduct represent reality for countless victims.

I then passed out the scholarship information and discussed its value to the awardees to assist in completing a bachelor's degree in criminal justice. One recruit, who had displayed body language that seemed to indicate his lack of interest in anything I had to say, suddenly seemed somewhat attentive when I talked about the scholarship. Rather than just pick up the information from his place on the table, he slowly slid the paper closer and carefully turned it over to read. Other recruits had immediately begun to read the information after they received the handouts, whereas he had left his copy facedown, until I suppose his curiosity overwhelmed him.

The statement on the handout read as follows:

Leslie Vaughn Prater was born on December 24, 1966, in Chattanooga, Tennessee. He was the son of Dwight and Loretta Prater, and the brother of Stefan Prater. He was a graduate of Tyner High School, where he was selected as a Senior Superlative of his 1985 graduating class. He had a very charismatic personality and strong leadership qualities. During his teenage years, Leslie developed a strong interest in the arts, particularly painting and drawing. Leslie attended Tennessee State University and the Art Institute of Atlanta. While living in Atlanta, he held a position as an illustrator and post-production manager with Medical Legal Illustrations. Eventually, he returned to Chattanooga where he resided until his tragic and untimely death on January 2, 2004, at the age of thirty-seven. Although his glowing smile and personality are no longer here to brighten the days of those who knew and loved him, his love of life and passion for helping people will live on through this scholarship. It is the family's sincere hope that the recipients of this scholarship will embrace justice and embark on a successful professional career to ensure that justice is enjoyed by all.

At the end of our session, Dwight and I were packing up our materials while the recruits were leaving the room for another break. One

academy participant approached me. He stated his name, and I immediately recognized it, even before he continued by saying, "I am the first
recipient of the Leslie Vaughn Prater Memorial Scholarship." Without
any warning from either of us, we embraced and fought back tears. To
me, it almost seemed as though Leslie was in the room. We talked for
several minutes, mostly about his plans for the future and my congratu-
lating him on graduating. I told him how much I appreciated his letter
to thank us for the scholarship. In that correspondence, he had stated
that it had been a financial struggle for him to stay in school and that
the scholarship allowed him to continue enrollment toward completing
his degree. He was going to be the first one in his family to graduate
from college. I was surprised that he was pursuing employment in Chattanooga. In his letter, he had mentioned his plans to work in Nashville.
He also shared that he believed that law enforcement would be a good
fit for his strengths of thinking on his feet, interacting well with people,
and helping others with problem solving. After initially reading his letter, I had a yearning to meet him, but I had accepted the reality that it
was unlikely that we would ever meet. My meeting him was a miracle,
in my opinion.

I stopped in the hallway to talk to the young man who had given
the unsolicited testimony confirming my description of Leslie as a
wonderful person. I told him how much we appreciated what he said
and that I was sincerely moved by his kindness. I also conversed with
a police officer whom I had taught when he was in high school. I had
no idea that he would be at the training center that day. He was the
same officer I had seen at the Bessie Smith Strut, but we acted as
though we didn't know each other. Because of all of the local public-
ity surrounding our case, he had to know about the lawsuit conclusion
and why I was there.

It had been approximately twenty-five years since our last communication. We had mutual fond memories of our former student-teacher
relationship. We hugged and he starting talking to me about his life
since high school. He had married, and he proudly showed me a picture
of his toddler, who looked exactly like him. I talked about my career
since teaching family life education at Hixson High School. I can definitely say that although I entered the building with sadness and anxiety,
I left with joy and a smile. Divine intervention is powerful.

The second and third presentations to academy recruits in Chatta-nooga were generally duplicates of the first one. As with the first one, a police administrator contacted me to discuss the academy's schedule and to see what date would best fit my schedule. It was important for me to have adequate advance notice because Dwight and I had to request vacation days from work to travel to Chattanooga. I always tried to schedule a Monday morning presentation, so we could have the weekend to travel and only needed to use one vacation day. As a longtime educator, I was aware that every class was different, even if it was the same course, using the same textbook, audiovisuals, and class assignments, because the students bring their own dynamics. Unlike my secondary school or university classroom presentations, however, there was little difference between the first and successive classes at the acad-emy. Participant demographics were similar, and cadets were required to be there. We used the same instructional materials for each session. The training officers were always cooperative and cordial. Presentations were taped, with a copy of the video remaining with the department and one provided for us.

My discussion in the PowerPoint presentation did vary somewhat with each workshop. Because Dwight and I participated in ongoing activities, there was always something additional to say about police brutality. Nationwide, new cases of police misconduct occurred, and I would mention those situations that received media attention, to pro-vide current information. With each presentation, my confidence grew, and anxiety became almost nonexistent. It never became easy to read Stefan's poem or show Leslie gravesite, but I managed to maintain a professional presence.

The third workshop satisfied the lawsuit agreement, but I knew that sensitivity training was still needed at the academy. I attended a city council meeting to publicly request permission to continue this service. I was told that Chief Cooper would make the decision. Subsequently, I contacted him, and he told me I could continue to conduct the work-shops as long as I wanted. However, budget constraints prohibited the initiation of another academy for some months. Chief Cooper retired at the end of March 2011, before there was another training session scheduled. When the next class of cadets was formed, I contacted the new police chief and asked about scheduling the sensitivity training.

He reminded me that the department had satisfied the directive in the lawsuit agreement. I responded that I had offered my service indefinitely and the previous chief had accepted the offer, but, as previously mentioned, I was not allowed to do any presentations during his tenure or during the tenure of his successor. Throughout the years after Chief Cooper's retirement, Chattanooga residents kept asking, "Why did you stop giving the presentations?" My response was "They won't let me."

My motive was to save lives, theirs and others, and increase mutual respect and trust among police officers and citizens. For years, various chiefs of police in Chattanooga were always implying that a major goal was to increase trust between the community and the department. Accepting my offer would have contributed to an establishment of trust, especially among Chattanoogans who wanted me to continue the workshops. Department personnel were probably still angry that our family had settled a wrongful death lawsuit against them and decided to never allow me to address their recruits again. On May 8, 2017, an article in the *Chattanooga Times Free Press* reported on the need to create trust between the community and the Chattanooga Police Department. Apparently, the department continues to struggle with that issue.

In addition to the academy sessions previously described, the second sensitivity training in Cape Girardeau had another component. Connie, the mother of Derek Hale, and I were co-presenters. Derek's death confirms what I have been redundant in stating: "This can happen to anyone." Although research consistently reports that men of color are usually the victims of these incidences, white families are also impacted. Police brutality is not an issue only for black people but an issue of human rights for all people. I have stated that I am an angry black woman. Connie is an angry white woman. Collectively, we are angry mothers. I believe that Connie's presence in the academy presentation gave more validity to the claim that all people are vulnerable. Many black people believe that society doesn't care about the life of young black males. Her son, who had served his country, was confronted by a rogue police officer. Maybe this officer was trigger happy. Who knows why he chose to end Derek's life? In these tragic situations of unarmed people being killed by police officers, when there is no apparent danger to the officers, and even sometimes when the victims are running away from the police, I believe that the officers had a choice.

Connie and I were only two mothers among many who had to bury a child because of police brutality. I had spoken to several other mothers as well, and I felt a need to share with the recruits some comments from a few others. I will refer to them as Mother 1, Mother 2, and Mother 3.

Mother 1: *I resent that my life has been changed forever and that I didn't have anything to do with it. I fight bitterness every day and I don't like the person I have become.*

Mother 2: *My son was killed ten years ago. I went to trial and won, but the police appealed. My life is shattered. Every day, I drive by the place where he was killed. I am considering moving to another city.*

Mother 3: *My son was killed four years ago. I am still in the process of a lawsuit. His body may have to be exhumed. I cry every day and the family is torn apart.*

Often, speakers will leave an audience with a few takeaways. I followed that pattern and provided the recruits with three statements to ponder. I hope recruits will recall my three messages:

1. Take the job seriously, more seriously than any other job you have ever had.
2. You will have power over life and death.
3. Look inside of yourself and think about how you would have handled these issues presented to you today. Ask yourself if you have a racial bias that would impact your behavior.

Before completing this chapter, I wanted to share with you some of the results of the research question "Why did you want to become a police officer?" Five groups participated in the research. I didn't distinguish between responses from Chattanooga recruits versus those from Cape Girardeau. The identity of each person's response remained anonymous. This summary will give you a sense of the motivation expressed by cadets planning a career in law enforcement. From my review of ninety-four responses, I felt encouraged that there were many potentially effective law enforcement professionals among those recruits. Many of the statements were very similar, and common themes emerged. I must admit concern, however, when persons equate community policing with the same actions practiced during their former military life. Responses seemed clustered within the themes of helping people and the community, desiring to get criminals off the street, a connection to the family or former military life, or satisfying a lifelong dream. Collectively, the majority of the responses included the word "help." The feedback listed below is exactly as written, without any editing.

- *I want to be a police officer because I believe it is a noble profession that needs people who care about the community, the citizens and upholding the law.*
- *To help people, bring communities together and put criminals in jail.*
- *I am interested in people. Whenever I am in a position to help someone, I do! This is a position I do not feel will bore me in the future. I am willing to put my life on the line for others, so I feel there is no better way to do so other than be a police officer.*
- *I was in foster care for most of my life and have been around a lot of things. I currently work with teens in foster care and I also am a mentor to these teens. So I choose this field to help others mainly children from taking the wrong path.*
- *I chose law enforcement because I want to serve the community and do good works in my savior's name. Because of growing up in the slums of Chicago, I didn't think that I was "man of cloth" material because of some worldly attributes I have from the world.*
- *To help others; to be the "friendly" folksy type cop; help protect my family and others and drive a 500 up car.*
- *The community I live in doesn't have very good police officers that will do their job and do it right. So, I decided to become a police officer to help my community and do my part in protecting them from crime and criminals.*
- *I worked as a Deputy Sheriff in the early 90's. However, due to the low pay, I had to quit for a better paying job. Now that I have my family raised, I want to return to the law enforcement field because I have always felt a calling to law enforcement and have always wanted to help others in their time of need and crisis.*
- *It is the job that is most like what I did in the military.*

- *To help the small town to take control of the drug and alcohol. To protect people so they can feel safe in their own homes and make it a better place for my grandchildren to grow in.*
- *Get drug addicts and sellers and crooks off the streets.*
- *I want to be a police officer because I want to fight crime, corruption, vice and violence. I'm here to fight it and I want to enforce it.*
- *To help those in need. To help to protect the innocent and get those who believe they are above the law off the streets.*
- *To help and protect my family and community and to educate young people and tell them that they should not be afraid of the police.*
- *I chose a career in law enforcement because I'm a third generation cop and I enjoy helping others.*
- *The reason I became a police officer was my mom and uncle tried awhile ago to become one and did not make it. I guess I am fulfilling their dream. I like the image that it projects. It has always been a dream of mine.*
- *My father is a police officer. I've been around police officers my entire life. The nobility, discipline, and camaraderie enticed me into making this choice.*
- *Crime in my family has been a constant and I have seen the effects on, not only them, but millions of people worldwide. I would like to do my part to help minimize that environment.*
- *There have been some bad things happen in my family and this is the way I feel I can contribute to the solution, instead of the problem.*
- *To aide in keeping the community safe, for the sake of my children.*
- *I would like to be a police officer because of people who abuse women and children, especially those who sexually assault children. I was sexually assaulted when I was younger and I do not want anyone else to go through that.*
- *As a kid growing up it was something that I wanted to be. As I grew older, it called for me.*
- *Something I've always wanted; goes along with military background; protect the weak and innocent.*
- *I was raised in a military home. I always wanted to serve my country in the armed services, but due to a medical condition I cannot*

get into the military. So, this is the best way for me to serve my country.

- *I would like to be a police officer because I like to fellowship with people and try to keep people honest. It's not about beating up people or being mean to people. Maybe you could be at the right place at the right moment to change a person's life to keep them from doing something wrong. I want to try to help people and keep people safe.*

The placement of the last response is deliberate. When I read that one, I thought, "He or she really gets it." As a researcher, one is always thinking about how one research project causes one to ask other questions. I would love to have been able to conduct a longitudinal study with those persons. For those who completed the academy and became full-time police officers, I would love to know if their anticipations were realized. I wish I could ask each, "Now that you have been a police officer, based on why you selected law enforcement as a career, were your expectations realized, and if not, what was different?"

I am hopeful that other opportunities to research those questions will arise, as I plan to continue presenting sensitivity training. I have been invited to return to the regional academy in Cape Girardeau, and I have entered into discussions with Dr. Pernell Witherspoon, a criminal justice faculty member at Lindenwood University in St. Louis, and a former Ferguson police officer. We are planning to develop joint workshops focused on sensitivity training. Our combined resources of background, knowledge, and experience can be invaluable in helping police departments develop effective community relationships.

10

NO JUSTICE, NO PEACE

Paths in Seeking Change through Public Policy

Let me begin this chapter by sharing the chorus from "We Are the Survivors." This was performed at the opening ceremony of the Parents of Murdered Children's Conference on August 8, 2008, in Irvine, California. I did not attend, but this was sent to me by attendee Dr. Marcia Riley.

> *We are the survivors, left behind to carry on.*
> *We are the survivors, joined together we are strong.*
> *We will speak out for our loved ones who were not given a choice.*
> *We are the survivors, hear our voice.*

This chapter is dedicated to the many surviving victims of police brutality, those seeking a path to justice. Although I focus mostly on mothers, I recognize that persons with other relationships to victims are suffering too. We are on the seemingly endless journey of searching for peace, while conceding that justice has been denied. As persons thrust into a foreign existence, we are navigating a web of pain, seeking closure but wondering if closure really exists or is just a myth. With the completion of this book, will I be able to close the door and attain closure? I suppose that is one of my fears. I have suppressed so many emotions in order to have the energy and concentration to focus on writing. Maybe that is why it has taken me thirteen years to get to this point. If closure is not on the other side of the door, what else could be waiting?

What is the main purpose of this concluding chapter? In listening to a news report on May 15, 2017, a statement from former president Bill Clinton answered that question. His comment was related to anti-immigration policies. At the graduation ceremony at Hobart and William Smith Colleges, he challenged graduates to "expand the definition of 'us' and shrink the definition of 'them.'" Applying those words to the issue of police brutality, that is exactly my hope. If effective community policing is to become a reality, we must bridge the gap between "us" and "them." The "us" represents families grieving from the results of police brutality and others who see a need for change in policing. The "them" represents police department personnel, the judicial system, and citizens who feel that police can do no wrong. If those divisions were lessened, there could be two positive outcomes: we could come together as a collective force against injustice, wherever it may reside, and we would give police officers the respect that is earned, and for which they yearn.

These are complex matters, without quick fixes. The suggestions I pose have emerged from literature reviews, talking to others, and personal experience, with some backed up by research. These recommendations alone will not erase conflict. In a number of communities, interactions between police and citizens represent a complex and potentially volatile environment, creating a condition that developed over many years. It may be two more generations before society "figures it out." In the meantime, we need to work together to live peaceably. In one of my sensitivity trainings, a police cadet wrote, "Peace is not the absence of conflict, but rather the presence of justice."

Television shows and movies about murders usually focus on the murderers, with little attention to the families of the persons killed. These grieving families include a growing number of individuals who seek out one another for empathy and understanding.[1] They seek justice, rather than revenge. Throughout history, there are examples of families avenging a murder by killing someone from the family of the murderer. The result was a blood feud that could last for generations, as with the Hatfields and McCoys.[2] As societies became more prosperous and more settled, they gained a strong incentive to resolve such conflicts peaceably. Unfortunately, gang members continue to practice "an eye for an eye."

In America, the victims' rights movement largely began among feminists in the 1970s, with the opening of the first rape-crisis centers. Surprisingly, the strongest resistance to victims' rights came from within the criminal justice system. The feeling was that empowering the crime victim would place a limit on the power of the state. Most cases were disposed of behind closed doors, with attorneys, prosecutors, and judges deciding punishments by bargaining. Many criminal cases are still settled in that manner, but justice isn't served until crime victims are served.[3]

Grief after homicide does not follow a predictable course for families. The intense grief experienced by survivors can last a lifetime. Discussing the murder is like trying to put together the pieces of a puzzle to make sense of it all. As much as they try, the pieces just don't fit. These families, or secondary victims, continually experience trauma. They seek help through counseling, support groups, and spiritual avenues. To help with the grief process and to control anger, some seek a way to turn emotions into positive action, rather than resorting to revenge.

There are some common experiences among families in which a child dies at the hands of law enforcement. Often, the cards seem stacked in favor of the police and it is unclear where to turn for help. When a family member is killed by someone other than a police officer, the judicial system is the family's friend. At meetings of Parents of Murdered Children (POMC), many family members gave testimonials expressing appreciation for the help, consideration, and understanding of police officers. I witnessed this also at the 2016 annual Rainbow of Mothers Gala in St. Louis. Sitting at the table with me was a mother who echoed these same sentiments. Initially, I had thought that her child was killed by police officers because most of the "Rainbow Mothers" had that experience. She told me, however, that her son was killed by a neighbor, not a police officer. She quickly clarified her circumstances, saying, "The killer was sentenced to life in prison, but that fact still did not bring my son back or give me peace." I sensed her deep hurt. Although the circumstances that ended our sons' lives and the consequences for the killers were different, in the end, no grief can be judged more or less than that of another.

I mentioned earlier that Rev. Al Sharpton and Congresswoman Maxine Waters attended the Rainbow of Mothers Gala. I was heartened by their expressions to family members. Rev. Sharpton made a statement that has continued to resonate with me. To paraphrase, he said that to the general public, deaths from violence are headlines, but to the mothers, this is their life without their sons and daughters. I believe that all of the mothers probably suffer from a stress-induced condition known as "broken heart syndrome" that results from grief and extreme anger.[4] I also appreciated that Congresswoman Waters gave us encouragement that changes could be forthcoming within the criminal justice system, especially if persons elected to office in 2016 are supportive of criminal justice reform. Unfortunately, Jeff Sessions, the new US attorney general, has clearly stated his position. He wrote, "Local control and local accountability are necessary for effective local policing. It is not the responsibility of the federal government to manage non-federal law enforcement agencies."[5] For persons suffering from police misconduct, it appears that seeking assistance from the current federal Department of Justice leaders will be fruitless.

Victims' stress is compounded by revictimization from media sensationalism immediately after the loved one's death. The constant news reports are hard to bear. One of the most extreme examples of media excess is the Michael Brown/Ferguson case. I empathize with his family every time I see one of those reports, especially those that show his body lying in the street in a pool of blood. Immediately after hearing of a child's death, why would a reporter ask a mother in shock, "How do you feel?" Journalists, because of their vast public influence, must understand that they can do damage as well as good. They must weigh the need to inform the public against the need for those involved to be treated with compassion. Being a sensitive human being can clash with being a loyal employee. Here is an amazing example of that concept. A school in Pennsylvania initiated a new policy that if a child's parents had an outstanding lunch account of more than $25, the child would receive a cheese sandwich instead of a hot meal. This applied to children in kindergarten through sixth grade. Students in grades 7–12 would not receive a replacement lunch. The "lunch lady" refused to abide by the policy and gave a hot meal to a first grader who was only eligible for a cheese sandwich. The employee was admonished and forced to take away that meal, which had to be thrown away. After observing the sad look on the child's face and tears in his eyes, she terminated her employment. She refused to carry out such a mean-spirited practice.[6] When faced with choices in conflict with your inner peace, maybe the rule is to consider how you would like to be treated in a similar situation, more commonly referred to as the Golden Rule.

Social media comments can also be very hurtful, especially those that make negative assumptions about your child and family without any factual information. This secondary victimization is traumatic for survivors. Strangers using social media as a method to hurt survivors only add to the pain. In some instances, the social media aggressors maintain their privacy. Survivors don't have that advantage. In our experience, although some of the social media comments were supportive of us, I had to stop reading most of the entries. Even if only one out of ten was mean-spirited, I was hurt and angered by that one comment. My blood pressure would escalate, and it was difficult to sleep. Those people didn't even know Leslie or us but would write cruel statements, often sprinkled with name-calling, and portray their false statements as facts.

Reporters can be valuable in helping families to bring attention to injustice. I do understand the role of the press and that the Constitution allows for freedom of speech. We need freedom of the press, as well as balanced sensitivity to situations. I am thankful for the freedoms embedded within the First Amendment of the Constitution and pray that those freedoms are one day extended to everyone. It is also good to remember that shouting "fire" in a crowded theater in which there is no fire is not without legal consequences. The First Amendment doesn't protect false speech that is likely to cause immediate harm to others. Oliver Wendell Holmes wrote, "The question in every case is whether the words used are used in such circumstances and are of such a nature as to create a clear and present danger."[7]

Families have no control over the written word or the outcome of the grievance. Law enforcement and criminal justice systems control the right to information and to seek justice through punishment of the perpetrator. Loss of control is even more pronounced when the perpetrator is never punished or acknowledged as being at fault. In that case, where is the closure for survivors? The tragedy is compounded by the fact that many family members have no prior experience with the criminal justice system. They are unfamiliar, even with terms such as "plea-bargain," "continuance," and "deposition." Some situations require family members to incur travel expenses because they also have little or no control over the location of deliberations. Families trying to navigate through these tragedies tend to experience longer bereavement periods because we must delay our grief process while coping with the intrusions of the outside world. Actually, in addition to grieving for our loved one, we are grieving the loss of ourselves. We can never be the same people. We don't know how to respond when people say to us, "You should get on with your life." Where is the road map for that journey?

Families caught up in this judicial drama have common experiences. I have categorized it as a scripted play, with the police department administrators, their officers, and other law enforcement personnel as the stars. Victims' family members are the extras. Our assigned role has mostly been to stand to the side, remain silent, and observe as the stars perform. It has only been recently that more families are rejecting these roles. When these wrongful deaths occur, the parts are distributed to the performers to begin the play. Act 1 usually begins with the police chief putting the officers on paid administrative leave and convening a press conference to state that they will thoroughly investigate the incident to get the facts and that they will be transparent. In the meantime, they want the community to remain calm and allow them to pursue their investigation. I practically heard those exact words in our case and in regard to the shooting death of thirteen-year-old Tyre King in Columbus, Ohio. Similar to twelve-year-old Tamir Rice, Tyre was in the possession of a toy gun and was killed by a white officer.[8] Sometimes police officials will promise to keep the family and community informed, but that may or may not happen.

Act 2 is for the department to begin investigating the victim's past and rush to give the press any negative situations to stereotype the victim. They dig deeply for anything "bad." Prior to the final act, there is a strategy to extend the intermission as long as possible. They drag out the investigation and wear down the family. When they finally release the results of their internal investigation, the last scene in the play, the finding is that the officers were justified in killing the victim. The officers are returned to their positions. As usual, their life goes on, until the next citizen's wrongful death. In subsequent cases, the same officer or officers may be involved. With each situation, the officers use the common defense "I felt threatened." When that occurs, the play is repeated. It is as though it's all in a day's work. The families are left with memories, a gravesite, and an open wound of a perpetual sense of loss.

Recently, more families have publicly opposed police departments' typical findings. It angers the family when the tendency is to blame the victim and elevate the officers to sainthood. Departments repeat this process because it keeps working for them. Usually, the outcome favors the officers, so why would they want to do anything different? Even in the face of ridiculous excuses, such as "I feared for my life," when the deceased was clearly unarmed and posed no threat to anyone, police officers are successfully defended. Even with one unarmed victim in the presence of several armed police perpetrators, these excuses still seem to work. Even if the person is already handcuffed or is unarmed and running away from the police when killed, these excuses serve as a successful defense. Sometimes this grief journey feels like riding a roller coaster with no straps around us for protection.

I wrote many of my feelings in a journal in 2004. I thought using journal writing as an emotional release would help me to keep my sanity. Unfortunately, on most days, I felt too depressed to even write. I didn't want to review the day and relive the pain. To my amazement, some of the feelings expressed remained constant over the years. Here are a couple of examples:

May 16, 2004. *It's Sunday morning again. I can hardly stand it. Sunday mornings were the time the telephone usually rang and when I said hello, there was a cheerful, "Hello mother dear," from Leslie. Oh, how I miss his voice, those conversations, and his presence. There is so much anger and rage bottled up inside of me. How could those cruel and ignorant cops take his life? What gave them the right to do that, just because they were wearing a uniform? I can't believe that the Blue Wall protects police regardless of what they do. It is maddening. A lot of people still tell us that they are praying for us. I always say to continue, because we need it and are far from justice. The Lord is our only refuge. I keep praying for strength, because I know that we have a long battle ahead of us. I keep hoping that some of the people who are "with us" in private will come out of the house and publicly state their positions. I keep praying for that.*

December 5, 2004. Lord help me. Everyone keeps telling me to "hang in there," but I feel that daily I am slipping. It is hard to think of anything except getting justice for Leslie's murder. Today was one of my grief days. I was depressed and had little energy to do much of anything. It was beautiful outside, but I couldn't get motivated to do anything, except to go to the post office. I feel so helpless. My anxiety about Christmas and the anniversary of Leslie's death gets worse with each passing day. I wish I could skip Christmas.

In discussing a family's response to police killings, attention is mostly focused on adults. Children are also influenced by these deaths. You may have observed children marching with their parents during some of the televised community protests. The heartbreak was real for brave nine-year-old Zianna Oliphant, from Charlotte, North Carolina. Zianna appeared before the Charlotte City Council on September 26, 2016, a week after police fatally shot African American Keith Lamont Scott. She gave a tearful testimony on racism and policing. She pleaded with authorities to stop the police from killing our fathers and mothers. She talked about children having to visit the graves of their parents because of these homicides. Zianna said, "We are black people and we shouldn't have to feel like this. We shouldn't have to protest because y'all are treating us wrong."[9]

In addition to parents, many victims of wrongful deaths are survived by spouses, siblings, other relatives, and friends, who are also grieving. Leslie's aunt Louise often speaks of the special relationship she had with Leslie. In expressing her feelings, she wrote, "I really feel as though he is still with me, for I loved him very much. More than words can say, he is embedded deep within my heart." In an effort to keep the anger, frustration, outrage, and sadness from consuming him, Leslie's brother, Stefan, confronted his feelings through writing, which allowed some of his suppressed emotions to escape. Also, he starred in a full-length feature independent film, *Officer Down*, produced by Rick Bakewell and dedicated to Leslie's memory. Stefan was cast in the role of a police officer. Through the movie, he gained insight into a more positive side of policing.

I suppose I am doing the same thing by writing this book. From a counseling theory perspective, Stefan and I used a suggestion from Gestalt psychotherapy. This technique proposes that individuals must find their own ways to deal with unfinished business.[10] In some of Stefan's expressions, his words were primarily directed to those four police officers, although he never met them. I am amazed at how clearly Stefan also captured many of my own and Dwight's feelings. I believe that he also expressed the sentiments that numerous other siblings would like to say to police officers who killed their brother or sister. Here is some of what he wrote:

Why did you feel it was necessary to beat and brutalize an unarmed, naked man? From the very way that the four of you behaved that night and the days that have followed since, I have strong doubts that any of you have a conscience. Not one of you has stepped forward to offer so much as an apology. It takes a coldhearted individual to take an innocent life, and not give it a second thought. The only thing Leslie was guilty of that night was indecent exposure. It was your job to get him to the nearest hospital to be evaluated. That was the right thing to do, instead you chose to act as the judge, jury and the executioner. What gives you that right? That's why we have a judicial system in place. One of you should have stood up as a man to say, "Stop, this is unethical and is against procedure." I don't respect you as men or as police officers. No one deserves to be treated the way my brother was treated on that fateful evening. I'm sure the four of you could care less about what you did, and how it has affected me, my family and Leslie's friends who loved him so much. You don't realize that you are lucky. How many people can say they received a week's paid vacation for murdering someone? During that same week and for the final time, I had to say good-bye to my big brother, whom I idolized. It is a travesty that you were not prosecuted and sent to jail. You still have your jobs. Most importantly, you still have your lives, which is something you took away from my brother. Leslie will never have the opportunity to enjoy life again.

Whether it were your parents, siblings, children, or any other of your loved ones, imagine someone doing to them what you did to Leslie on January 2, 2004. Just imagine someone abusing their body and then holding them facedown and restricting their breathing. Try to picture them gasping for their last breath, with their bruised, battered, and naked body lying lifeless on the ground. Now, imagine that the perpetrators of this violent act were the same individuals hired to protect and serve the community. You should all be ashamed, especially the two older officers. You were supposed to set an example for the younger officers. You failed and failed miserably. What is the danger to you when confronting a nude, unarmed, helpless man in need of your help? The entire Chattanooga Police Department should be ashamed for trying to masque what really took place that evening. We need to rid police departments of rogue and vigilante officers.

It is my true feeling that, if our justice system started holding officers responsible for their crimes, this nonsense might come to a halt. Raising the standards and requirements to become an officer might help, such as requiring a college degree. Based on the actions of some officers, annual mental evaluations would be helpful in identifying persons who should not be on the force. I know some good police officers, as well as some US (United States) marshals, Federal Bureau of Investigation (FBI) agents, and federal judges who all work to uphold the law honestly and ethically. Through my employment, I have had the opportunity to know and inter-act with these individuals. From my conversations with them, they have all agreed that your behavior was inhumane and unnecessary. They said, "It's individuals like you who make their jobs much harder." I completely agree. We need more police officers who believe in protecting and serving everyone. You probably thought that Leslie was a "thug," but he was not. He was a lovely kindhearted person, who had lots of family and friends who loved him. You may not have known that on Jan. 2nd, but I imagine you know it now.

Do you think it is a coincidence that the city settled? They settled be-cause they knew we had a strong case. I care nothing about the money. I would give it all back to have my brother here again; or to hear him laugh the way he did the morning of Jan. 2nd. I was blessed to spend the last two weeks of his life with him. That's something that you can't take away from me. You robbed him of his life, but you can never take away the memories of the times we had together.

Every time I look at my mother's face or hear the tremble in her voice, I see all of the pain and damage that you have caused. We all love our mothers and are very protective of them. It angers me to a point I can't explain, when I see how sad your behavior has made her. On a daily basis, I'm forever haunted by Leslie's murder. Every time you close your eyes, you should see his face. When you're spending time with your family dur-ing the holiday, think about Leslie and the fact that you have damaged us beyond repair. Leslie will never have another Christmas, Christmas Eve birthday or any day, for that matter. It didn't have to be that way, if only you had done your jobs that night. My brother deserved the respect that you would want someone to bestow upon you. He did not deserve to be treated like an animal. He was a human being, who deserved to live to have his day in court. You had no right to end his life. He should not be lying in a coffin, buried in a cemetery. He should be enjoying life the way you are. Think about that the next time you are having a good time. You may not be going to a physical prison, but it is my hope that you will forever live in a mental prison.

Although my contacts have mostly been with mothers, fathers grieve also. At the Rainbow of Mothers event, there was one father who asked if he could be included in the recognition ceremony. Of course, he was welcomed and embraced. Dwight is one who loves deeply and grieves deeply, but without few outward verbal expressions. As a very private person, he hasn't openly discussed a lot of his emotions associated with Leslie's death, not even with me. I invited him to write about any feelings that he would like for me to include in this book. Dwight's thoughts are uniquely his and not the result of discussions with other fathers. This is what he wrote:

Losing a loved one is a trying experience. Losing a son is especially hard, since there are many goals that were put forward, that are now afterthoughts. These goals that were planned will never be attempted or reached. Stefan has lost his only sibling through the intentional actions of others, and I hurt for him. There is so much that I miss. I miss the relationship and the bonds of love; I miss the smiles and sometimes the frowns; I miss the visits and the gatherings; and I miss the possible achievements that could have been, similar to Kenney Chesney's song, "What you could have been." There is a realization that there will not be grandchildren from Leslie to carry on a legacy. There are holes in my life that can never be filled. People say things like, "You can have closure." I assure you, there is no closure to a death that was perpetrated through the evil intent of others.

When Leslie died, many people lost a good friend. On Saturday, December 6, 2006, at 9:29 a.m., I received an e-mail from David. The subject was Les. This is an excerpt of what he wrote:

I was sitting thinking at Christmas who had shaped my life and inevitably Leslie's name came to mind. You see, Leslie and I would wander in and out of each other's lives from seventh grade until he passed a couple of years ago. Since moving from Chattanooga many years ago, I had just recently found out of his passing, while looking for his number on the Internet. My prayers will continue to go out to your family.

Your son taught me lessons about racism at an early age. Later in life, I called him up and asked him if he thought I was a racist, solely because I had recently been called one by a black man. Not that I thought I was, but maybe I was sending out the wrong "vibe" and I did not want to be misunderstood. This started a very somber and seldom seen flow of conversation from Les. He wanted to make sure, first and foremost, that I knew I wasn't a racist. He summed it up to me in one phrase, "racism occurs when you no longer have the desire to understand tolerance." It is never about race, it is control.

I just had a rush of memories typing that last paragraph. We would go water skiing on Chickamauga Lake, taking turns dragging each other until our hands were the shape of the handles. I went to Atlanta to meet his co-workers when he was doing medical illustrations. I was both jealous and amazed by his artistic ability. I intended moving to Atlanta years later and only living a couple of blocks away from the Art Institute, and thinking of him daily. He introduced me to the works of Earl Klugh and other jazz musicians. He was the first black person to be a guest at my grandmother's home. My father loved your son, and I can still recall that peaceful feeling of looking over and seeing Les waving hysterically to me at my father's funeral 18 years ago. I just wanted you to know that with all the complexities in life that we all have to overcome; your son has influenced some of the greatest dialog and life lessons that continue to influence not only me, but generations of both friends and family.

Sometimes we feel that we are alone, but there are sparks of support. Thankfully, there are some people whose actions demonstrate the words of Edmund Burke. In 1770, he addressed the House of Commons and said, "The only thing necessary for the triumph of evil is for good men to do nothing. Injustice and oppression must not win." In the Letters to the Editor from the July 11, 2004, edition of the *Chattanooga Times Free Press*, a person wrote in reference to Leslie's homicide. The letter stated, "It's time for the murder of unarmed citizens to end in our community. And time to demand that our elected officials and the TBI [Tennessee Bureau of Investigation] stop being accessories, after the fact, by being involved in the cover-ups." A couple of weeks later, on the July 26, 2004, editorial page, another person stated that he was disgusted by the inhumane and brutal treatment of Leslie. In his concluding paragraph, he wrote, "Now, are we tax-paying residents of our great city and Hamilton County going to allow such conduct from the men on our police force?" Based on what we experienced, the answer was "Yes."

A couple from Alabama sent Dwight and me a note, postmarked June 30, 2004. We knew them but had not seen or talked to them in ten years. I want to stress that compassion, concern, and love should have no boundaries of race. This is a white couple who did not withhold their support because we were of a different race. I wish more Americans, on both sides of the spectrum, would follow their lead. Their words were comforting and seemed to be just what we needed to get through that day when the letter arrived.

I can't begin to imagine how horrible the last few months must have been for you. Your loss has weighed heavily on my heart. My husband and I are asking the Lord to continue to give your family strength and courage as you go through this ordeal that no parent should ever have to face. We are also praying for justice for your son and your family.

On August 31, 2004, I received an e-mail from a former police officer who had previously lived in Hamilton County and had worked for the Sheriff's Department. The subject of the communication was "I'm sorry for your grief." He wrote, "I'm very sorry for what you have endured with the lies and cover ups that the Chattanooga Police Department has been doing for many years, and still will until someone like you stands up for the rights of your son."

We have been fortunate that our support has come from so many sources. To our surprise, one of our neighbors wrote a song about Leslie. After a dinner party at their home, the song was performed for us and other guests. "A Song for Leslie Prater" is an original creation of lyrics and guitar music by Dr. Dale Haskell, first performed on October 22, 2015.

He was a gentle spirit, with a smile that lit up the room.
It never dawned on us he could be gone so soon.
He was somebody's brother. He was his parents' beloved son.
Leslie was somebody, and he died too young.
It should not have gone the way it did. The police were involved.
Leslie Vaughn Prater's passing wounded us all.

Leslie Prater's passing wounded us all.
Nine-one-one was called that night when Leslie needed help.
People paid to protect and serve got busy protecting themselves.
They took him into custody. In a heartbeat, a good man dies.
They violated Leslie's rights. Then, cover-up and lies.
It happened in Chattanooga, several years ago.
Being angry is not wrong. They say it's changin', but change is slow.
Stories like Leslie's keep comin' round, again and again.
Law enforcement uses force on dark-skinned men.

What happens when family members feel that there is little support? What happens when the support is short-lived? What happens when family members feel there is no treatment for the pain? With these sudden deaths, family members are overwhelmed, and the ability to use adaptive coping mechanisms is compromised. There is no schedule to the traumatic death experience. There is no specified length of time in which to adjust to life without the deceased. There was no time to prepare for the loss, so the total experience is overpowering. There was no chance to say good-bye and there was unfinished business. Also, traumatic death events often serve as reference points in time for the people who experience them. Depending on your age, most of you can remember where you were and what you were doing when you heard the news of the shooting of President John F. Kennedy, or the explosion of the space shuttle *Challenger*, or the September 11, 2001, downing of the Twin Towers in New York.

For survivors of victims from police brutality, there is a common experience of withdrawal of support. In addition to grief, survivors must deal with feelings of fear and vulnerability, anger, rage, shame, blame, and the denial that this could happen to someone they love. Questions about the death will be asked repeatedly in an effort to seek understanding and confirmation that this cannot be true. Also, the lack of familiarity and support by law enforcement, the criminal justice system, and media intrusion complicate bereavement. The delays in resolution of the murder, lack of adequate punishment for the crime, and lack of acknowledgment by society increases the feelings of loss of control.[11] I was fortunate in that I had some knowledge of the criminal justice system, although personal involvement in a wrongful death lawsuit was new to me.

The death can provoke posttraumatic stress disorder (PTSD), with repeated intrusion of traumatic memories, numbing of general responsiveness, and increased physiological arousal.[12] The Mayo Clinic's staff defines PTSD as a mental health condition triggered by a terrifying event, either experiencing it or witnessing it. Symptoms may include flashback, nightmares, and severe anxiety, as well as uncontrollable thoughts about the event. Many people have difficulty adjusting to traumatic events, but do cope. When symptoms get worse and interfere with functioning, that is a signal that you may have the disorder.[13] PTSD can develop in response to one or more traumatic events such as deliberate acts of interpersonal violence, severe accidents, disasters, or military actions. Devoting time and energy to civic work and trying to build bridges between police and the community through advocacy, writing, and training is my way of avoiding symptoms of PTSD. Families who buried loved ones because of police misconduct have been accused of only being interested in receiving money from a lawsuit. We did not choose sacrificing Leslie's life as a scheme to make money. I don't believe any of the other families did either. We must voice objections to violence through actions of police brutality.

Only recently, based on video footage, have some persons admitted that a police officer could provide an untruthful statement or participate in wrongdoing. Police officers are human, just like other people. There are police officers guilty of lying and committing crimes, just like other humans. Some of these wrongful actions are caught on camera. Subsequently, some of these taped interactions may be posted on the internet, even in real time. This happened in the case of thirty-two-year-old Philando Castile. His girlfriend was in the car with him when he was fatally shot by a police officer during a routine traffic stop in Minnesota. The interaction was live-streamed on Facebook.[14] Also, consider the timely video posted by Rakeyia Scott, the wife of victim Keith L. Scott, killed in Charlotte, North Carolina.[15] She recorded footage before and after the shooting.

In chapter 2, I addressed the question of whether police brutality was a myth or reality. Now, there are follow-up questions: "Is police brutality a social disease, adversely affecting a group of people?" "Should the Centers for Disease Control declare a health crisis in certain communities nationwide because of the disease of police brutality?" Actually, there is a social movement toward linking violence with health outcomes, although not specific to police brutality. If police brutality is a social disease, then treatment is needed. There was some good news related to treatment. The United States Department of Justice, under the leadership of former president Barack Obama and former attorney general Loretta Lynch, aggressively investigated several large urban police departments for systematic civil rights abuses, such as harassment of racial minorities, false arrests, and excessive use of force. The report of the Chicago Police Department found that there was a reasonable cause to believe that the department engaged in a pattern of using deadly force in violation of the Fourth Amendment of the Constitution.[16]

Ferguson, Missouri, is not a large community, but its police department was among those investigated. Because racial minorities tend to experience these abuses more than others, we cannot ignore Dr. Cornell West's admonition that race matters.[17] Of course, there are always people who believe that such a tragedy could never happen to them. Consider this anonymous statement a warning: "If it can happen to somebody, it can happen to anybody, and if it can happen to anybody, nobody is safe." I interpret this to mean that it could happen to you.

Some people feel protected within the comfort of complacency and believe that they could never become a victim of police brutality. They choose to remain silent. I confess that I was one of those persons, so I am not condemning anyone for their behavior. I didn't have the courage to speak out either, but I was blasted out of my comfort zone when Leslie was killed. Maybe I was like the Lion in the *Wizard of Oz*, because I received courage immediately.

These murders are just too horrible to think that any of us could be victims, or that it could happen to anyone we know. As often as these deaths are occurring, none of us can afford to ignore the reality that, yes, it could happen to you or someone you know, or, even worse, someone you love. Think about the warning of Pastor Martin Niemöller, a Protestant pastor and social activist. He spent seven years in a Nazi concentration camp. In a speech on January 6, 1946, he said,

> First they came for the Socialists, and I did not speak out because I was not a Socialist. Then they came for the Trade Unionists, and I did not speak out because I was not a Trade Unionist. Then they came for the

Jews, and I did not speak out because I was not a Jew. Then they came for me and there was no one left to speak for me.[18]

Some police officers and their supporters identify anyone who questions police misconduct as a police hater. This is untrue. For our family and others in our situation, we don't even hate the officers who killed our loved ones. I admit that I am still confused by their actions and am struggling with forgiveness. As I have stated before, I certainly don't believe that all officers are bad people. I do believe that a conciliatory approach is an effective method for resolving police-community conflicts. Good officers are those honest professionals who are sincere about protecting all people. They conduct themselves with the highest degree of integrity. Unfortunately, their good works are overshadowed by the abusive actions of a few others. We should not ignore the fact that these "others" do exist. Denial is not the answer. Continuing with that approach will cause our communities to crumble from within. Because our nation is composed of multiple communities, the collective impact is that our nation could crumble.

We've heard the expression, "A few bad apples will spoil the whole barrel." Why not get rid of them? What happens to the "bad apples" guilty of police misconduct? Some of them become "gypsy cops" and move from one department to another because of misconduct or poor performance.[19] Others remain in place and possibly move up through the ranks. As a society, we protect them, promote them, and eventually glorify them at their retirement reception.

There are two facts we must embrace. We need police officers, and communities need to feel safe. In America, we have persons with great minds who have succeeded in overcoming all kinds of challenges. We must get this problem solved. We have figured out how to get men on the moon, but can't determine how to live peaceably in our local communities. In seeking solutions, the first step is to admit that there is a problem.

The rejection of denial is the first step toward some semblance of healing and progress toward solutions, requiring years of sincere involvement on both sides. There is an "elephant in the room" that many refuse to even see. That elephant is racism. Yes, I just played the race card. As I said earlier, the race card is already in the deck and has been for hundreds of years, permeating every component of our society. Why would anyone think that policing would be immune? Employment, education, housing, entertainment, health disparities, personal income, and any other social entity you can envision have issues with racism. Denying that race is a factor can only make matters worse.

Effective leadership is crucial for police departments. I question the effectiveness of chiefs of police who resort to excuses and refuse to acknowledge problems of police misconduct. Consider a statement by a former Chattanooga chief of police. His statement was in response to the firing of two officers and suspension of another after disciplinary hearings found the men used excessive force in two instances. There were no deaths involved. In explaining the officers' misconduct, he attributed their actions as akin to having an adrenaline rush following a police pursuit. He said, "When emotions run high, poor decisions can be made. With repetitive training, we are trying to train them through this time, through those natural human tendencies."[20] I suppose those feelings are why he decided that Leslie's death was an accident and subsequently refused to hold those officers accountable. Killing because of a possible adrenaline rush is not justifiable.

The climate within a police department is influenced by the leader. Other factors are involved as well, such as the attitudes of individual officers, the legacy of the department, police union intervention, and the actions of the surrounding community. However, the leadership of the chief is key, and words do matter. On January 13, 2012, the *Chattanoogan.com* posted a quote from the Hamilton County sheriff. His statement was in reference to the problem with gangs. He said, "We need to run them out of town, put them in jail, or send them to the funeral home." In my opinion, his remarks were a green light for officers to "shoot to kill" any persons perceived as gang members and ask questions later. The public should recall that unfair profiling does occur. Recall the earlier description of black males in chapter 3 as the "symbolic assailant." Thus, innocent black men could be labeled as gang members. Fortunately, there are police administrators expressing statements that are helpful. An Ohio police chief went on Twitter to post a message in response to the killing of unarmed Terence Crutcher in Tulsa. On September 21, 2016, this chief wrote, "As an officer, I am so sick and drained of some cops doing things like this.

You are making us all look bad. STOP."[21] My response is "Hallelujah, he gets it."

As acknowledged previously, the work of a police officer is stressful and the compensation does not compare to the extreme personal risks that many face daily. Policing can be dangerous and challenging in many ways. Clearly, everyone who would like to wear the uniform and badge is not suited for this profession. Officers who cannot fulfill their responsibilities without submitting citizens to unnecessary violence should not be in these positions. If they refuse to protect everyone, regardless of their personal biases, then they should seek employment elsewhere. In making this assertion in a public presentation, I was approached by a local police chief who agreed with me.

My dream is for police departments to be 100 percent free of brutality, to uphold the Constitution, and to discontinue these acts of "street justice." A number of departments may be short staffed, but is it more important to fill slots, or have the right persons on staff? I would think that a smaller, effective department would be more desirable than a large ineffective one. I would also agree with the sentiments expressed by Earl Ofari Hutchinson. He stated, "Black cops are no antidote to police violence." Black officers have been involved in police brutality as well. One of Leslie's killers was a black officer. Hutchinson further stated, "A black cop killing an unarmed black under highly questionable circumstances is no longer an oddity. The irony is that black leaders have long clamored for more black cops. They believe they would be less likely to brutalize other blacks than racist white cops. This is pure fiction."[22]

Among certified police officers, there are more males than females. Reports are that women officers are substantially less likely than their male counterparts to be involved in problems of excessive force. If this is true, it would appear that one strategy of solving excessive-force situations is to employ more women and fewer males, but there is no quick fix. People are now questioning that premise after a female officer shot and killed unarmed Terence Crutcher. She was arrested and charged with manslaughter but acquitted by a jury.[23] On the other hand, male officers cost two and a half times more than female officers in payments of excessive-force liability lawsuits. Male officers are eight and a half times more likely to have excessive-force complaints sustained against them, and they have more citizen complaints. Men have more upper-body strength, but physical prowess is less related to job performance than communication skills, suggesting that males are not necessarily better officers, by whatever measure. Now the question is, why are women attracted to this profession in fewer numbers than men? Unfortunately, part of the reason is that in policing, women face discrimination, harassment, and intimidation, especially as they move up the ranks.[24]

When there is a breakdown between police and community relations, there is no easy remedy. The concept of community policing has been proposed as one strategy, but there is no universal "fix" that would apply to all communities. Actions that may work in one residential area could be disastrous in another. Some feel that community policing is merely putting more officers on the streets in the community to intimidate the residents, similar to military occupation. I have seen empty police vehicles strategically placed in neighborhoods to scare residents, but that doesn't work. Some misguided administrators identify community policing as merely establishing a satellite station in the middle of a high-crime area.

Community policing is multifaceted, but one must consider that each community is unique and the long-term strategic plans must be tailored to the needs of that community. From the review of literature and knowledge of some activities that have not worked, I propose some common themes in developing successful community policing strategies. No community policing initiative is going to be successful without mutual trust between residents and police officials. This takes time, especially if there is a long history of mistrust. Elected officials, community leaders, and police personnel must believe in the process, which requires training for all departmental employees. Established partnerships with grassroots organizations are essential, and activities should be focused on problem solving of specific concerns. Another important element in success is to establish a citizen review board that is independent of police control.

Police can improve public opinion by increasing informal contacts with citizens. This should be institutionalized as part of their ongoing policing activities. Participating in community activities is one helpful suggestion. In Cape Girardeau, the chief of police, Wes Blair, is a board member with the Chamber of Commerce. Many departments already do some of this through their Christmas "Shop with a Cop" program for children. Some departments assist in collections for local food pantries. Another example is a department that sponsors "Coffee with a Cop" informal meetings in different neighborhoods. This structure facilitates informal dialogue between police officials and residents. I have already mentioned the Drug Abuse Resistance Education (DARE) program as an excellent public relations strategy, even if it doesn't prevent all youth from experimenting with drugs. There are programs in which police officers take children shopping for clothing at the beginning of the school year. Those programs were funded from department fundraising or personal donations from officers. There are numerous examples of humanitarian efforts by police officers, and no one should assume that all officers are bad. In some communities, there have been other positive programs involving officers. Some officers participate in youth sporting programs. There was a joint effort in Chattanooga between police departments and real estate developers to encourage police officers to purchase housing in targeted urban communities with an attractive financial incentive. These are just a few other ideas focused on increasing positive interactions between the police and community. We need more of these innovative ideas as part of twenty-first-century policing. More police chiefs and their officers should follow the recommendation of Terrence Cunningham, the president of the International Association of Chiefs of Police (IACP). In addressing the issue of building trust between police and minorities at the 2016 annual meeting, he said, "The first step is for law enforcement to acknowledge and apologize for the actions of the past and the role that our profession has played in society's historical mistreatment of communities of color."[25]

In matters of sudden loss of life, research has shown that communities need to be proactive.[26] The circumstances are not exclusive to deaths caused by police, but the recommendations can apply. Departments can develop effective ways to intervene in these situations, and should already have policies and procedures in place. I am referring to fair, effective policies based on integrity and honesty. A policy in which police officers are instructed to immediately get together without any supervision or recording, create their collective reality to explain their killing of an unarmed citizen, and report that creative writing exercise on one "use-of-force" report is an outrageous policy. What is more outrageous is when the outcome of their cover-up process is accepted as factual. That is what happened in our case.

Here is one idea in reference to police interactions with mentally ill citizens: After many tragic endings to police confrontations with the mentally ill in Memphis, the police decided to handle certain calls with more compassion and education. Doctors, social workers, the police department, and two universities collaborated to create the Memphis Model, including a Crisis Intervention Team (CIT).[27] The Memphis Crisis Intervention Team (CIT) is an innovative police first responder program that has become nationally known as a pre-arrest jail diversion for those in a mental illness crisis. The program provides law enforcement–based crisis intervention training for helping individuals with mental illness. Research has shown CIT to be effective in developing positive perceptions and increased confidence among police officers, providing very efficient crisis response times, increasing jail diversion among those with mental illness, improving the likelihood of treatment continuity with community-based providers, and decreasing police injury rates.[28] I would surmise that death rates from police officers killing unarmed mentally ill citizens have probably decreased as well. This model could also work for unarmed persons who are acting strangely when approached by the police. The model has been approved by the National Alliance on Mental Illness as best practice since 1996. My concern about the program is that it is voluntary instead of mandatory for all police officers to complete the CIT training. There is still other work to be done in Memphis. The Department of Justice (DOJ) was invited by the mayor and police director to initiate a partnership between Memphis and the DOJ's Community Oriented Policing Services (COPS) program to complete a comprehensive review of the police department.[29]

If a city has a single focus of ending gang violence, rather than including gang violence within a comprehensive plan for effective policing, that could be problematic. Concerns about gang members victimizing citizens are legitimate. When groups of police officers assault and kill unarmed citizens who are not harming them or others, what is the distinction between that group of police officers and other people identified as gang members? There are people who fear walking in their own neighborhood because of the actions of gang members. But there are also people afraid of doing the same because of the actions of the police. In another opinion piece posted on *Chattanoogan.com* on April 18, 2005, a father wrote, "As the parents of biracial young men (part African-American), my family and I decided to leave Chattanooga, because of the police abuses my sons have often encountered. At times, it appeared they needed a pass or something to freely move around, as the slaves must have had to endure during slavery. It wasn't even safe to walk around in one's own neighborhood after dark."[30]

Education and training are key components in seeking a decrease in police brutality. I want to be very clear that decreasing police brutality saves lives of both residents and police officers. This is a point that needs repeating. Also, decreasing police brutality increases the likelihood that residents will partner with police officers in solving crimes. I saw an interesting televised report to illustrate this point. An officer was trying to apprehend a person who had just committed a crime and was running away from the scene. Fortunately, the officer did not choose to execute the man by shooting him in the back, as abusive officers might have done. Two men witnessing the physical altercation were initially busy recording the incident because they thought it was another case of police brutality. It was only after the officer pleaded, "Help me," that the two men realized that they were mistaken and rushed to the aid of the officer. With the help of those two African American bystanders, the suspect was apprehended, without any injuries to anyone. This shows the depth of mistrust of officers. The question to ponder is "Why was it an automatic assumption that the police officer was being abusive?" Just think about that.

Different types of training are needed in preparing police officers. Unlike many other professions, these professionals might face life-and-death situations at any moment. At the end of the day, they should return home to their families. Families of those whom police encounter would also like their loved ones to come home. Inadequate training is happening in some departments, both in the absence of topics covered and in the amount of time devoted to certain topics. Also, the training should be updated. Training must be progressive and consider the changing demographics. Social scientists and grassroots residents could assist departments with that training.

Training needs to go beyond how to shoot a gun, write a ticket, and use handcuffs. Training modules should also include the proper use of

"pepper spray" or a Taser, if the department continues to use those potentially lethal devices. Pepper spray is an inflammatory agent derived
from cayenne peppers that inflames the mucous membranes causing
the eyes to sting. The spray can temporarily paralyze the larynx, causing gagging and choking. Research reported by Amnesty International
suggests that pepper spray may be particularly harmful in the case of
people who are agitated and under the influence of drugs or to people
with respiratory problems caused by asthma or heart disease. Critical
thinking and common sense are also crucial assets. Activities designed
to screen candidates in those attributes can address some of this, but
not all. Either you have these skills or you don't, because no screening
scenarios can anticipate everything that could possibly occur in the field.

Diversity and sensitivity training, grouped with instruction regarding
community relations, proper police conduct, racial profiling, and effective conflict resolution are definitely aids to a comprehensive training
experience. You can't train a person to be compassionate, but I do believe that intervention may increase sensitivity to certain situations. For
example, people with physical or mental disabilities may not be able to
obey every command that an officer issues. It should not be justified to
kill an unarmed person because of not following the command of "put
up your hands." Timothy, my late cousin, was a victim of polio as a child.
He recovered and lived to be an adult, but the condition left him unable to raise his hands above his waist. He never encountered aggressive
police. He might have been killed merely because he would not have
been able to raise his hands above his head. In addition, the training is
too rigid in some instances, without any allowances for reasonable exceptions. Even in a situation of imminent danger, officers who decide to
shoot don't have to shoot to kill. In reference to interacting with citizens
without killing them, and all things being equal, police officers should
use the same strategies with black people that they use with most white
people. It is interesting that even when officers know that white people
are armed, many still survive police contact, as opposed to blacks, especially black men. So, the difference in outcomes is more than just
elevated training.

For reasons that some understand, and others do not, I chose to
conduct sensitivity training for police departments. Officers need to
understand the real consequences of their actions when a homicide

could have been avoided. I represent the face and voice of so many mothers, and I structured my training sessions in such a way that I could be of most value, based on my professional and personal experiences. Although I feel that the cadets benefited from my presentations, I realize that not all police chiefs would welcome me, merely because of our family's wrongful death lawsuit. Still, I am not deterred by that attitude and plan to continue offering the training in places where I am welcomed and as often as my resources of time, energy, and availability of travel will allow.

Dr. Lorie Fridell, from the University of South Florida, is another academic working in this field. She developed a training program that is getting attention. It is a training program for police departments seeking to address their officers' implicit biases and unconscious sources of prejudiced behavior. After police-involved killings of black males in Ferguson, Missouri, and elsewhere, and the ongoing impact of the Black Lives Matter movement, the call for improved, less biased policing in the United States continues to be heard. A Gallup poll released in 2015 found that Americans' trust in the police is at a twenty-two-year low and communities of color remain particularly leery.[31] I called Dr. Fridell and congratulated her on this innovative training, which has been successful in cities around the country.

Aggressive officers may not perform according to their training even after becoming certified. Here is one example: Officers in Chattanooga were terminated because of misconduct in the beating of a resident, which was caught on a video recording. They appealed to get reinstated. When their hearing was scheduled, I traveled to Chattanooga to attend the hearing sessions. One of the officers, who didn't deny his abusive actions, said, "What I did was no different than what other officers do, and they weren't fired." It was so sad that he didn't recognize or acknowledge wrongdoing—but he was telling the truth. How he treated that citizen was confirmation of the reputation of that police department. The victim of his abuse was still living, while other officers had killed Leslie and other citizens and were not terminated.

Can police officers resist the temptation to abuse the rights and privileges of their position? Does the departmental culture encourage its employees to resist or tolerate certain types of misconduct? The police supervisors' style can have an impact on the patrol officer. In addition to classroom training, the quality of field supervision is important. That experience significantly influences the patrol officer's behavior. An active style of leading by example seems to be most influential. Patrol officers were twice as likely to use force if that negative behavior was modeled by the supervisor. Consider the actions demonstrated in the movie *Training Day*.[32] Other policing leadership styles are traditional, innovative, and supportive.[33]

In addition to providing the best training for new officers, there are other suggestions for curbing brutality. Stronger in-service training and recognizing educational achievements of officers can have positive influences on their behavior. Early intervention with counseling or more training is recommended to address performance problems. In a study to investigate early warning (EW) systems, intervention resulted in reductions in citizen complaints and involvement in use-of-force incidents. EW is only one effective management tool. The enforcement of disciplinary standards and a climate of accountability are additional effective strategies.[34]

There needs to be accountability and oversight. Amnesty International suggests that this should include prosecutions, discipline, monitoring and tracking officers involved in repeated complaints, external oversight, and national data collection on police use of force. Unfortunately, there is yet to be a national tracking program. *The Brown Watch: News for People of Color* keeps track of many of these police abusive situations.[35] Local, state, and federal authorities should ensure that excessive force will not be tolerated, that officers will be held accountable for their actions, and that those responsible for abuses will be brought to justice. Police departments should be required to keep detailed records on use of force, in-custody deaths and injuries, number and type of complaints filed, and their disposition and outcome.

The fight for justice is ongoing. Yes, it is a fight, but not one that will be won with guns, other instruments of violence, or physical confrontations. After nearly fourteen years of being without Leslie's physical presence, and participating in numerous activities opposing police brutality, I remain constant in seeking solutions to end this horrible epidemic of police misconduct. Carefully screening applicants to employ the right people is a positive strategy toward solutions. Fighting violence with more violence is not the answer. These incidences of some people killing police officers must stop. Those murders are just as horrible as those of police officers killing citizens for no reason. I believe there are nonviolent measures that can address both situations.

Dr. Martin Luther King Jr. wrote a letter from the Birmingham, Alabama jail on April 16, 1963. The letter is valid today and reads as follows:

Injustice anywhere is a threat to justice everywhere. Perhaps it is easy for those who have never felt the stinging darts of segregation to say, "Wait," but when you have seen vicious mobs lynch your mothers and fathers at will and drown your sisters and brothers at a whim; when you have seen hate-filled policemen curse, kick and even kill your Black brothers and sisters; when you see the vast majority of your twenty million Negro brothers smothering in an airtight cage of poverty in the midst of an affluent society, then you will understand why we find it difficult to wait.[36]

Dr. King further stated in his letter that the ultimate measure of a man is not where he stands in moments of comfort and convenience but where he stands at times of challenge and controversy. The situation in which we are faced is that unarmed citizens continue to be murdered by law enforcement officers. As long as people are unwilling to face the challenge of the obvious controversy that emerges when one speaks out against police brutality, nothing will change. No, it will never be over as long as we, as a society, continue to accept this injustice and abuse and there is no accountability for those crimes.

Over the years, people have kept inquiring, "When will the book be completed?" At first, I would respond with a self-imposed deadline date, which I never reached. Finally, I just said, "When I have said all that I want to say." Considering the book's title, it seemed as though I would never finish, because these tragedies continued to occur. When something else would happen, I wanted to include that victim's story in the book. Sadly, unless things change, there will be more of these unjust homicides.

In closing, I am sharing a poem that Stefan wrote for inclusion on Leslie's funeral program. He speaks for all who love Leslie. We feel so blessed that he wrote this memorial tribute to his brother. The poem's title is inscribed on Leslie's gravestone, and it is always read at his memorial services and sensitivity workshops I conduct. Like so many families, we are continuing to seek peace.

There Will Never Be Another You

Memories of you are all I have to get me through the day
Emptiness fills my soul now that you have gone away
I'm searching for any piece of you that I can hold on to
One thing is for certain my brother, there will never be another you.
As your little brother, I always let you lead the way
Throughout my life, you held my hand
Making sure that I never went astray
Who'll be my guiding soldier, now that you're not here to look up to
There's no one else my brother, because there will never be another you.
Certain people are out to portray you as a man who was filled with hate
But as your little brother, it's up to me to set the record straight
Anyone who knew you, knew that you were a man full of life and filled
with love, my brother, it's the real you, we'll be thinking of
You touched the lives of your family and friends for 37 years
We're all trying to be strong, even as we're fighting back the tears
There will never be another like you, my brother
For your life played like a melody reminiscent of a jazz tune
It was just over a week ago, you and I were able to be together
We had so much fun and laughter, I wanted those moments to last forever
Your smile brightened the day of all your friends and all your family
There's no other, like you my brother Les,
I love you and you will forever live inside of me
We love you and miss you.

—Stefan D. Prater

NOTES

PROLOGUE

1. Nancy Friday, *My Mother/Myself: The Daughter's Search for Identity* (New York: Random House, 1977).

2. Keith Brown, *Sacred Bond: Black Men and Their Mothers* (Boston: Little, Brown, 1998).

3. Clifton L. Taulbert, *When We Were Colored* (New York: Penguin Books, 1989).

INTRODUCTION

1. Margaret D. Hughes, "You're My Guest in Thought," http://www.heaven sent2002.com/Friends.html.

2. "Shooting of Oscar Grant," *Wikipedia*, http://en.wikipedia.org/wiki/ Bart_Police_Shooting_of Oscar_Grant.

3. Elizabeth Kübler-Ross, *On Death and Dying* (New York: Macmillan, 1969).

4. "Man Charged in Shooting of Two Dogs," *Chattanooga Times Free Press*, December 15, 2009.

5. Kadiatou Diallo with Craig Wolff, *My Heart Will Cross This Ocean* (New York: Ballantine, 2003).

6. Lezley McSpadden with Lyah Beth LeFlore, *Tell the Truth and Shame the Devil: The Life, Legacy, and Love of My Son Michael Brown* (New York: Simon & Schuster, 2016).

7. "Triangulation (social science)," *Wikipedia*, https://en.wikipedia.org/wiki/Triangulation_(social_science).

8. Norman K. Dezin, *The Research Act in Sociology* (Chicago: Aldine, 1970).

9. Kathleen M. DeWalt and Billie R. DeWalt, *Participant Observation: A Guide for Fieldworkers* (Walnut Creek, CA: AltaMira Press, 2002).

CHAPTER I

1. Centers for Disease Control and Prevention, "Heart Disease Facts," www.cdc.gov.heartdisease.facts.htm.

2. Centers for Disease Control and Prevention, "Women and Heart Disease Fact Sheet," https://www.cdc.gov/dhdsp/data_statistics/fact_sheets/fs_women_heart.htm.

3. Annie Kelly, "Traffic Accidents Are the 'Biggest Killer of Young People Worldwide' Report Says," *Guardian*, May 2, 2012, https://www.theguardian.com/global-development/2012/may/02/traffic-accidents-biggest-killer-young-people.

4. Scott Travis, "Homicide Leading Cause of Death of Young Black Men, Says FAU Research," *Sun Sentinel*, April 10, 2013, http://www.huffingtonpost.com/2013/04/10/leading-cause-of-death-young-black-men-homicide_n_3049209.html.

5. Ben Brumfield, "Massive Florida Sinkhole That Swallowed a Man Reopens," August 20, 2015, CNN, http://www.cnn.com/2015/08/20/us/florida-sinkhole-seffner/index.html.

6. "The 43 Victims of Oso's Landslide," *Seattle Times*, March 21, 2015, http://www.seattletimes.com/seattle-news/the-43-victims-of-osos-landslide/.

7. "Sandy Hook Elementary School Shooting," *Wikipedia*, https://en.wikipedia.org/wiki/Sandy_Hook_Elementary_School_shooting.

8. "Overland Park Jewish Community Center Shooting," *Wikipedia*, https://en.wikipedia.org/wiki/Overland_Park_Jewish_Community_Center_shooting.

9. Alan Wolfelt, "The Mourner's Bill of Rights," *Griefwords*, http://griefwords.com/index.cgi?action=page&page=articles%2Fmourners.html&site_id=7.

10. Rick Wilking, "Missouri Legislature Upholds 'Stand Your Ground,' Concealed Carry Law Requiring No Permits," September 16, 2016, *RT News*, https://www.rt.com/usa/359604-missouri-stand-ground-guns.

11. "Stand-Your-Ground Law," *Wikipedia*, https://en.wikipedia.org/wiki/ Stand-your-ground_law.

12. Greg Botelho and Holly Yan, "George Zimmerman Found Not Guilty of Murder in Trayvon Martin's Death," July 14, 2013, CNN, http://www.cnn .com/2013/07/13/justice/zimmerman-trial/index.html.

13. Tonyaa Weathersbee, "The Extermination of Jordan Davis: An Empty Verdict, a Hollow Victory," February 16, 2014, http://www.cnn.com/2014/02/16/ opinion/weathersbee-dunn-davis-verdict/index.html.

14. Eliott McLaughlin and John Couwels, "Michael Dunn Found Guilty Of 1st Degree Murder in Loud Music Trial," October 1, 2014, http://www.cnn. com/2014/10/01/justice/michael-dunn-loud-music-verdict/index.html.

15. Katheryn K. Russell, "What Did I Do to Be So Black and Blue? Police Violence and the Black Community," in *Police Brutality: An Anthology*, ed. Jill Nelson (New York: W. W. Norton, 2000), 135–48.

16. Robin D. G. Kelly, "'Slangin' Rocks . . . Palestinian Style': Dispatches from the Occupied Zones of North America," in Nelson, *Police Brutality*, 21–59.

17. C. K. Ferreri, "It's 2016 and Lynchings Are Still Happening," *Odyssey*, December 12, 2016, https://www.theodysseyonline.com/2016-lynchings-still-happening.

18. Michael Muskal, "Black Man Found Hanging in Mississippi: Why This Story Haunts the Nation," *Los Angeles Times*, June 1, 2017, http://www.latimes .com/nation/la-na-mississippi-history-20150320-story.html.

19. Donald Ayotte, "In Delaware, They Lynch Negros," *RedState*, July 1, 2013, http://www.redstate.com/diary/delawarewindjammer/2013/07/01/in -delaware-they-lynch-negros/.

20. "Murder of James Byrd Jr.," *Wikipedia*, https://en.wikipedia.org/wiki/ Murder_of_James_Byrd_Jr.

21. Dr. F. K. King, MD, "Autopsy Report of Leslie Prater," March 24, 2004, Office of Hamilton County Medical Examiner, Chattanooga, Tennessee.

22. "Homicide," *The Free Dictionary*, http://legal-dictionary.thefreediction-ary.com/homicide.

23. Candice Combs, "Autopsy Reveals Struggle," *Chattanooga Times Free Press*, March 27, 2004.

24. Office of the Medical Examiner, Dr. Bruce Levy, Forensic Medical Case MEC04-0088, January 26, 2004.

25. *Webster's Ninth New Collegiate Dictionary*, s.v. "abrasion," "contusion," "laceration" (Springfield, MA: Merriam-Webster, 1990).

26. Dahlia Lithwick, "Dying of Excitement," *Slate*, June 11, 2015, http:// www.slate.com/articles/news_and_politics/jurisprudence/2015/06/excited_ delirium_deaths_in_police_custody_diagnosis_or_cover_up.html.

27. David Kleinman, "Excited Delirium," *EMSWorld*, March 1, 2009, http://www.emsworld.com/article/10320570/excited-delirium.

28. "Leslie Vaughn Prater Death Ruled Homicide," *Chattanoogan*, March 26, 2004, http://www.chattanoogan.com/2004/3/26/48548/Leslie-Vaughn-Prater-Death-Ruled-Homicide.aspx.

29. "Shooting of Michael Brown," *Wikipedia*, https://en.wikipedia.org/wiki/Shooting_of_Michael_Brown; "Death of Eric Garner," *Wikipedia*, http://en.wikipedia.org/wiki/Death_of_Eric_Garner.

30. "*Selma* (film)," *Wikipedia*, http://en.wikipedia.org/wiki/Selma_(film).

31. Candice Combs, "Autopsy Reveals Struggle," *Chattanooga Times Free Press*, Saturday, March 27, 2004, A6.

32. "Henderson Family Files Suit over Fatal Traffic Stop Shooting," *Chattanoogan*, April 28, 2004, http://www.chattanoogan.com/2004/4/28/51173/Henderson-Family-Files.

33. "Abner Louima," *Wikipedia*, https://en.wikipedia.org/wiki/Abner_Louima.

34. Jason Rydberg and William Terrill, "The Effect of Higher Education on Police Behavior," *Police Quarterly* 13 (2010): 92–120.

35. "Shooting of Michael Brown."

36. Katie Moisse, "1 in 68 Kids Has Autism, CDC Says," ABC News, March 27, 2014, http://abcnews.go.com/blogs/health/2014/03/27/1-in-68-kids-has-autism-cdc-says/.

37. To see an example of the arm bar technique, review the YouTube video at www.youtube.com/watch?v=w_Zub3HsCLw.

CHAPTER 2

1. Ashley Frantz and Holly Yan, "South Carolina Shooting: Officer Charged and Fired; Protesters Demand Justice," April 9, 2015, http://www.cnn.com/2015/04/08/us/south-carolina-officer-charged-with-murder/index.html.

2. Holly Yan, Khushbu Shan, and Emanuella Grinberg, "Ex-Officer Michael Slager Pleads Guilty in Shooting Death of Walter Scott," May 2, 2017, http://www.cnn.com/2017/05/02/us/michael-slager-federal-plea/index.html.

3. "Police Brutality Law and Legal Definition," *USLegal*, http://definitions.uslegal.com/p/police-brutality/.

4. "Increasing Police Brutality: Americans Killed by Cops Now Outnumber Americans Killed in Iraq," *Global Research*, http://www.globalresearch.ca/increasing-police-brutality-americans-killed-by-cops-now-outnumber-americans-killed-in-iraq-war/5361554.

5. Kevin Johnson, "Police Brutality Cases since 9/11," *USA Today*, December 18, 2007.

6. Nat Parry, "Is Police Brutality Color-Blind?" *Consortium News*, August 22, 2014, http://consortiumnews.com/2014/08/22/is-police-brutality-color-blind.

7. Amnesty International, *USA: Race, Rights, and Police Brutality*, August 31, 1999, Index Number AMR 51/147/1999, https://www.amnesty.org/en/docu ments/AMR51/147/1999/en/.

8. David Freed, "Police Brutality Claims Are Rarely Prosecuted," *Los Angeles Times*, July 7, 1991.

9. Seth Morris, "23 Years after Rodney King, Victims of Police Violence Get Even Less Justice," *Vanity Fair*, February 2015, http://www.vanityfair. com/news/2015/02/rodney-king-23-years-even-less-justice.

10. "Chief Dodd Says Attack on Prisoner by Officers Sean Emmer, Adam Cooley 'One Of The Worst I've Ever Seen,'" *Chattanoogan*, June 26, 2013, http://www.chattanoogan.com/2013/6/26/254032/Chief-Dodd-Says-Attack.

11. Joy Lukachick Smith, "Chattanooga Reaches $88,000 Settlement with 2 Fired Police Officers," *Chattanooga Times Free Press*, January 15, 2014, http:// www.timesfreepress.com/news/2014/jan/15/city-settles-with-fired-cops.

12. Shelly Bradbury, "Police Chief Says Fired Cops Shouldn't Work as Officers Again," *Chattanooga Times Free Press*, April 26, 2015.

13. Allison T. Chappell and Alex. R. Piquero, "Applying Social Learning Theory to Police Misconduct," *Deviant Behavior* 25 (2004): 89–108.

14. "City Police Officer Fired after Disciplinary Hearing," *Chattanoogan*, October 26, 2005, http://www.chattanoogan.com/2005/10/26/74827/City-Police -Officer-Fired-After.aspx.

15. Robert Anglen and Dan Horn, "Police Review Themselves When Citizens Complain: Officers Exonerated on 90% Of Minor Issues," *Cincinnati Enquirer*, July 8, 2001.

16. "Trio Pleads to Reckless Homicide in Death of Man at Flea Market," *Chattanoogan*, September 12, 2006, http://www.chattanoogan.com/2006/ 9/12/92600/Trio-Pleads-To-Reckless-Homicide-In.aspx.

17. Katheryn K. Russell, "What Did I Do to Be So Black and Blue? Police Violence and the Black Community," in *Police Brutality: An Anthology*, ed. Jill Nelson (New York: W. W. Norton, 2000), 135–48.

18. Carolyn. M. McKinstry, *While the World Watched* (Carol Stream, IL: Tyndale House Publishers, 2011).

19. Wil Haygood, *The Butler: A Witness to History* (New York: Atria Books, 2013).

20. "Medgar Evers," *History*, http://www.history.com/topics/black-history/ medgar-evers.

21. Robin D. G. Kelley, "'Slanging Rocks . . . Palestinian Style': Dispatches from the Occupied Zones of North America," in *Police Brutality: An Anthology*, ed. Jill Nelson (New York: W. W. Norton, 2000), 21–59.

22. Russell, "What Did I Do."

23. Budimir Babovic, "Police Brutality or Police Torture," *Policing: An International Journal of Police Strategies and Management* 23, no. 3 (2000): 374–80.

24. ACLU, *Fighting Police Abuse: A Community Action Manual*, https://www.aclu.org/other/fighting-police-abuse-community-action-manual.

25. Simon McCormack, "What's Happening in Baltimore Didn't Just Start with Freddie Gray," *Huffington Post*, April 29, 2015, http://www.huffington-post.com/2015/04/28/freddie-gray-baltimore-history_n_7161962.html.

26. John McWhorter, "Police Kill Too Many People—White and Black," *Time*, July 14, 2016, http://time.com/4404987/police-violence/.

27. Valerie Richardson, "White Teen Killed by Black Cop in Gilbert Mirrors Ferguson," *Washington Times*, November 27, 2014, http://.washingtontimes.com/news/2014/Nov/27/white-teen-gilbert.

28. David Rudovsky and Lawrence Rosenthal, "The Constitutionality of Stop-and-Frisk in New York City," *University of Pennsylvania Law Review* 162 (2013): online 117.

29. Ibid.

30. David Jacobs and Robert M. O'Brien, "The Determinants of Deadly Force: A Structural Analysis of Police Violence," *American Journal of Sociology* 103, no. 4 (1998): 837–62.

31. Renford Reese, *American Paradox: Young Black Men* (Durham, NC: Carolina Academic Press, 2004).

32. Steven A. Tuch and Ronald Weitzer, "Racial Differences in Attitudes toward the Police," *Public Opinion Quarterly* 61 (1997): 642–63.

33. Jill Nelson, ed., *Police Brutality: An Anthology* (New York: W. W. Norton, 2000).

34. Russell, "What Did I Do."

35. Chappell and Piquero, "Applying Social Learning Theory."

36. Thomas Barker, "Peer Group Support for Police Occupational Deviance," *Criminology* 15 (1977): 353–66.

37. German Lopez, "Cleveland Police Shooting of Tamir Rice: City to Pay $6 Million after 12-year-old's Death," *Vox*, November 24, 2014, updated April 25, 2016, www.vox.com/2014/11/24/7275297/tamir-rice-police-shooting.

38. Charlotte Alter, "Florida Cops Used Mugshots of Black Men for Target Practice," *Time*, January 16, 2015, http://time.com/3671503/florida-police-black-men-mugshots-target-practice/.

39. Brian Lazenby, "Jury Set in Former Police Officer's Trial," *Chattanooga Times Free Press*, February 11, 2004.

40. Candice Combs, "Mistrial for Former Officer," *Chattanooga Times Free Press*, February 14, 2004.

41. "Gaynor Found Not Guilty in Henderson Shooting," *Chattanoogan*, April 27, 2005, http://www.chattanoogan.com/2005/4/27/66066/Gaynor-Found-Not-Guilty-In-Henderson.aspx.

42. "Law Enforcement Honored for Service," *Chattanooga Times Free Press*, May 14, 2009, http://www.timesfreepress.com/news/local/story/2009/may/14/law-enforcement-honored-service/219631/.

43. Jerome H. Skolnick, *Justice without Trial: Law Enforcement in Democratic Society* (New York: Macmillan College Publishing, 1994).

44. Patricia Williams, "Obstacle Illusions: The Cult of Racial Appearance," in Nelson, *Police Brutality*, 149–56.

45. See http://www.innocenceproject.org.

46. "Innocence Cases," Death Penalty Information Center, https://death-penaltyinfo.org/innocence-cases.

47. Alan Blinder, "Alabama Man Freed after Decades on Death Row," *New York Times*, April 3, 2015, https://www.nytimes.com/2015/04/04/us/anthony-ray-hinton-alabama-prison-freed-murder.html?_r=0.

48. Ron Daniels, "The Crisis of Police Brutality and Misconduct in America: The Causes and the Cure," in Nelson, *Police Brutality*, 240–60.

49. Jacobs and O'Brien, "The Determinants of Deadly Force."

50. Russell, "What Did I Do."

51. Richard Austin, "Under the Veil of Suspicion," in Nelson, *Police Brutality*, 206–24.

52. Katheryn Russell-Brown, *The Color of Crime: Racial Hoaxes, White Fear, Black Protectionism, Police Harassment, and Other Macroaggressions* (New York: New York University Press, 1998).

53. Kenneth Meeks, *Driving While Black* (New York: Broadway Books, 2000).

54. Arrick L. Jackson and John E. Wade, "Police Perceptions of Social Capital and Sense of Responsibility: An Explanation of Proactive Policing," *Policing: An International Journal of Police Strategies and Management* 28, no. 1 (2005): 49–68.

55. Michelle K. Lersch, "Malpractice: A Critical Analysis of Citizen's Complaints," *Policing: An International Journal of Police Strategies and Management* 21, no. 1 (1998): 80–96.

56. Ishmael Reed, "Another Day at the Front," in Nelson, *Police Brutality*, 89–205.

57. Black Youth Project, *Report: White on White Crime Exceeds That of Black on Black Crime*, August 18, 2014, http://blackyouthproject.com/report-white-on-white-crime-rate-exceeds-that-of-black-on-black-crime/.

58. Janet Reno, Speeches of Attorney General Reno, 1993–2001, National Press Club, April 15, 1999, https://www.justice.gov/archive/ag/speeches/1999/04-15-1999b.pdf.

59. Bob Martin, *Both Sides of the Fence* (Bloomington, IN: Author House, 2006).

60. "Workers at Former Clark Bros. Make Startling Discovery," *Chattanoogan*, October 11, 2004, http://www.chattanoogan.com/2004/10/11/57006/Workers-At-Former-Clark-Bros.-Make.aspx.

61. Martin, *Both Sides of the Fence*.

62. "Lynching of Ed Johnson," *Wikipedia*, https://en.wikipedia.org/wiki/Lynching_of_Ed_Johnson.

63. Emily Yellin, "Lynching Victim Is Cleared of Rape, 100 Years Later," *New York Times*, February 27, 2000.

64. For more insight into this idea, see Robert Staples, *Urban Plantation: Racism and Colonialism in the Post Civil Rights Era* (Oakland, CA: Black Scholar Press, 1987).

65. D. P. Laville-Wilson, "Perceptions of Police Abusive Behavior: Factors Influencing Citizens' Attitudes of Police Violence," *American Journal of Sociology* 103 (1998): 837–62.

66. Marvin D. Free, *African Americans and the Criminal Justice System* (London: Routledge, 1996).

67. Stanley Crouch, "What's New: The Truth as Usual," in Nelson, *Police Brutality*, 157–68.

68. Craig Hemmens and Daniel Levin, "Resistance Is Futile: The Right to Resist Unlawful Arrest in an Era of Aggressive Policing," *Crime and Delinquency* 46 (2000): 472–96.

69. William H. Frey, *Diversity Explosion: How New Racial Demographics Are Remaking America* (Washington, DC: Brookings Institute Press, 2014).

70. "Shooting of Trayvon Martin," *Wikipedia*, https://en.wikipedia.org/wiki/Shooting_of_Trayvon_Martin.

71. "T. J. Holmes Pulled Over: 'Driving While Black Ain't No Joke!'" July 30, 2012, http://www.huffingtonpost.com/2012/07/30/tj-holmes-pulled-over-driving-black-no-joke_n_1718981.html.

72. Abby Goodnough, "Harvard Professor Jailed; Officer Accused of Bias," *New York Times*, July 21, 2009, http://www.nytimes.com/2009/07/21/us/21gates.html.

73. Michael E. Dyson, "Special to CNN: Professor Arrested for Housing while Black," *Anderson Cooper 360*, July 22, 2009, http://ac360.blogs.cnn.com/2009/07/22/professor-arrested-for-housing-while-black/.

74. "The White House Beer Summit," *Boston.com*, www.boston.com/news/politics/gallery/073009_beer_summit_obama/.

75. Peter Holly, Abby Phillip, and Abby Ohlheiser, "Alabama Police Officer Arrested after Indian Grandfather Left Partially Paralyzed," *Washington Post*, February 12, 2015, https://www.washingtonpost.com/news/morning-mix/wp/2015/02/11/alabama-cops-leave-a-grandfather-partially-paralyzed-after-frisk-goes-awry/?utm_term=.4fe7503dc040.

76. Jessica King and AnneClaire Stapleton, "Charlotte Police Kill Ex-FAMU Player Who May Have Been Running to Them for Help," September 16, 2013, http://www.cnn.com/2013/09/15/justice/north-carolina-police-shooting/index.html.

77. Julie Craven, "Michael Slager, The Cop Who Killed Walter Scott, Wasn't Convicted Because Black Lives Don't Matter," *Huffington Post*, December 5, 2016, http://www.huffingtonpost.com/entry/michael-slager-black-lives-matter_us_58420019e4b017f37fe4c266.

78. "Sean Bell Shooting Incident," *Wikipedia*, https://en.wikipedia.org/wiki/Sean_Bell_shooting_incident.

79. "Shooting of Michael Brown," *Wikipedia*, https://en.wikipedia.org/wiki/Shooting_of_Michael_Brown.

80. "Increasing Police Brutality."

81. Nick Wing, "We Pay a Shocking Amount for Police Misconduct, and Cops Want Us to Just Accept It. We Shouldn't," *Huffington Post*, May 29, 2015, http://www.huffingtonpost.com/2015/05/29/police-misconduct-settlements_n_7423386.html.

82. Robert E. Worden, "Situational and Attitudinal Explanations of Police Behavior: A Theoretical Reappraisal and Empirical Assessment, "*Law and Society Review* 23 (1989): 687–711.

83. Lopez, "Cleveland Police Shooting of Tamir Rice."

84. Cato Institute, *National Police Misconduct Reporting Project*, www.policemisconduct.net/statistics.

85. David Feige, "The Myth of the Hero Cop," *Slate*, May 25, 2015, http://www.slate.com/articles/news_and_politics/politics/2015/05/the_myth_of_the_hero_cop_police_unions_have_spread_a_dangerous_message_about.html.

CHAPTER 3

1. Steve Tobak, "Want a Great Job? Then Shave," *CBS News Moneywatch*, www.cbsnews.com/news/want-a-great-job-then-shave.

2. "Blonde Stereotype," *Wikipedia*, https://en.wikipedia.org/wiki/Blonde_stereotype.

3. "Ebonics (word)," *Wikipedia*, https://en.wikipedia.org/wiki/Ebonics_(word).

4. "Oakland Ebonics Resolution," *Wikipedia*, https://en.wikipedia.org/wiki/Oakland_Ebonics_resolution.

5. *Webster's Ninth New Collegiate Dictionary*, s.v. "discrimination" (Springfield, MA: Merriam-Webster, 1990).

6. Wornie Reed, "Framing the Discussion of Racism," in *Africana Cultures and Policy Studies: Scholarship and the Transformation of Public Policy*, ed. Zachery Williams (New York: Palgrave Macmillan, 2009), 55–69.

7. Patricia Bidol, *Developing New Perspectives on Race: An Innovative Multi-Media Social Studies Curriculum in Racism Awareness for the Secondary Level* (Detroit: New Detroit, 1970).

8. "Fourteenth Amendment to the United States Constitution," *Wikipedia*, https://en.wikipedia.org/wiki/Fourteenth_Amendment_to_the_United_States_Constitution.

9. "Fourteenth Amendment," *The Free Dictionary*, http://legal-dictionary.thefreedictionary.com/fourteenth+amendment.

10. "Affirmative Action," *Dictionary.com*, dictionary.reference.com/browse/affirmative+action.

11. Jessie Daniels, "White Women and Affirmative Action: Prime Beneficiaries and Opponents," *Racism Review*, March 11, 2014, http://www.racismreview.com/blog/2014/03/11/white-women-affirmative-action/.

12. "The Black Codes," *International World History Project*, history-world.org/black_codes.htm.

13. Nkechi Taifa, "Justice or Just Us: Fifty Years of the Criminal Punishment System," in *The Black Policy Paper on the March on Washington at 50: A Deposit Was Made, But the Check Still Bounced*, ed. Z. Williams and M. Sanyika (East Elmhurst, NY: Institute of the Black World 21st Century, 2015), 59–62.

14. Nicole Puglise, "Black Americans Incarcerated Five Times More Than White People—Report," *Guardian*, June 18, 2016, https://www.theguardian.com/us-news/2016/jun/18/mass-incarceration-black-americans-higher-rates-disparities-report.

15. Steven Tuch and Ronald Weitzer, "Racial Differences in Attitudes toward the Police," *Public Opinion Quarterly* 61 (1997): 642–63.

16. ACLU, "Racial Profiling: Definition," https://www.aclu.org/racial-profiling-definition.

17. Jason Horowitz, Nick Corasaniti, and Ashley Southall, "Nine Killed in Shooting at Black Church in Charleston," June 17, 2015, https://www.nytimes.com/2015/06/18/us/church-attacked-in-charleston-south-carolina.html?_r=0.

18. Alan Blinder and Kevin Sack, "Dylan Roof Is Sentenced to Death in Charleston Church Massacre," *New York Times*, January 10, 2017, https://www.nytimes.com/2017/01/10/us/dylann-roof-trial-charleston.html.

19. Christopher Waldrep, *Racial Violence on Trial: A Handbook with Cases, Laws, and Documents* (Santa Barbara, CA: ABC-CLIO, 2001).

20. "Anti-miscegenation Laws," *Wikipedia*, https://en.wikipedia.org/wiki/Anti-miscegenation_laws.

21. Tim Lewis, "Ruth Negga: 'There Are Films That Really Mark You. *Loving* Is One of Those for Me,'" *Guardian*, January 29, 2017, https://www.theguardian.com/film/2017/jan/29/ruth-negga-loving-interview-rising-star-oscar-nomination.

22. Southern Poverty Law Center, "Ku Klux Klan: A History of Racism," February 28, 2011, https://www.splcenter.org/20110301/ku-klux-klan-history-racism.

23. Ibid.

24. Carolyn M. McKinstry, *While the World Watched* (Carol Stream, IL: Tyndale House Publishers, 2011).

25. Adam Gabbatt, "Ku Klux Klan to Rally in Memphis in Protest at Park's Name Change," *Guardian*, March 20, 2013, https://www.theguardian.com/world/2013/mar/20/ku-klux-klan-memphis-rally.

26. Jolie Lee, "KKK Raising Money for Ferguson Police Officer," *USA Today*, August 19, 2014, https://www.usatoday.com/story/news/nation-now/2014/08/19/ku-klux-klan-ferguson-police-michael-brown/14275115/.

27. Joseph A. Baldwin, "Theory and Research Concerning the Notion of Black Self-Hatred: A Review and Reinterpretation," *Journal of Black Psychology* 5, no. 2 (1979): 51–77.

28. John H. Griffin, *Black Like Me* (Boston: Houghton Mifflin, 1961).

29. Greg Botelho, "Rachel Dolezal's Brother: She's Making Up More and More Lies," June 18, 2015, http://www.cnn.com/2015/06/17/us/washington-rachel-dolezal-naacp/index.html.

30. "*Imitation of Life* (1934 film)," *Wikipedia*, https://en.wikipedia.org/wiki/Imitation_of_Life_(1934_film).

31. "What Is Cyberbullying," Stopbullying.gov, https://www.stopbullying.gov/cyberbullying/what-is-it/index.html.

32. Katheryn K. Russell, "What Did I Do to Be So Black and Blue? Police Violence and the Black Community," in *Police Brutality: An Anthology*, ed. Jill Nelson (New York: W. W. Norton, 2000), 135–48.

33. Kenneth Meeks, *Driving While Black* (New York: Broadway Books, 2000).

34. Jerome H. Skolnick, *Justice without Trial: Law Enforcement in Democratic Society* (New York: Macmillan College Publishing, 1994).

35. "Shooting of Trayvon Martin," *Wikipedia*, https://en.wikipedia.org/wiki/Shooting_of_Trayvon_Martin.

36. Skolnick, *Justice without Trial*.

37. Renford Reese, *American Paradox: Young Black Men* (Durham, NC: Carolina Academic Press, 2004).

38. For those still perplexed about the existence of racial profiling, I recommend Gregory Williams, *Life on the Color Line: The True Story of a White Boy Who Discovered He Was Black* (New York: Dutton Publisher, 1995). Williams and his brother were privileged white children who became oppressed black children overnight. When Dr. Williams was ten years old, his mother left the family with his younger brother and sister. He and his other brother were left with his alcoholic father. Dr. Williams later discovered that his father had been passing for white but was actually the son of a black mother. When his father could no longer care for the two boys, he took them from Virginia as white boys to Indiana to live with his mother. The boys had no idea of their black heritage until they arrived in Indiana and became two black boys. The story of Dr. Williams is an amazing example of racial profiling and white privilege.

39. "King: 'Can We All Get Along,'" ABC News, http://abcnews.go.com/US/video/Rodney-King-16589937.

40. McKinstry, *While the World Watched*, 280.

CHAPTER 4

1. Elizabeth Kübler-Ross, *On Death and Dying* (New York: Macmillan, 1969).

2. "Terence Crutcher Was Turning His Life Around before Fatal Tulsa Police Shooting, Family Says," *Chicago Tribune*, September 21, 2016, http://www.chicagotribune.com/news/nationworld/ct-tulsa-police-shooting-20160921-story.html.

3. Naomi Martin, "Inmate Death at Orleans Parish Prison First under Federal Oversight," *Times Picayune*, March 14, 2014, http://www.nola.com/crime/index.ssf/2014/03/inmate_death_at_orleans_parish.html; Richard Webster, "Dying at OPP: A Look at 5 Lawsuits against the New Orleans Jail," *Times Picayune*, September 30, 2014, http://www.nola.com/crime/index.ssf/2014/09/dying_at_opp_a_look_at_5_lawsu.html.

4. Dean Meminger, "Exclusive: Inmate Died in Prison, Was Buried before His Bronx Family Was Notified," *NY1*, May 19, 2016, http://www.ny1.com/nyc/all-boroughs/criminal-justice/2016/05/19/ny1-exclusive--inmate-buried-upstate-without-bronx-family-being-notified.html.

5. Brendan O'Connor, "Seven Months Later, Still No Answers for Family of Man Who Died by Suicide in Solitary Confinement," *Jezebel*, October 17, 2016, http://jezebel.com/seven-months-later-still-no-answers-for-family-of-man-1787820640.

6. Ibid.

7. John Bacon, "Sandra Bland's Family Settles Wrongful Death Case for $1.9M," *USA Today*, September 15, 2016, https://www.usatoday.com/story/news/nation/2016/09/15/sandra-blands-family-reportedly-settles-wrongful-death-case-19m/90400160/.

8. Margaret E. Noonan and Scott Ginder, "Mortality in Local Jails and State Prisons, 2000–2011—Statistical Tables," US Department of Justice, Office of Justice Programs, August 2013, NCJ 242186, https://www.bjs.gov/content/pub/pdf/mljsp0011.pdf.

9. Margaret Noonan, Harley Rohloff, and Scott Ginder, "Mortality in Local Jails and State Prisons, 2000–2013—Statistical Tables," Bureau of Justice Statistics, August 2015, https://www.bjs.gov/content/pub/pdf/mljsp0013st.pdf.

10. Andrea M. Burch, "Arrest-Related Deaths, 2003–2009: Statistical Tables," US Department of Justice, Bureau of Justice Statistics, November 2011, https://www.bjs.gov/content/pub/pdf/ard0309st.pdf.

11. Mark Puente, "Justice Department to Probe Allegations of Police Misconduct in Baltimore," *Baltimore Sun*, October 3, 2014, http://articles.baltimoresun.com/2014-10-03/news/bs-md-justice-investigation-20141003_1_police-misconduct-justice-department-baltimore-sun.

12. Ezra Klein, "Since 2011, Baltimore Has Lost or Settled More Than 100 Cases Related to Police Brutality," *Vox*, April 28, 2015, https://www.vox.com/2015/4/28/8508125/baltimore-police-brutality.

13. Keith L. Alexander, "Baltimore Reaches 6.4 Million Settlement with Freddie Gray's Family," *Washington Post*, September 8, 2015, https://www.washingtonpost.com/local/crime/baltimore-reaches-64-million-settlement-with-freddie-grays-family/2015/09/08/80b2c092-5196-11e5-8c19-0b6825aa4a3a_story.html?utm_term=.c7517e31dddb.

14. Carolyn Sung and Catherine E. Sholchet, "Freddie Gray Case: Charges Dropped against Remaining Officers," July 27, 2016, http://www.cnn.com/2016/07/27/us/freddie-gray-verdict-baltimore-officers/index.html.

15. Colleen Curry and Luis Martinez, "Ferguson Police's Show of Force Highlights Militarization of America's Cops," August 14, 2014, http://abcnews.go.com/US/ferguson-police-small-army-thousands-police-departments/story?id=24977299.

16. "Shooting of Walter Scott," *Wikipedia*, https://en.wikipedia.org/wiki/Shooting_of_Walter_Scott.

17. Brian A. Reaves, "Local Police Departments, 2013: Personnel, Policies, and Practices," US Department of Justice, Office of Justice Programs, May 2015, NCJ 248677, https://www.bjs.gov/content/pub/pdf/lpd13ppp.pdf.

18. Urbana Police Department, "Serious Uses of Force and In-Custody Deaths," *Urbana PD Policy Manual*, http://www.urbanaillinois.us/sites/default/files/attachments/305_Serious_Uses_of_Force_and_In-Custody_Deaths_0.pdf.

19. Tony Rogers, "Covering the Cops: Reporting on One of Journalism's Most Exciting and Stressful Beats," *ThoughtCo*, April 24, 2017, https://www.thoughtco.com/covering-the-cops-2073873.

20. "Walter Scott Shooting: Michael Slager Testifies He Felt Total Fear," *Crimesider*, CBS News, November 29, 2016, http://www.cbsnews.com/news/walter-scott-shooting-michael-slager-testifies-he-felt-total-fear/.

21. Disability Rights California, *The Lethal Hazard of Prone Restraint: Positional Asphyxiation*, April 2002, Publication #7018.01, http://www.disabilityrightsca.org/pubs/701801.pdf.

22. Bill Whitaker, "Officer Betty Shelby on Terence Crutcher," *60 Minutes*, April 2, 2017, http://www.cbsnews.com/news/terence-crutcher-unarmed-black-man-shooting-60-minutes-2/.

CHAPTER 5

1. See the Albert Ellis Institute website at http://albertellis.org/.

2. Gerald Corey, *Theory and Practice of Counseling and Psychotherapy*, second edition (Monterey, CA: Brooks/Cole Publishing, 1982), 170–83.

3. F. Brinley Bruton, Alexander Smith, Elizabeth Chuck, and Phil Helsel, "Dallas Police 'Ambush': 12 Officers Shot, 5 Killed during Protest," *NBC News*, July 8, 2016, http://www.nbcnews.com/storyline/dallas-police-ambush/protests-spawn-cities-across-u-s-over-police-shootings-black-n605686.

4. Jennifer Rowland, "Four Officers Acquitted in King Beating, Riots Break Out," UPI, April 29, 1992, http://www.upi.com/Archives/1992/04/29/Four-officers-acquitted-in-King-beating-riots-break-out/3290195933043/.

5. *The L.A. Riots 25 Years Later*, History, http://www.history.com/specials/the-l-a-riots-25-years-later.

6. "Los Angeles Riots Fast Facts," CNN, http://www.cnn.com/2013/09/18/us/los-angeles-riots-fast-facts/index.html.

7. Eric Nicholson, "Several Local Police Departments Are Banning Tasers as Evidence Mounts They Kill People," *Dallas Observer*, September 23, 2013.

8. Dennis K. McBride and Natalie B. Tedder, *Efficacy and Safety of Electrical Stun Devices* (Washington, DC: Potomac Institute for Policy Studies, 2005).

9. "Man Dies after Traffic Stop Involving Taser," *Chattanooga Times Free Press*, June 28, 2008.

10. Michael Cass, "19 Stuns from Tasers Not Excessive in Patrick Lee's Death, Jury Says," *Tennessean*, May 19, 2009.

11. Scott R. Maier, "A Cross-Market Assessment of Newspaper Error and Credibility," *Journalism and Mass Communication Quarterly* 82 (2005): 533–51.

12. Brenna R. Kelly, "Man Dies after Brawl with City Police Officers," *Cincinnati Enquirer*, December 1, 2003.

13. "Coroner Rules Cincinnati Death a Homicide," *CNN.com*, December 3, 2003, http://www.cnn.com/2003/US/Midwest/12/03/died.in.custody/index .html?iref=newssearch.

14. Mike O'Neal, "Chief Pledges Death Probe to Be Open," *Chattanooga Times Free Press*, January 4, 2004.

15. Martin Robbins, "How Dangerous Is Pepper Spray?" *Guardian*, November 22, 2011, https://www.theguardian.com/world/the-lay-scientist/2011/ nov/22/how-dangerous-is-pepper-spray.

16. Duane W. Gang, "Wallace Declines Top Police Post," *Chattanooga Times Free Press*, January 21, 2004.

17. Duane W. Gang, "Council Confirms Parks' Nomination as Police Chief," *Chattanooga Times Free Press*, February 4, 2004.

18. Candice Combs, "Police Train for Violence: Academy Conditions Officers to Make Life-Saving Choices," *Chattanooga Times Free Press*, February 2, 2004.

19. "Man Dies while Being Taken into Custody," *Chattanooga Times Free Press*, January 3, 2004.

20. John Phillips, "Is Silence Really Golden during a Traffic Stop?" *Car and Driver*, July 2008, http://www.caranddriver.com/columns/is-silence-really -golden-during-a-traffic-stop.

21. Jessica King and AnneClaire Stapleton, "Charlotte Police Kill Ex-FAMU Player Who May Have Been Running to Them for Help," September 16, 2013, http://www.cnn.com/2013/09/15/justice/north-carolina-police-shooting/ index.html.

22. Manny Fernandez and Matthew Haag, "Police Officer Who Shot 15-Year-Old Texas Boy Is Charged with Murder," *New York Times*, May 5, 2017, https://www.nytimes.com/2017/05/05/us/roy-oliver-charged-murder -dallas-police-shooting-jordan-edwards.html.

23. Thomas H. Holmes and Richard H. Rahe, "The Social Readjustment Rating Scale," *Journal of Psychosomatic Research* 11, no. 2 (1967): 213–18.

24. Jaweed Kaleem, "Michael Slager, Officer Who Fatally Shot Walter Scott in South Carolina, Pleads Guilty in Federal Case," *Los Angeles Times*, May 2, 2017, http://www.latimes.com/nation/la-na-michael-slager-walter-scott- 2017-story.html.

CHAPTER 6

1. "Chattanooga Police Department," *Wikipedia*, https://en.wikipedia.org/wiki/Chattanooga_Police_Department.

2. Courtney Howard, "Date Rape, Distracted Driving and Other Potential Prom Night Dangers," *Sovereign Health*, 06-18, https://www.sovteens.com/addiction/date-rape-distracted-driving-other-potential-prom-night-dangers/.

3. Dennis Cauchon, "D.A.R.E. Doesn't Work: Studies Find Drug Program Not Effective," *USA Today*, October 11, 1993.

4. Steven Hawkins, "Education vs. Incarceration," *American Prospect*, December 6, 2010.

5. Michael J. Klarman, *From Jim Crow to Civil Rights: The Supreme Court and the Struggle for Racial Equality* (New York: Oxford University Press, 2004).

6. April V. Taylor, "More Black People Killed by Police Than Were Lynched during Jim Crow," *San Francisco Bay View*, October 5, 2014.

7. Malcolm Gladwell, *David and Goliath: Underdogs, Misfits, and the Art of Battling Giants* (New York: Little, Brown, 2013).

8. Rebecca D. O'Brien, Michael H. Saul, and Pervaiz Shallwani, "New York City Officer Won't Face Criminal Charges in Eric Garner Death," *Wall Street Journal*, December 4, 2014.

9. Mark Zaretsky, "Emma Jones Relives '97 East Haven Police Shooting of Son, Malik in Ferguson Case," *New Haven Register*, August 8, 2014.

10. See http://stolenlives.org/.

11. Alan Feuer, "Ex-Officer Convicted in Choking Death Is to Leave Prison," *New York Times*, April 15, 2005.

12. See National Lawyers Guild, https://www.nlg.org/.

13. See October 22 Coalition, http://www.october22.org/.

14. National Lawyers Guild, Anthony Baez Foundation, October 22 Coalition, *Stolen Lives: Killed by Law Enforcement*, second edition (New York: October 22 Coalition, 1999).

15. "Gaynor Found Not Guilty in Henderson Shooting," *Chattanoogan*, April 27, 2005, http://www.chattanoogan.com/2005/4/27/66066/Gaynor-Found-Not-Guilty-In-Henderson.aspx.

16. "Black Lives Matter," *Wikipedia*, https://en.wikipedia.org/wiki/Black_Lives_Matter.

17. "Johnnie Cochran," *Wikipedia*, https://en.wikipedia.org/wiki/Johnnie_Cochran.

18. Bergstein and Ulrich, LLP, "Monell, Monell, Monell," *Wait a Second!* (blog), November 1, 2007, http://secondcircuitcivilrights.blogspot.com/2007/11/monell-monell-monell.html.

19. Larry McShane, "Freddie Gray's Family Has Reached 6.4M Settlement: Report," *New York Daily News*, September 9, 2015.

20. Richard Fausset, "Walter Scott Family Reaches a $6.5 Million Settlement for South Carolina Police Shooting Case," *New York Times*, October 8, 2015.

21. *Marek v. Chesny*, 473 US 1 (1985), http://caselaw.findlaw.com/us-supreme-court/473/1.html.

22. "Injunctive Relief," *Legal Dictionary*, https://legaldictionary.net/injunctive-relief/.

23. "Chattanooga Police Officer Resigns after He Is Caught Shoplifting from Wal-Mart," *Chattanooga Times Free Press*, January 30, 2016, http://www.timesfreepress.com/news/local/story/2016/jan/30/chattanoogpolice-officer-resigns-after-he-cau/347472/.

CHAPTER 7

1. Lezley McSpadden and Lyah B. LeFlore, *Tell the Truth and Shame the Devil: The Life, Legacy, and Love of My Son Michael Brown* (New York: Reban Arts, 2016).

2. "Cape Couple's Son Dies in Tennessee in Police Custody," *Southeast Missourian*, February 18, 2004.

3. Neil Nagraj, "Senator's Daughter Carjacked in Washington, D.C.," *Daily News*, December 3, 2009, http://www.nydailynews.com/news/national/tennessee-senator-bob-corker-daughter-carjacked-washington-suspects-custody-article-1.432070.

4. See http://stolenlives.org/.

5. Frank Harris III, "In East Haven, Echoes of '97 Police Shooting," *Hartford Courant*, February 2, 2012.

6. Joe L. Kincheloe, Shirley R. Steinberg, Nelson M. Rodriguez, and Ronald E. Chennault, *White Reign: Deploying Whiteness in America* (New York: St. Martin's Press, 1998).

7. Emily Zulz, "A Local Form of Terrorism," *Daily Eastern News*, February 27, 2008, 1.

8. "Five Alabama Cops Fired for Taped Beating," May 21, 2009, http://www.cbsnews.com/news/5-alabama-cops-fired-for-taped-beating/.

9. See http://www.pomc.com/.

10. Victoria Bekiempis, "Nearly 1 in 5 Americans Suffers from Mental Illness Each Year," *Newsweek*, February 28, 2014.

11. Mark Bliss, "Pain in Our Eyes," *Southeast Missourian*, front page, 5a, November 30, 2016, http://www.semissourian.com/story/2364444.html.

CHAPTER 8

1. K. M. Blum, "Making Out the Monell Claim under Section 1983," *Touro Law Review* 25, no. 3 (2012); Bergstein and Ulrich, LLP, "Monell, Monell, Monell," *Wait a Second!* (blog), November 1, 2007, http://secondcircuitcivilrights.blogspot.com/2007/11/monell-monell-monell.html.

2. Pete Edwards, "The Brandon Miller Shooting," *People News*, March 2004, http://www.thepeoplenews.com/march04/.

3. Pete Edwards, "Grand Jury Scandal," *People News*, http://www.the peoplenews.com/june04.

4. T. J. Greaney, "Cape Native's Death Questioned," *Southeast Missourian*, November 28, 2006.

5. William Norman Grigg, "Death Squad in Delaware: The Case of the Murdered Marine," *Tennessee Tribune*, December 4–10, 2008.

6. "Delaware Settles Fatal Police Shooting for 875K," *Claims Journal*, December 15, 2010.

7. Marcia Riley, "Another Senseless Murder in a Texas Jail," *Tennessee Tribune*, December 4–10, 2008.

8. Danny Gallagher, "Dead Inmate Combative with Officers: Rangers Report Says," *McKinney Courier-Gazette*, February 20, 2008.

9. Tiara M. Ellis, "Jail Inmate on Suicide Watch Dies after Being Restrained," *Dallas Morning News*, July 3, 2007.

10. Noreen Hyslop, "Jury Awards $1M in '08 Shooting," *Southeast Missourian*, August 19, 2012.

11. Holly Brantley, "Officer Charged with Involuntary Manslaughter," *KFVS News*, February 27, 2008, http://www.kfvs12.com/story/7932479/officer-charged-with-involuntary-manslaughter.

12. Al Jones, "Family of Pace U. Football Player Killed by Police Files Civil Rights Suit," *CBS New York*, April 20, 2011, http://newyork.cbslocal.com/2011/04/20/family-of-danroy-henry-pace-university-football-player-killed-by-police-filing-civil-rights-lawsuit/.

13. "The Negro Family: The Case for National Action," *Wikipedia*, https://en.wikipedia.org/wiki/The_Negro_Family:_The_Case_For_National_Action.

14. Ray Rivera and Trymaine Lee, "Many Questions on Killing of Pace Student by Police," *New York Times*, October 18, 2010.

15. Ashley Southall, "No Charges for Officer Who Killed Pace University Student in 2010," *New York Times*, April 7, 2015, https://www.nytimes.com/2015/04/08/nyregion/no-charges-for-officer-who-killed-pace-university-student-in-2010.html.

16. "Brutality Claim in D. J. Henry Case," *ESPN*, October 20, 2010.

17. Lisa W. Foderaro, "$6 million Settlement over Police Shooting of Danroy Henry," *New York Times*, March 14, 2016, https://www.nytimes.com/2016/03/15/nyregion/6-million-settlement-over-police-shooting-of-danroy-henry.html.

18. Marie Rohde, "Slain Man's Mom Must Pay Legal Fees," *Journal Sentinel*, October 6, 2008, http://archive.jsonline.com/news/milwaukee/32467209.html/.

19. "Revisiting the Scene of Jonathan Ferrell's Death," *Charlotte Observer*, https://www.youtube.com/watch?v=QxLgQJLa1M0 (video created by Todd Sumlin).

20. Aamer Madhani, "No Charges for Milwaukee Officer Who Shot Man 14 Times," *USA Today*, December 22, 2014.

21. Justin Fenton, "Judge Affirms Baltimore Officers' Use of Lethal Force on Mentally Ill Man," *Baltimore Sun*, July 28, 2015.

22. "The Murder of Maurice Donald Johnson by Baltimore Police: Mother Marcella Holloman Speaks," YouTube, posted September 3, 2013, https://www.youtube.com/watch?v=rOqOMDtuOhU.

23. Valerie Bell, "Why I Am Marching on Mother's Day for My Son," *The Blog, Huffington Post*, May 6, 2016.

24. See https://justice4alanblueford.org/tag/the-alan-blueford-center-for-justice/.

25. "Collette Flanagan Speaks about Her Son's Murder by Dallas Police," *Dallas Weekly*, September 24, 2013, https://www.youtube.com/watch?v=RNnV_Oqn0TM.

26. Megan Cassidy, "Family of Man Killed by Phoenix Police: Don't Focus on Race," *AZCentral*, December 4, 2014, http://www.azcentral.com/story/news/local/phoenix/2014/12/05/family-man-killed-phoenix-police-focus-race/19934383/.

27. Crimesider Staff, "Hadiya Pendleton Murder: Teen Girl Who Performed at President Obama's Inauguration Fatally Shot at Chicago Park, Report Says," *CBS News*, January 30, 2013, http://www.cbsnews.com/news/hadiya-pendleton-murder-teen-girl-who-performed-at-president-obamas-inauguration-fatally-shot-at-chicago-park-report-says/.

28. Jack Dunphy, "Mothers of the Movement," *PJ Media*, July 29, 2016, https://pjmedia.com/blog/mothers-of-the-movement/.

CHAPTER 9

1. Dave Altimara, "For Police, Nepotism a Common Danger," *Hartford Courant*, February 12, 2011.

2. Kenneth Meeks, *Driving While Black* (New York: Broadway Books, 2000).

3. Bob Martin, *Both Sides of the Fence* (Bloomington, IN: Author House, 2006).

4. Norm Stamper, *Breaking Rank* (New York: Nation Books, 2005).

CHAPTER 10

1. Eric Schlosser, "A Grief Like No Other," *Atlantic*, September 1997, https://www.theatlantic.com/magazine/archive/1997/09/a-grief-like-no -other/376944/.

2. "Hatfield-McCoy Feud," *Wikipedia*, https://en.wikipedia.org/wiki/ Hatfield%E2%80%93McCoy_feud.

3. *Crime Victims' Rights in America: An Historical Overview*, https://vic timsofcrime.org/docs/ncvrw2013/2013ncvrw_5_landmarks.pdf?sfvrsn=0.

4. Mayo Clinic, "Broken Heart Syndrome," http://www.mayoclinic.org/ diseases-conditions/broken-heart-syndrome/home/ovc-20264165.

5. Office of the Attorney General, "Memorandum for Heads of Depart-ment Components and United States Attorneys," https://assets.documentcloud .org/documents/3535148/Consentdecreebaltimore.txt.

6. Nicole Lyn Pesce, "Pa. Lunch Lady Quits over New Rules Humiliat-ing Poor Students," *New York Daily News*, September 22, 2016, http://www .nydailynews.com/life-style/lunch-lady-quits-new-rules-humiliating-poor-kids -article-1.2801656.

7. Ken Paulson, "Not Many Exceptions to Free-Speech Guarantee," *First Amendment Center*, November 18, 2011, http://www.firstamendmentcenter .org/not-many-exceptions-to-free-speech-guarantee/.

8. Mark Berman, "Columbus Police Officer Fatally Shoots Tyre King, 13-Year-Old with a BB Gun," *Washington Post*, September 15, 2016, https:// www.washingtonpost.com/news/post-nation/wp/2016/09/15/columbus-police -fatally-shoot-tyree-king-13-year-old-with-a-bb-gun/.

9. Phil Helsel, "I'm Not Shy: Charlotte Girl Zianna Oliphant Discusses Emotional Speech to City Council," NBC News, September 27, 2016, http:// www.nbcnews.com/news/us-news/i-m-not-shy-charlotte-girl-gives-emotional -speech-race-n655776.

10. Gerald Corey, "Gestalt Therapy," in *Theory and Practice of Counseling and Psychotherapy* (Monterey, CA: Brooks/Cole Publishing, 1982), 97–117.

11. Lula M. Redmond, "Sudden Violent Death," in *Living with Grief after Sudden Loss: Suicide, Homicide, Accident, Heart Attack, Stroke*, ed. Kenneth J. Doka (Washington, DC: Hospice Foundation of America, 1996), 53–71.

12. Therese A. Rando, "Complications in Mourning Traumatic Death," in *Living with Grief after Sudden Loss: Homicide, Accident, Heart Attack, Stroke*, ed. Kenneth J. Doka (Washington, DC: Hospice Foundation of America, 1996), 139–59.

13. Mayo Clinic, "Post-Traumatic Stress Disorder (PTSD)," http://www .mayoclinic.org/diseases-conditions/post-traumatic-stress-disorder/home/ovc -20308548.

14. Yaron Steinbuch and Joe Tacopino, "Woman Records Horrific Scene after Boyfriend Is Fatally Shot by Police," *New York Post*, July 7, 2016.

15. Richard Fausset and Yamiche Alcindor, "Video by Wife of Keith Scott Shows Her Pleas to Police," *New York Times*, September 24, 2016.

16. United States Department of Justice, "Justice Department Announces Findings of Investigation into Chicago Police Department," *Justice News*, January 13, 2017.

17. Cornell West, *Race Matters* (New York: Vintage Books, 1994).

18. "Martin Niemöller," https://en.wikiquote.org/wiki/Martin_Niem%C3% B6ller.

19. "Gypsy Cop," *Wikipedia*, https://en.wikipedia.org/wiki/Gypsy_cop.

20. Candice Combs, "Two Officers Gone, 1 Suspended for Recent Acts," *Chattanooga Times Free Press*, December 31, 2004, 1, 9.

21. Laura Bult, "Ohio Police Chief to Tulsa Cop Who Killed Terence Crutcher: You Are Making Us All Look Bad," *New York Daily News*, September 21, 2016, http://www.nydailynews.com/news/national/ohio-police-chief -tulsa-making-bad-article-1.2800940.

22. Earl O. Hutchinson, "Killer Cops," *Salon*, November 1, 2000, http:// www.salon.com/2000/11/01/cops_2/.

23. Faith Karimi, Eric Levenson, and Justin Gamble, "Tulsa Officer Acquitted in Fatal Shooting of Terence Crutcher," CNN, May 18, 2017, http://www cnn.com/2017/05/17/us/tulsa-police-shooting-trial/index.html.

24. Kim Lonsway, "Men, Women, and Police Excessive Force: A Tale of Two Genders," National Center for Women and Policing, April 2002, http:// womenandpolicing.com/PDF/2002_Excessive_Force.pdf.

25. John Bacon, "Top Cop Sorry for 'Historical Mistreatment' of Minorities," *USA Today*, October 18, 2016, https://www.usatoday.com/story/news/na tion/2016/10/18/top-cop-sorry-historical-mistreatment-minorities/92348646/.

26. Kenneth J. Doka, ed., *Living with Grief after Sudden Loss: Homicide, Suicide, Accident, Heart Attack, Stroke* (Washington, DC: Hospice Foundation of America, 1996).

27. See http://www. citinternational.org.163-memphis.

28. Ibid.

29. Katie Fretland and Yolanda Jones, "DOJ Is Conducting a Comprehensive Review of the Memphis Police Department," *Memphis Commercial Appeal, USA Today Network*, October 25, 2016.

30. "Racial Bias Survey Ignores Serious, Escalating Problem," http://www.chattanoogan.com/2005/4/18/65603/Racial-Bias-Survey-Ignores-Serious.aspx.

31. Joseph Erbentraut, "Police Department Bias Trainings Are More in Demand Than Ever," *Huffington Post*, October 19, 2015, http://www.huffington-post.com/entry/police-bias-training-programs_us_561ecc70e4b050c6c4a437f9.

32. Antoine Fuqua (dir.), *Training Day* (2001; Burbank, CA: Warner Home Video, 2007), DVD.

33. Robin S. Engel, *How Police Supervisory Styles Influence Patrol Officer Behavior*, National Institute of Justice Report 194078, June 2003, https://www.ncjrs.gov/pdffiles1/nij/194078.pdf.

34. Samuel Walker, Geoffrey P. Alpert, and Dennis J. Kennedy, "Responding to the Problem Police Officer: A National Study of Early Warning Systems, Final Report," National Institute of Justice (NIJ), September 2000.

35. See http://www.brown-watch.com.

36. Martin Luther King Jr., *Why We Can't Wait* (New York: Harper and Row, 1964).

INDEX

ABOUT THE AUTHOR

Loretta P. Prater, PhD, retired in 2012 as professor and dean of the College of Health and Human Services at Southeast Missouri State University, where she provided administrative oversight for the Department of Criminal Justice and Sociology and a Regional Police Academy. Prior to moving to Missouri, she held academic assignments at Eastern Illinois University and the University of Tennessee at Chattanooga. Dr. Prater received her doctorate in child and family studies from the University of Tennessee at Knoxville. As a social scientist interested in family dynamics over the life span, her research, national presentations, and publications have focused on topics addressing the health and well-being of children and families, including issues related to police brutality and the relationship between policing and the community. During her professional career, she has received numerous awards and has published book chapters and journal articles. She has a passion for and personal interest in social justice. Dr. Prater has served on numerous boards in various communities and states. She has served as president of the Southeast Missouri Chapter of the United Way. She currently is a member of the Family and Community Trust Board of Missouri and is the chairperson of the Community Advisory Council for the Missouri Foundation for Health.